WALKING THE RETREAT

THE MARCH TO THE MARNE: 1914 REVISITED

Also by Terry Cudbird:

Walking the Hexagon
An Escape around France on Foot

WALKING THE RETREAT

THE MARCH TO THE MARNE: 1914 REVISITED

TERRY CUDBIRD

Signal

Signal Books
Oxford

First published in 2014 by
Signal Books Limited
36 Minster Road
Oxford
OX4 1LY
www.signalbooks.co.uk

A catalogue record for this book is available from the British Library.

ISBN 978-1-909930-02-5 Paper

Production: Tora Kelly
Cover design: Baseline Arts, Oxford
Cover illustrations: © Military Images/Alamy; Baseline Arts, Oxford
Half title page image: Peasant girl feeding passing French troops in 1914.
(Library of Congress, Washington DC)
Maps: Mike Reading, Hello Design
Printed and bound in India by Imprint Digital Ltd.

CONTENTS

MAPS

Carving of General Joffre and a French soldier, monument commemorating the Victory of the Marne, Mondemont. (Terry Cudbird)

INTRODUCTION: THE FIRST BATTLE OF THE MARNE
SEPTEMBER 1914

The *route départementale* rose smoothly up a steep incline deep in rural France. I had not seen another human being for some time. Ploughed fields and woods divided the landscape into a patchwork quilt. It was early in March and crests of hard-packed snow still covered the verges. The light was flat late in the afternoon. Nothing remarkable here, I thought. A narrow farm road led to a ridge. To my left the ground fell away quite steeply to a valley floor. Away to the east orderly fields gave way to dense vegetation, crossed by water channels, suggesting marshy ground. Just visible even further to my right stretched the bleak plain of *la Champagne pouilleuse* (the "infertile Champagne"), dead flat as far as the eye could see, earth stripped of vegetation, wisps of its light chalk soil raised by the wind.

The bitter northern wind stung my face forcing me to wrap my scarf more tightly around my neck for protection. I turned round and was surprised to see what looked like a massive carved menhir of recent date. Its bulk and height looked incongruous, towering over some small buildings, the walls of an old manor house and ancient woods. On top of the hill it must have been visible for miles around. Clearly someone was trying to make sure no visitor would forget it. Enormous carved figures covered the bottom half facing down hill; nine military men, generals most of them to judge by their head gear. The largest in the centre had his left arm around an ordinary soldier in a longer heavier coat than his august colleagues. The inscription above told me that I had found the monument to commemorate the Battle of the Marne, September 1914.

So here they were: the men I had first read about in Barbara Tuchman's Pulitzer prize-winning book *The Guns of August*. Joseph Jacques Césaire Joffre, the French Commander-in-Chief, stands in the centre. The son of a *vigneron* from Rivesaltes near Perpignan, he was a man of some bulk who clearly enjoyed his food. Stolid and unflappable, his staff knew they could always find him at lunch time in some station buffet. The soldier next to him represents a *poilu*, or hairy one, because he had no time to shave. There were around one million of them fighting from the gates of Paris to the Vosges Mountains in Alsace. It was Joffre's job to manoeuvre them into the right positions, but they were seen as the real heroes. On either side are the generals who were most directly involved, starting on the right with Joseph Galliéni, the Military Governor of Paris, and Michel-Joseph Manoury whose Sixth Army opened the battle by launching an attack on the German right flank. When the attack faltered some reinforcements were rushed to the front in a fleet of taxis. Next to him stands a figure in a different uniform and most noticeably a peaked cap, rather than the pillbox *képi* beloved of the French army. He outranks all the others; Field-Marshal Sir John French, commander of the British Expeditionary Force, a choleric cavalryman who stood on his dignity and struggled to get his tongue round the French language. Then comes Louis Franchet d'Esperey, the fierce and energetic leader of the Fifth Army, known as Desperate Frankie to the British. To the left of Joffre is Ferdinand Foch, future Allied commander-in-chief in 1918. His army occupied the central position and kept the Germans back against all the odds. After Foch come two generals whose armies stretched from Vitry-le-François across the plain and all the way north along the Côtes de Meuse to the fortress of Verdun—Ferdinand Langle de Cary commanding the Fourth Army and Maurice Sarrail the Third Army, both loyal Republicans.

*

When I got back home I started to study the first month of the Great War in more detail. One question above all others kept coming to mind as I read. Why did the German Army, which entered the war with such a high reputation, fail to knock France out of it in the first weeks of the conflict? That had been its plan— to defeat France quickly before focusing its main effort on Russia. The Germans invaded Belgium, aiming to outflank the French and British Armies. The French on the other hand concentrated the bulk of their forces along the frontier between the Meuse river and the Vosges Mountains. The Allied dispositions seemed to favour the German plans.

In the fighting of August 1914, known as the Battle of the Frontiers, badly prepared French attacks on the German centre in Lorraine and the Ardennes resulted in terrible losses for the French Armies. Further west the French Fifth Army was driven back at Charleroi in southern Belgium. The British Expeditionary Force (BEF) had to fight the numerically superior German First Army at Mons and then retire. The threat from the weight of the German right wing and the early losses caused the Allies to fall back. Their retreat lasted for two weeks from 23 August until 5 September. During this period the French changed their strategy in Lorraine to a defensive one, using well-fortified positions to repel German attacks. This posture enabled them to move substantial forces from the east and create a new army west of Paris on the German right flank. The Allied retreat came to a halt south of the Marne, when the French launched an attack on the German First Army out of Paris, supported by the other French Armies and the BEF. The Battle of the Marne lasted from 6 to 9 September. It ended when the Germans decided to withdraw because they feared an Allied thrust through the yawning gap between their First and Second Armies. The German Armies retreated to prepared defensive positions north of the River Aisne, from which the Allies were unable to dislodge them. Gradually both sides dug into the ground, creating a line of trenches from the Channel to the Swiss frontier. The Germans had failed to knock the French out of the war.

The retreat to the Marne was a planned withdrawal, not a rout. The Allied armies suffered heavy losses in the Battle of the Frontiers but they were not defeated. The bulk of their formations, together with their guns and equipment, were intact. The Germans took plenty of prisoners but not in the numbers they might have expected. Conditions during the retreat were chaotic at times with units separated from each other and supplies disrupted, but there was a plan—to fall back, recover, re-group and eventually strike back. The front line was fluid and permeable, with the German cavalry frequently moving ahead of scattered Allied units. Generally, however, the Allies kept ahead of the German Armies and they fought a series of delaying actions—at Le Cateau, Guise, Villers-Cotterêts—so that the majority of their forces could get away. If you read the diaries of Allied soldiers and officers you often come across discouragement, fear and anxiety, but never a sense that the game was up. Sometimes the troops ran but mostly they trudged south following orders. When France's new force was assembled outside Paris the retreating soldiers turned round and attacked the scattered spearheads of the German Armies.

In military terms the word retreat can describe many different circumstances. If we compare the retreat of 1914 with Napoleon's famous retreat from Moscow in 1812 the difference is obvious. Napoleon had to leave Moscow because he was running short of food and supplies, the winter was coming on and the Russian armies in the field had not been annihilated. As the weather took its toll and the Russians harried them, Napoleon's army melted away. It is estimated that 450,000 soldiers crossed the Niemen in June 1812 and only 30,000 returned. The retreat to the Marne in 1914 was totally different. The Germans thought they were victorious because they were pushing the Allies back and therefore the counter-attack on 6 September came as a surprise. Those who anticipated a German victory parade in Paris totally misread the situation. Unlike in 1940 there was no point at which the Allies had been totally outmanoeuvred; no decisive breakthrough, like the panzers' dash for the Channel. One eminent historian of this period, John Terraine, wrote a book on the march to the Marne with the title "Retreat to Victory", which sums it up very well.

Historians have questioned whether the German war plan was realistic. With little motor transport the Germans were dependent on horses, thousands of which died, many from lack of fodder. The Germans outran their supply lines with many of their troops not getting enough food. On the Marne they were 140 kilometres from the nearest railhead under their control. They had superior heavy artillery but in some cases it could not keep up with the rapid advance. Their forces were too few to accomplish all the tasks assigned to them. Two army corps plus two brigades had to be left to guard the French fortress of Maubeuge and the Belgian fortified camp of Antwerp and also to garrison Brussels. Maubeuge only fell on 7 September, too late for the troops engaged there to make a difference on the Marne. The Belgians made a sortie from Antwerp between 9 and 12 September to keep the Germans occupied. The Germans had all their reserves in the front line and could not easily call on fresh troops from Germany. This lack of manpower was compounded by the German Chief of Staff Helmuth von Moltke's decision to send two army corps east to East Prussia to help counter the Russian advance. They arrived after the decisive victory the Germans won at Tannenberg (25-29 August).

There was also rivalry between the generals in charge of the different armies. Von Moltke had to conduct operations with the Kaiser literally breathing down his neck. He was not a strong leader and even at Luxembourg was too far from the front. He gave way too easily to the demands of the Royal Princes— Crown Prince Wilhelm and Rupprecht of Bavaria—for fruitless attacks in Lorraine, when the right wing near Paris needed support. Alexander von Kluck commanding the First Army nearest the French capital was not willing to subordinate his movements to those of Karl von Bülow and the Second Army. There was a substantial gap between these two armies even before the Battle of the Marne. Von Kluck assumed he was chasing a defeated army and his forces were spread out in a headlong pursuit southwards. As a result he did not perceive the threat to his right flank from the French Sixth Army advancing from Paris. He underestimated his opponents.

While the German Armies were better equipped and better trained and led than the French, the latter had closed the gap in operational efficiency which had existed in the Franco-Prussian war of 1870. The French mobilization went smoothly. The French 75 mm field guns were acknowledged to be the best in the three armies. The French fielded as many men as the Germans and their use of railways to move troops from Lorraine to Paris ensured they had numerical superiority when the Battle of the Marne opened. Joffre had a much better understanding of operational realities than von Moltke because he kept in constant touch with the moving front line. He was in total control of his generals and was not hindered by interfering politicians. The French government gave him a free hand within the battle zone. He was ruthless in weeding out poor performers. He recognized his early mistakes and devised and implemented a strategy to counter the German invasion. He was also adept at cajoling the British into cooperation.

All these reasons for the German failure carry some weight. Yet it seems to me that historians have not given due emphasis to one crucial factor which plucked survival from the jaws of defeat—the resilience of the French and British soldiers during a retreat which tested men to the limits of endurance and beyond. They had to contend with physical hardships: long forced marches, lack of sleep and food, scorching heat, bleeding feet and a series of murderous engagements which resulted in the highest monthly losses in the whole war. They also withstood the psychological pressure of constantly moving backwards and wondering whether defeat was just around the corner. At the end of a two week retreat they fought a major battle on which the future of France depended. All this makes their achievement in denying victory to the German Army the more remarkable.

So I set out with the intention of discovering for myself what this retreat would have been like, both by reading contemporary accounts but also by walking it for myself. I decided to follow the exact route taken by one French Second Lieutenant, André Benoit, a reservist recalled to the army and not totally fit like many others. He was part of the Fifth French Army which retreated from Charleroi in Belgium to its battle position near Provins in the Champagne region. This army, with the BEF on its left, was on the exposed left flank of French forces, in constant danger of encirclement by the Germans. It had to retreat the longest distance and therefore its march is particularly significant. André Benoit wrote a detailed account of his part in the retreat (*Trois mois de guerre au jour le jour: 1914, journal d'un fantassin*, Three Months of War from Day to Day: 1914, Diary of a Soldier). He is at the centre of my story, but I have tried to recreate not only his experience but also that of ordinary soldiers and their junior officers throughout the British, German and French Armies. In doing so I have concentrated on the march itself, rather than the engagements fought along the way. There are several up-to-date accounts of Mons, Le Cateau, Villers-Cotterêts, Charleroi and Guise, which are listed in the bibliography and there did not seem to be much point in replicating these. I have tried to characterize the types of fighting the soldiers experienced without going into the details of every encounter with the German Armies. As far as the Battle of the Marne itself is concerned, I have given a brief account to complete the story without repeating the details available in several recent studies. My principal theme is the human experience of this great retreat rather than military manoeuvres, battle tactics or weaponry.

The most powerful image of the Great War is a trench with men surrounded by mud, living in cramped and often insanitary conditions, periodically subjected to intense shelling and enduring bouts of tedium alternating with the adrenalin rush of going over the top. The most famous battles of the war—the Somme, Verdun and Passchendaele, for example—were fought between fortified positions over restricted areas. They were battles of attrition, in which one side tried to wear down the other. Yet all this only applies to the fighting between late 1914 and the beginning of 1918. For several months at the beginning and end of the war the armies were on the move. The war started with one army trying to outmanoeuvre the other and ended in 1918 with two thrusts by the Germans— on the Somme and the Marne—and an Allied counter-attack, a methodical advance against a retreating German Army until the Armistice intervened. My aim in this book is not only to describe the endurance of the men who retreated to victory in 1914, but also to add another dimension to our picture of what soldiers of the Great War had to undergo.

It is now time to join André and his comrades as they travelled to the frontiers of France, ready to march forward and expecting to be home by Christmas. Before I set out to follow André on foot I had to work out a walking route. André's diary mentions many villages through which he marched. It describes a multitude of natural features he observed as he went along. It says where he stopped each night. He does not always describe exactly which road or track his unit took, although he always makes it clear where he crossed the many rivers in northern France. Certainly he did not follow modern marked footpaths. For the most part he probably strode along minor roads. Sometimes he says he went across the fields, which probably meant he used farm tracks between different areas of crops, through woodland or between hedgerows. I studied the 1:25000 walking maps for his route and picked out a continuous line of tracks and roads which would enable me to see all the settlements and countryside he traversed. I did not know if the way I had chosen would all be open but that added to the sense of adventure. I packed my rucksack which, when full, weighed about thirteen kilos; half the weight of an infantryman in 1914. What I packed was also very different—no long coat or heavy woollen trousers; no tent; no entrenching tools; no cooking pots and certainly not a rifle. My clothes were lightweight and ideal for summer weather. My boots were comfort itself compared with the hob-nailed variety worn one hundred years ago. A sun hat and sun creams also made the weather more bearable than it was for the Tommies and the *poilus*. I had decided to sleep in comfortable beds; not on the ground. When all this planning was done I bought a ticket for the Eurostar and took a train to Namur in Belgium where my discovery of the retreat to the Marne started.

(For further details of the walking route I followed see www. walkingtheretreat1914.com)

1: THE OUTBREAK OF WAR
1-7 AUGUST 1914

Mobilization

At the end of July 1914 André Benoit was on holiday at his parents' home in Charly-sur-Marne, a village overlooked by rows of vines in the Marne valley. He was 25 years old and had just failed the *agrégation*, his mathematics exams at Lille University. No doubt he was wondering what to do next, when the decision was taken out of his hands. He had already done two years' military service ending in September 1913. Starting as a private, he had been promoted to corporal after six months and then immediately transferred to an officer's training course. He passed out eleventh out of a class of fifty-seven and in April 1913 was appointed reserve 2nd lieutenant in the 67th Infantry Regiment based in Soissons. The Army record for 1911 says he was nearly six feet tall, with chestnut hair, blue eyes, and had a scar on his left hand. At 7 pm on Friday 31 July 1914 he received a yellow telegram ordering him to report immediately to his regiment. He quietly got on with his preparations and took a night train, changing at Château-Thierry. On his way he met a lieutenant in the gendarmerie who told him: "I don't know what's going on. All the telegrams have passed through my hands. We have to cover the frontier regions. In a few days, or maybe a few weeks, we will be back in our homes."[1]

The French government announced the mobilization of the Army on 1 August 1914 at 4 pm. Bells sounded from parish churches throughout the country summoning young men to the colours. In France there had been fears that a significant number of men would evade the draft. In fact the figure was 1.5 per cent.[2] After just over a week there were few single men between twenty and forty years of age left in any village in France. The majority of those mobilized were reservists and all had to be clothed, equipped and accommodated; no mean task as 2nd Lieutenant Robert Porchon of the 106th Infantry Regiment based at Châlons-sur-Marne remarked. No wonder he found all the hotels full when he arrived in the town. "At last we found the corner of a stable and three bales of hay," he wrote.[3] Sergeant Albert Omnès of the 47th Infantry Regiment said that, once the bells sounded in St. Malo, there was a real rush to the barracks. Several days of feverish activity followed.[4]

A number of witnesses suggest that the first week of August was a period of heightened emotion in France, Britain and Germany. The atmosphere was febrile; laughter and noisy demonstrations interrupted silence and tears. The emotions unleashed by the declaration of war were powerful but mixed.

André Benoit in the uniform of a Second Lieutenant in the 67th Infantry Regiment. (Courtesy of Dr. Monique Burtin and Mme. Anne Moreau-Vivien)

Sometimes these have been interpreted as evidence of enthusiasm for war but this would be a mistake.

The young educated sons and daughters of the bourgeoisie made noisy demonstrations in Paris and some other large French cities. French soldiers drew cartoons of the Kaiser on the side of their "pleasure trains for Berlin". Some sang popular songs fuelled by alcohol, no doubt partly out of relief that the period of waiting was over. In reality, however, the prevailing mood was more sober. Naturally enough, in days before TV and the internet, many scurried to the local *mairie* for news. Peasants in rural France worried how the harvest would be finished in their absence. Mothers and fathers burst into tears as their sons departed for the front. The prevailing sentiment seems to have been that Germany planned to attack France and had to be resisted. Resolution is perhaps a more appropriate word to describe the emotions of August 1914 than enthusiasm. Brigadier de Gendarmerie Célestin Brothier remarked, "I would not say that the population of Maulevrier [in the Loire valley] has accepted the mobilization with joy, but with a cold resolution, courageously and without any sense of bravado."[5] On 1 August 2nd Lieutenant Robert Deville of the 17th Regiment of Field Artillery met a reservist he knew at the Gare du Nord in the packed crowd trying to get to the trains. His friend said, "As soon as the Germans attack we have to respond with a good heart and not hold back." Deville remarked that this simple message was much more appropriate than the cries of "à Berlin!" shouted by a few red-faced drunkards."[6] Marc Bloch, a sergeant in the 272nd Infantry Regiment and later a great medieval historian and hero of the Resistance, summed up the mood eloquently:

One of the most beautiful memories the war has given me was the sight of Paris during the first days of mobilization. The city was quiet and somewhat solemn. The drop in traffic, the absence of buses, and the shortage of taxis made the streets almost silent. The sadness that was buried in our hearts showed only in the red and swollen eyes of many women. Out of the spectre of war, the nation's armies created a surge of democratic fervour. In Paris there remained only those who were leaving—the nobility—and those who were not leaving, who seemed at that moment to recognize no obligation other than to pamper the soldiers of tomorrow. On the streets, in the stores and streetcars, strangers chatted freely; the unanimous goodwill, though often expressed in naïve and awkward words and gestures, was nonetheless moving. The men for the most part were not hearty; they were resolute, and that was better.[7]

Soissons was a prosperous industrial town on the River Aisne with a famous cathedral, some forty kilometres north of Charly. No doubt André knew it well.

Nowadays the town still bears the scars of being near the front line between 1914 and 1918, when eighty per cent of the buildings were destroyed including much of the great church. The local economy has declined in recent years and unemployment is over twenty per cent. There are some distinctive old buildings left and post-1918 reconstruction projects, like the art deco market hall and war memorials, are not without interest. Yet somehow the life seems to have been knocked out of the place. When he reported for duty to the old Charpentier barracks on 1 August André was told he would be attached to a company working in the depot. We can imagine his crestfallen expression. "Disappointment. What? The war will start without me."

Nevertheless he got on with his administrative duties, issuing military record books, updating the regimental registers and allocating accommodation to the hundreds of new arrivals. Frequently he had to go to the railway station to direct other reservists arriving there. Some of them were drunk and noisy. He tried to look dignified but was conscious of his youthful appearance. One of the old sweats planted himself in front of André and said: "You're not joking, lieutenant, you're already a soldier?" He also had to stand guard at the covered market. All the panels advertising KUB soup cubes had been taken down because, he says with a touch of irony, they might have helped the enemy.[8]

This story about KUB had a more sinister side. Feeling against all things foreign and fear of spies became a positive mania in the newly combatant countries. Célestin Brothier recalled scare stories that German spies were blowing up bridges and railway lines deep inside France. Léon Daudet of the extreme nationalist movement Action Française had accused Maggi of Switzerland, manufacturer of the offending stock cubes, of being a front for a German spy network. Maggi was also a competitor for many smaller French businesses. On 2 August many of Maggi's outlets were pillaged and the police refused to intervene on the grounds that the firm was German.[9]

A few days later André's luck changed. He met a captain in the 267th Reserve Infantry Regiment who was looking for a second lieutenant to join them on active service. André accepted like a shot, particularly as his relationship with his existing captain was becoming difficult.[10]

André was not the only young man looking for adventure that August. Seventeen-year-old Carl Zuckmayer, later a well-known playwright and exile from Germany because of his Jewish ancestry, left school and volunteered for the German Army in 1914:

> Becoming a soldier, serving my year, had always been a threatening and embarrassing idea during my days at the Gymnasium... Now it meant the exact opposite: liberation! Liberation from middle-class narrowness and fussiness, from the necessity to go to school and swot, from the doubts

ARMÉE DE TERRE ET ARMÉE DE MER

ORDRE
DE MOBILISATION GÉNÉRALE

Par décret du Président de la République, la mobilisation des armées de terre et de mer est ordonnée, ainsi que la réquisition des animaux, voitures et harnais nécessaires au complément de ces armées.

Le premier jour de la mobilisation est le *Dimanche Deux Août 1914*

Tout Français soumis aux obligations militaires doit, sous peine d'être puni avec toute la rigueur des lois, obéir aux prescriptions du **FASCICULE DE MOBILISATION** (pages coloriées placées dans son livret).

Sont visés par le présent ordre **TOUS LES HOMMES** non présents sous les Drapeaux et appartenant :

1° à l'**ARMÉE DE TERRE** y compris les **TROUPES COLONIALES** et les hommes des **SERVICES AUXILIAIRES;**

2° à l'**ARMÉE DE MER** y compris les **INSCRITS MARITIMES** et les **ARMURIERS** de la **MARINE.**

Les Autorités civiles et militaires sont responsables de l'exécution du présent décret.

Le Ministre de la Guerre,   *Le Ministre de la Marine*

Proclamation of the French mobilization: the French order was signed on 1 August and therefore the first day of mobilization was 2 August 1914. (Wikimedia Commons)

about choosing a profession and from all the things we perceived—consciously or unconsciously—as the saturation, closeness and rigidity of our world… We shouted out freedom while we were jumping into the straight-jacket of the Prussian uniform.[11]

We should not be deceived, however, by the exalted language of some young Germans who swore allegiance to "our Nation, our Fatherland and God"[12]; nor by the festive atmosphere in the Café Vaterland, a popular meeting place on the Potsdamer Platz in Berlin for those who supported the war.[13] It was not typical of all students let alone the rest of the German population. Such enthusiasm was confined to the towns and was perhaps more obvious in Germany, because it was a more urban country than France. Farmers were worried about the harvest. Some were concerned that their savings would not be safe. There were panics about food supplies. Manual working-class men and women were generally more reticent in their demonstrations of support. The mass of the population courageously accepted the sacrifices ahead, but without great enthusiasm.[14] The so-called "spirit of 1914" was largely a propaganda tool used after the event.[15]

In Germany and Britain young men volunteered to join the Army, although not obliged to do so. Lieutenant Alan Hanbury-Sparrow of the 1st Battalion, Royal Berkshire Regiment, boarded a train at Aldershot, thinking how those who waved goodbye must envy him. "Now we are to find out what war is really like, and now we are to find out if we are really men."[16] In Britain the professional and commercial classes in the towns were much more likely to volunteer than agricultural workers in the countryside. In many European countries the press had a wider circulation among the urban population and the newspapers were generally supportive of the decisions to go to war.

While there is little evidence of real enthusiasm for war, in none of the three countries was there significant opposition among the population as a whole. In both France and Germany the socialists supported the government; a handful of unionists and supporters of the left took the opposite view. A few pacifist groups and a minority of Liberal and Labour supporters in Britain were opposed to war after the decision to intervene had been made. On 4 August President Raymond Poincaré praised the *union sacrée*, the unity of all French men and women, in the National Assembly. For the moment the solidarity of the French, British and German populations seemed likely to last, but for how long? It was perhaps the decision of the French to bury the ideological hatchet in the face of German aggression which was the most remarkable. The rifts between industrialists and unions, between conservatives and radicals, between the Church and the Republic had been healed for the moment. In the first few days of the war there was a definite return to religion with more communicants appearing at mass. Mass also began to be widely celebrated within the French Army.

The soldiers of 1914

Who were these men of 1914? André Benoit's regiment belonged to the French Fifth Army. Its total strength was 290,000 men, 8,800 officers and 108,000 horses. Over 200,000 of these men were in the infantry, but the army also had its own artillery and cavalry units. One whole army corps was detached fairly early on, leaving four army corps and a number of units under the direct control of the commander-in-chief—two divisions of colonial troops from Constantine and Algiers, three Reserve Divisions recruited broadly in the regions around Arras, Rouen and Reims, and the 1st Cavalry Corps which originated from Paris and Picardy. Of the four main corps the 18th came from south-west France with its HQ in Bordeaux and its recruitment area stretching from the foothills of the Pyrenees in the south to La Rochelle in the north. The 1st had its base in Lille and drew its men from Nord-Pas-de-Calais and Arras. The 3rd Corps came from Normandy, around Rouen, Le Havre and Caen, but with a recruitment area stretching up the Seine towards Paris. Lastly the 10th was based in Brittany, but with recruitment spilling over into the Cotentin Peninsula in Normandy. Although most regiments were based in a particular town, usually the prefecture or sub-prefecture of a *département*, they tended to draw their men from a fairly wide area. It was the policy of the Third Republic to integrate the army into the local community and prevent it from becoming a caste apart as it had been before 1870.[17]

These regions had very distinct characters in 1914. It was only in the last thirty years that the majority of their inhabitants had started to speak French instead of their local language or *patois*. Some of those from the south-west would still have spoken Gascon, a branch of the Occitan family of languages spoken in the south. Most of the Bretons came from eastern Brittany where Breton was not used by many, but some would have spoken a *patois* called Gallo. Those from the countryside in the extreme north-west of France would have spoken Flemish. The Catholic Church still catechized quite a few people in Flemish in that region. Even when all these men spoke French they would have spoken with strong regional accents. Jacques Brunel de Pérard was attached to the 43rd Artillery Company (3rd Corps) from Caen. He remarked how much he enjoyed hearing the local *patois* to which he had grown accustomed during holidays in his family's house in Arromanches. "Nos est pis que l'betail, les quiens s'battent itou, mais y ne s'tuent point. M'est avis que c'est pas leur faute à trétous, mais a leu chefs…" (We are worse than cattle. Dogs fight as well but don't kill each other. My opinion is that it is not the fault of our men at all. The leaders are to blame…). These Normans in his battery loved their native land.[18]

The south-west was predominately agricultural with wine being the principal product, except for the ports on the coast of which Bordeaux was the most important. Normandy was dairy country, except for the textile industry around Rouen and ports such as Le Havre. The north-west was of course heavily industrialized with a large coalfield and metallurgical industries. Political and religious traditions varied too, with Brittany, Normandy and rural Flanders being more Catholic and conservative in politics, while the south-west was a stronghold of the radical Republicans and the industrial area of the north had seen the growth of socialist politics. Despite these differences all the soldiers were determined to defend France and their homes. The unity of France in the twentieth century was forged in the crucible of war.

France was not unique in having army units with strong regional affiliations, however. The same point could be made about the British and the Germans. Regimental traditions among the regulars of the smaller British Army were particularly strong. The French Army of 1914 also included colonial troops from North Africa, of whom a significant number were Muslim inhabitants of that region.[19] British Empire troops did not play a significant role until later in the war.

The British Expeditionary Force of 100,000 men was unique in containing a significant proportion of regular soldiers (about forty per cent), but all three armies which fought on the Western Front in 1914 also depended heavily on reservists, meaning men who had once served in the Army, who attended some sort of annual training and who could be recalled when required. Reservists in the British Army would originally have served longer than their French and German counterparts, probably for eight years, but they found coping with long marches and battlefield conditions equally demanding. In addition to 800,000 regular soldiers, most of whom were conscripts, France mobilized reservists from three classes, each having served for two years up to 1911, 1912 and 1913 respectively. The three-year service law was only passed in 1913. A total of 621,000 men joined the regulars and 655,000 went into 25 reserve divisions. To these totals must be added 184,000 territorials. The German Army on both fronts of 2.15 million men contained 1,250,000 reservists. In addition the German High Command could call on one million so-called *ersatz* reserve troops.[20]

The infantrymen in the three armies were expected to carry packs and equipment weighing between 25 and 28 kilos. The German load was the heaviest because they carried more entrenching tools. The French *poilu* had to carry a saucepan, a can for eating, a tent, a rolled up cape, ammunition, a very small spade and a rifle, among other things.[21] Unless these foot soldiers were very fit they struggled to march the fifty kilometres a day often demanded of them. In his blue uniform with red trousers the French *poilu* stood out much more than the Germans dressed in field grey or the British in khaki, and was therefore an easy target for German marksmen. There had been a debate in France before the war about changing uniforms to the duller *horizon bleu* colour used later on. The right-wing press attacked the proposed changes as a betrayal of France's glorious military traditions. The new uniforms for officers would destroy their authority over their men it was said.[22]

What sort of life did these men have?

Life expectancy before the war was 49.4 years for men in France, five per cent higher than in Germany and five per cent lower than in England and Wales. Infant mortality had a huge effect on these figures, because rates of more than 100 babies dying per 1,000 live births were much higher than today. Pre-war England and Wales had a rate of 105, France 120 and Germany 165. The latter figure was partly linked to the fact that breast feeding was far less common in Germany. Mortality was higher among the poor of 1914. Respiratory ailments like tuberculosis and digestive diseases were major killers. Drinking water was still suspect, as the Tommies were told when they went to France. There had been major improvements in housing in cities before the war, with more piped water and mains sewerage. The transmission of disease was much better understood too.[23] However, many of the soldiers would have been used to cramped and dirty living conditions in France, Germany and Britain. Nutrition for ordinary soldiers' families was often poor by today's standards. One hot meal a day was normal, perhaps a soup consisting of vegetables and occasionally a few fragments of meat, probably bacon. A great many soldiers were not fit compared with professionals today. Many of them came from neighbourhoods where violence and drunkenness were common. In all, 9,230 British soldiers were fined for drunkenness between 1912 and 1913.[24] In addition, the working day was generally much longer at over ten hours.

Yet despite these hazards population was growing rapidly in Britain and Germany, but not in France where the birth rate only just exceeded the death rate. This phenomenon meant that France needed to conscript many more of its young men in 1914 than Germany—85 per cent compared to 53 per cent[25]—to produce an army on the Western Front of comparable size. Conscription was a much more universal experience for the French in 1914.

The soldiers reflected the characteristics of the different societies from which they came. Agricultural employment was much more important in 1914 than it is today. But whereas 41 per cent of France's working population was employed in agriculture and 34 per cent of Germany's, the corresponding figure for the UK was only 12 per cent. Some 33 per cent of France's population worked in industry compared with 38 per cent in Germany and 44 per cent in the

UK. Some 54 per cent of these French industrial workers toiled in small firms, not the larger enterprises of the great industrial centres like Rouen, the Pas-de-Calais and Lorraine. Yet the biggest difference between the three countries was in employment in the service sector: UK 44 per cent, France 26 per cent, Germany 28 per cent. Overall the UK was the richest country with a higher standard of living in 1914. Relative wages in real terms were 15 per cent lower in Germany and 28 per cent lower in France. Perhaps this explains why only 10 per cent of British women worked before the war, compared with 40 per cent in France.[26] The smaller firms in which many French workers were employed did not pay as well and the same applied to agriculture. Many of the landless agricultural labourers in France depended on charity.

It is a commonplace that French agriculture in 1914 seemed archaic in many respects. There were still large numbers of peasants on farms of only a few hectares. About 75 per cent of farms were owned by those who worked on them, but they only accounted for 53 per cent of the land area.[27] These small farms were very common in the south. In the north, meanwhile, larger farms produced for the market in the industrial towns and Paris. They had more accumulated capital to make the transition from subsistence agriculture to specialization. Improved transport links aided this process. There was substantial growth in cattle rearing to provide meat for the towns. Incomes in these farms were roughly double what they were elsewhere.

The French countryside in 1914 still had a very substantial population, but it was gradually becoming more dependent on the towns, large and small. Over half the French population lived in towns with fewer than 2,000 inhabitants[28] and many of the "industrial" workers there would have been skilled craftsmen, like André Benoit's father and maternal grandfather in Charly who were both carpenters. Although population was moving to the larger centres in search of jobs in the new industries, 80 per cent stayed within the *département* where they were born.[29] This was certainly true of Benoit's family, some of whom were living in Charly before the French Revolution.[30]

Something like 25 per cent of young men called up in France were deemed unfit for military service, either because of health, size or mental capacity. Between 6 and 10 per cent were exempted on a permanent basis.[31] In the Nord-Pas-de-Calais region the average weight of conscripts before the war was 62 kilos (under 10 stone) and the average height 1.68 metres (5ft 5in.), fairly typical for France as a whole.[32] Average height in Germany and Britain was slightly greater. Two per cent of French conscripts were illiterate in 1914, but a third had a totally inadequate education.[33] Generally illiteracy was more of a problem in rural areas, except for the heavily industrialized areas like the north-west.[34]

A French infantryman in 1914: note his short stature relative to the size of his Lebel rifle which measured just under six feet with a fixed bayonet. (Library of Congress, Washington DC)

Officers and men

In all three armies there was a marked social divide between the officer corps and the common soldiers, which reflected the divisions in society at large, divisions due to relative wealth and access to education, particularly secondary education. But it was even more obvious in Britain and Germany than in France. British officers in 1914 came almost exclusively from the aristocracy and the well-to-do middle class. Private Frank Richards, a reservist in the Second Battalion, Royal Welch Fusiliers, marched into Le Cateau at midnight on 25 August and immediately went with two mates to look for food. They entered a café where officers and men were buying food and drink together. Richards says: "This was the only time during the whole of the War that I saw officers and men buying food and drink in the same café."[35] Church of England chaplains in the British Army tended to be identified with the ruling classes to which they personally belonged unlike their Roman Catholic counterparts. In France, unlike in Britain, priests were conscripted like everyone else and perhaps they were closer to the ordinary soldier as a result. By 1916 the social exclusivity of the British officer class started to break down in the new mass army in which fifty per cent of officers were promoted from the ranks.

Traditionally the German officer corps was drawn from the aristocracy. As the army expanded Kaiser Wilhelm II's government made it possible for educated members of the middle classes to become officers, but they were expected to toe the government line politically and prove themselves reliable.[36] In France too the bulk of the officer corps (about 55 per cent) came from the aristocracy and the wealthy bourgeoisie, being trained either at the famous military academy at St. Cyr or the École Polytechnique for engineers. Before the war, however, the remainder of the officers came from the ranks, having either passed through a military college called St. Maixent for NCOs (35 per cent) or been promoted directly.[37] A higher proportion of junior officers came from the ranks. For example, in the 5th Division sixty per cent of lieutenants were commissioned by this route.[38]

There was no doubt that the British and German officer corps were better trained and enjoyed greater prestige than those in France. The radical Republicans, who ran most French governments in the generation before the war, were suspicious of army officers, traditionally Catholic and conservative and potentially a threat to Republican values. In effect the politicians conducted a campaign against them, inflicting several petty humiliations which reduced the number of recruits and their intellectual quality. In the aftermath of the Army's false conviction of Alfred Dreyfus for spying, the government was determined to control the officer corps and ensure it did not interfere in politics. Army officers were not well paid[39] and their pensions were less generous than those of other public servants. To keep their jobs they needed to avoid making political enemies. As a result of this pressure Roman Catholic families were less willing to send their sons to St. Cyr and the number of entrants dropped by a half between 1897 and 1907. In 1903 the Army was 13,000 officers short.[40] In the 5th Division there was a huge deficit in the number of lieutenants required.[41] The problem was also acute among the reserves where there was a serious shortage of competent captains and lieutenants. The German reserve units were much better led.

NCOs

The French Army also suffered from an acute shortage of non-commisssioned officers. It had less than half the number serving in Germany, both in the regular army and the reserves.[42] Compared with Germany there were also far fewer civilians doing non-combatant jobs. French NCOs had a very poor reputation, often considered ignorant brutes with limited skills. Like the officers, French NCOs suffered poor pay and pensions. In Germany and Britain a soldier could enjoy a satisfactory career as an NCO, even if it was impossible to enter the officer corps. In Britain soldiers might be promoted up to corporal during their first eight-year enlistment and even to sergeant if they stayed on for a further period. In France talented NCOs were promoted to be junior officers. The Germans had the best complement of NCOs, who did many of the jobs carried out by officers in the other two armies. They provided the competent leadership at platoon level which was lacking in France.[43]

Infantry training

It is also clear that the French infantry were not as well trained as their German and British counterparts. Most of them had no experience of firepower and lacked the know-how to cope with it. They were amateurs in comparison. There were insufficient training camps and the first year of a conscript's life in barracks was occupied with square bashing and menial duties. Those who joined the Army in 1913 had to face the Germans with almost no combat training at all. Only one-third of the active Army attended a training camp in any one year. Training of reserves was also poor. In 1908 the National Assembly cut the number of reservist training days from 69 to 49.[44] Many reservists did not turn up for what training there was. Forty per cent of reservists had received no training at all and were totally unfit. Because of their better training the German reserves could make a front line contribution from day one, something beyond most of their French counterparts. Reports on annual manoeuvres were highly critical.

For example, in September 1913 General Galliéni noted hopeless attacks on prepared positions. Cooperation between infantry and artillery was poor.[45]

The impact of artillery and machine guns

This lack of training was particularly critical because of the firepower of modern weapons. In 1914 French soldiers faced a German Army which had much more heavy artillery and regarded it as a strategic asset. The French saw their artillery mainly as a flexible mobile support to attacking infantry. The French 75 mm rapid firing field gun was the best among the three armies on the Western Front and the French army had plenty of them. Dubbed "black butchers" by the Germans, they showered troops with shrapnel. German 105 and 150 howitzers were able to inflict severe casualties on French infantry, however, and because of their superior range the French found it difficult to take counter-measures. Many of the French soldiers remarked in their diaries that their comrades were often killed by guns that they could not see, by German heavy weapons well dug in and concealed on reverse slopes. In addition they knew that if a German plane appeared overhead, a not infrequent occurrence, then shells would surely follow. At least in 1914 the French had almost as many planes for reconnaissance as the Germans, around one hundred and fifty. The British added thirty to the Allied strength. In the war of movement these planes played a vital role.[46]

The Germans had more machine guns than either the British or French Armies at the beginning of the war. Each German infantry regiment of three battalions had three machine gun companies with six guns each; therefore six guns per battalion. They were concentrated in these specialist units for maximum fire power. The British started the war with two machine guns in each battalion, a third as many as the Germans. In the French Army the ratio of machine guns per battalion was around 1:3 at the outset of hostilities, but this weapon was controlled at divisional level

French infantry tactics

There has been much discussion of the doctrine of the offensive in France and much misunderstanding. It was long said that the French Army believed attacking infantry with sufficient determination would carry all before it. It was a question of morale and will power. Colonel de Grandmaison and Ferdinand Foch taught this doctrine at the École de Guerre. The image of the French infantry in red trousers advancing towards German machine guns, with fixed bayonets and bugles playing, appears in many popular histories.

The reality is more complex. Foch, for example, understood perfectly well that courage without preparation and skill was useless. Cooperation between infantry and artillery was essential. Faced with superior German heavy artillery and machine guns the French infantry proved unwilling to dig into the ground to avoid the worst effects of enemy fire. In attack it should have worked forward in dispersed formations, making use of features in the landscape, before concentrating its firepower to deliver a final assault. This implied a level of skill and experience of close cooperation between different arms which many French units did not possess. No one doubted the French soldiers' willingness to use their bayonets, but they rarely got close enough to the Germans to do so. In the opening battles infantry made mass attacks against prepared positions with dreadful consequences, not because they believed they would work, but because officers and men did not have the training and experience to do anything else. At a strategic level Joffre had decided to take the war to Germany rather than adopt a defensive posture. Given the level of training of his troops this was unwise.

In the end the Radical Republic got the army it deserved, but the *poilus* paid the price in the opening two months of the war when over 400,000 soldiers were lost, some through ignorance and fear. It was not a theoretical belief in attack with the bayonet whatever the circumstances that led to this carnage, but lack of training, lack of firepower, lack of enough NCOs and junior officers and unwillingness to dig in. It is also worth remembering that the German Army not infrequently attacked in massed formations with similar consequences.

Why did they go to war?

As several million young men headed for the frontiers of their countries it is also worth asking what they thought they were fighting for. What was at the bottom of this conflict of which no one predicted the catastrophic consequences for Europe and the world? The debate on the origins of the Great War and the fruitless search for who was to blame rages on one hundred years later. Libraries are full of books on the subject and still they keep coming. It would not be appropriate here to examine in detail the events leading up to the war. For those who want to know more I have recommended three particular recent books.[47]

The theme of this book is the experience of soldiers in the first weeks of fighting on the Western Front. The negotiations of diplomats sometimes seem to have taken place in a different world from that of the troops whose fate they determined. Yet it is not right to see diplomacy operating in isolation. Foreign policy was subject to many influences and there was a public debate in the press and elsewhere about foreign affairs. No doubt this debate informed the opinions of the soldiers of 1914 and to some extent influced their morale.

The military were not a caste apart with an entirely different mindset. To a greater or lesser degree they reflected the views of the social background from which they came. Some officers in the French, British and German Armies at the beginning of the war were career soldiers, although many were reservists called back from civilian occupations. As we have seen, they came on the whole from a different social class from the men under their command. No doubt their higher levels of education enabled them to understand some of the issues behind the conflict. The ordinary soldiers in the French and German Armies were all conscripts and represented a cross section of the population in all its diversity. Those in the British Army were a mixture of long service soldiers and reservists. Whatever the personal history of all these men they were more open to the influences of the civilian world than the standing armies of previous generations. Age no doubt influenced the views of those who had served for a long time. Many in the British and French Armies but also in the German had seen action in colonial wars. Several senior officers in their sixties in the French and German Armies had fought each other as young men in the Franco-Prussian war of 1870.

Here it is only possible to offer an outline of the main issues which would have framed their thinking. In a sense, the answer to the question of what the soldiers thought is straightforward. Of those few who published diaries few commented on the origins of conflict in any depth. They felt their country was threatened, they had been given orders to join their regiments and there did not seem to be any alternative. Some refused to fight, either out of fear, resistance to government diktats or conscience, but very few. There was almost no support for left-wing militants within the French Army as some had feared. No doubt the vast majority of troops in each army felt right was on their side. They were stoical, determined to defend their homes and not to let their comrades down. Whether citizens of the Republic, servants of the King or soldiers of the Kaiser and the Fatherland, troops marched to the front out of a sense of duty, with regret but determination. Most believed they would be home victorious by Christmas; a few disagreed.

French hostility towards Germany

In France, however, many felt a deep-seated hostility to the new Germany. To understand this we have to go back to the Franco-Prussian war of 1870 which produced a shift in the balance of power in Europe. Historically France was the oldest and most powerful nation state on the continent, which it dominated briefly under Napoleon. After his fall it was the rogue state which had to be watched and contained by Britain, Prussia, Austria and Russia. In the mid-century new nationalist movements threatened the stability of the old order. Italy was unified by 1870 but the greatest threat to the balance of power came from Prussia. Rapid industrialization and population growth meant that this kingdom, which originated on the eastern marches of Germany, was the dominant player in Central Europe by the 1860s. Its position was confirmed when it defeated the Austrian Empire in a brief war in 1866. Prussia's Iron Chancellor Otto von Bismarck provoked France into a foolish declaration of war in 1870 over a dispute about the future of the Spanish monarchy.

Many in France thought they would teach the upstart Prussians a lesson. In fact the much better-equipped and organized Prussian Army rapidly invaded France, where their opponent's mobilization was a shambles. Two of France's armies were surrounded at Metz and Sedan and forced to surrender. The Emperor Napoleon III was taken prisoner, never to return to France again. Although new forces were raised to confront the invader their resistance was over by the end of the winter and Paris was surrounded. The King of Prussia was proclaimed as German Emperor in the Galerie des Glaces at Versailles. In the end the French government was forced to sign a humiliating treaty which included a huge war indemnity and the cession of Alsace and eastern Lorraine to the new Germany. It was the end of an era. The main question for European diplomats was no longer how to restrain France from further adventures but how to cope with the reality of German power.

The outcome of the Franco-Prussian war left a legacy of bitterness in France, fuelled by the loss of the two provinces. Gambetta, the leader who rallied France to further resistance in 1870, famously said that the French must not speak about Alsace but must, on the other hand, never forget it. The novels of Erckmann-Chartrian, the drawings of Hansi and many other artistic and literary productions kept alive sympathy for Alsace-Lorraine among the middle classes. Children were taught about the injustice of the German occupation of the lost provinces. The statue of Strasbourg in the Place de la Concorde in Paris was draped in black from 1871 to 1918.

The nationalist revival in France

A more aggressive French nationalism developed in the late nineteenth century, based on the cult of those who had spilt their blood for France over the centuries. We see it in the writings of Maurice Barrès and the growth of the extreme right-wing Action Française movement led by Charles Maurras. It provided a fertile breeding ground for anti-Semitism and the fear of German spies which culminated in the false imprisonment of the Jewish army officer Alfred Dreyfus. Some of the war diaries which I will examine contain references to German barbarians who behaved like beasts. André Benoit was born in 1888. He would have grown up aware of this resentment against Germany.

We can see this more aggressive nationalistic attitude manifesting itself politically during the second Moroccan crisis of 1911. To some extent France had sublimated its resentment against Germany by seeking a new empire overseas in Africa and Asia. The bargain underlying the Entente Cordiale of

1904 between France and Britain was that Britain would have a free hand in Egypt in return for France being able to pursue its own designs on Morocco. In a previous crisis in 1905 France wanted to control the Moroccan army and police. Germany opposed this but France got its way, supported by Britain and Russia. In April 1911 the French sent a large force to the sultanate and the Germans responded by despatching an aged gunboat to Agadir. During this crisis it seemed that the opposing parties were willing to contemplate all-out war. Part of the blame lies with the hawks in the French Foreign Office. Fortunately the French Ambassador in Berlin, Jules Cambon, appealed to Joseph Caillaux, the French Prime Minister, who opened a back channel to the German government. The crisis was settled when Germany acquiesced in a French Protectorate of Morocco in return for proper protection for German business interests and a portion of territory in the French Congo. Subsequently Caillaux's back stairs dealing became public knowledge. He was criticized for giving too much away and was forced to resign.

French policy continued in this vein with the arrival in office of Raymond Poincaré as both Prime Minister and Foreign Secretary in January 1912. Subsequently he was elected President in 1913, a position which he held until 1920. Normally the President of the Third Republic was a figurehead but Poincaré stretched the constitutional authority of his office in the realm of foreign affairs to the limit. In effect he directed policy by direct contacts with officials and by ensuring that weak men unlikely to oppose his wishes were appointed as Foreign Secretary. Poincaré was one of the Lorrainers, a leader of the nationalist current which grew more influential in intellectual and government circles in France in the last few years before the war, although not widely supported by the general population. He was brought up in Bar-Le-Duc, a small town in Lorraine, and as a boy of eleven he remembered the Prussian occupation of his town. He was willing to deal with the Germans but believed they were all bullies. This perception was reinforced for Poincaré and his supporters by German oppression of the Alsatians. For example, in October 1913, a German officer in Saverne made insulting remarks about Alsatians. Some Alsatians staged a protest and were arbitrarily locked up by the German Army. In 1913 the future of Alsace-Lorraine remained as divisive an issue between France and Germany as it had been in 1870. While the two countries might reach a diplomatic understanding over a particular issue they could not build a long-term relationship because that would have required France to accept the loss of Alsace-Lorraine permanently; something it was not prepared to do. Few of the French soldiers of 1914 were interested in the more exalted nationalist ideas promoted by Parisian politicians and intellectuals. Most of them knew nothing about the sufferings of Alsace-Lorraine. Yet the bitterness and suspicion of Germany remained. It would come to the surface when the war started.

The Franco-Russian alliance and its consequences

To escape from the diplomatic isolation of 1870, when France faced Prussia alone, the French government opened discussions with Russia and by 1894 had signed a full defensive alliance which formed a cornerstone of French foreign policy up to the Great War. The inheritors of the legacy of the French Revolution had teamed up with the autocrat of all the Russias. The alliance was confirmed when Tsar Nicholas II made a very successful state visit to Paris. Over the years which followed France underwrote Russian industrialization and the re-equipment of its armed forces with massive loans. By 1914 roughly a quarter of all foreign investment in Russia came from France. There was considerable awareness within France of the importance of the Russian alliance for national security. France had a smaller population than Germany and it was growing more slowly. If it was to survive another war it needed a continental partner with a large army.

One might question, however, whether all those who applauded the Tsar on his state visit understood the implications of the commitments being made on their behalf. Between 1908 and 1914 Russian policy was consistent in supporting South Slav aspirations for freedom from Ottoman rule in the Balkans. By July 1914 it was prepared to mobilize its forces to protect Serbia from Austrian aggression following the assassination of the Archduke Franz Ferdinand on 28 June. The Franco-Russian alliance treaty was ambiguous about whether France would have to go to war to support this aggressive Russian policy. Poincaré made it clear that France would support Russia even at the risk of war. After 1912 consultations between the Russian and French General Staffs were frequent. The French were constantly pressing the Russians to launch an immediate attack on Germany in the event of war. Their intelligence already told them that Germany planned a lightning strike in the west before turning on Russia and they wanted support in this eventuality. The French were financing the construction of railways in western Russia to transport Russian soldiers to the front.

Given the constantly shifting allegiances of the Third Republic, however, Poincaré could not count on support for his policy lasting for ever. In 1913 he had secured the passing of a military law which extended national service from two years to three. Germany also increased army numbers with its own bill in 1913. But the French three-year service law was not popular and only just survived in the National Assembly in the following year. There were those, like the great socialist leader Jean Jaurès, who were opposed to Poincaré's policy. "Are we going to unleash a world war," Jaurès asked French journalists on the eve of the Great War, "because Izvolsky [Russian Foreign Minister] is still furious over Aehrenthal's [Austrian Foreign Minister] deception on the Bosnian affair?"[48]

Franco-Russian musical box of 1897 commemorating the Franco-Russian Alliance and featuring Tsar Nicholas II and the French President Félix Faure. It plays the *Marseillaise* and the Russian national anthem. (Historial de la Grande Guerre - Péronne (Somme) et © Yazid Medmoun)

The assassination of the Archduke and the crisis which followed in a sense solved the problem for Poincaré of how to continue with his tougher policy towards Germany. He was not interested in whether Serbia was complicit in the assassination, as Austria-Hungary alleged. While Germany was supporting Austrian demands for action Poincaré went ahead with a pre-planned state visit to St. Petersburg on 20 July. He openly expressed solidarity with his Russian allies and warned the Austrian Ambassador that Serbia had friends. He left on 24 July and immediately afterwards Russia started partial mobilization of its forces. Back in France on 28 July he was convinced that war could not be avoided. Russia mobilized fully on 30 July and from that crucial step everything else followed.

German self-confidence

So this is how the world might have looked to the French soldiers of 1914: suspicion of Germany, support for the Russian alliance and pride in the new French empire. What were the pre-occupations of their German opponents? No doubt there was pride in the pre-eminent position that the new united Germany occupied in Europe after 1870. A country long divided was now a Great Power. There was a feeling that the remarkable economic growth of Germany and its achievements in industry, science and the arts should be respected and given due recognition. Middle-class nationalist opinion, expressed for example through the National Liberals in the Reichstag, had an impact on government policy. The acquisition of colonies--Weltpolitik as it was sometimes called—was popular and in the mind of nationalist Germans Britain was the main opponent. They openly criticized British oppression of the Boers while seeking to build up Germany's African empire. Whether it was a question of the partition of Africa or competition for influence in China, Germany wanted a place at the table. It was also this current of opinion which supported Admiral Tirpitz's programme to create a sizeable German fleet of battleships and heavy cruisers, started in 1898. The Navy League channelled this enthusiasm among the wider German public and helped Tirpitz secure the necessary backing among governing circles.

German insecurity and isolation

Mixed up with this new self-confidence was a strain of insecurity in German thinking about its place in the world. Germany was the country in the middle of Europe threatened by states on its eastern and western borders. Bismarck dealt with this problem by creating a set of alliances and understandings which continued to isolate France. Germany became the arbiter of European disputes and in a sense punched below its weight to make its new strength more acceptable to its neighbours. The key planks of Bismarck's diplomacy were the Triple Alliance of Germany, Austria-Hungary and Italy and the defensive Reinsurance treaty with Russia. He also cooperated with Britain in settling international questions—for example at the Congress of Berlin in 1878 after the war between the Ottoman Empire and Russia. Bismarck's leadership among European leaders came to an end in 1890 when he was dismissed by the new Kaiser Wilhelm II.

One of the first decisions of the new Chancellor Leo von Caprivi was to allow the defensive treaty with Russia to lapse. The mood among the new leaders in Germany was to create freedom of action on the world stage and not to be bound by the web of undertakings negotiated by the old Chancellor which sometimes seemed so baffling that only he could hold them together. Why should Germany, it was asked, protect Russia from Austria and vice-versa? Germany in effect had decided to go it alone. Yet this new found freedom created fresh difficulties. German attempts to demand more respect for its interests led to hostility from other powers, which was eventually its undoing.

The Franco-Russian entente originally held together because both parties frequently found themselves opposed to British imperial policy, rather than because of concern about Germany. The Entente Cordiale and the Anglo-Russian Convention of 1907 were a further means of adjusting imperial interests rather than specifically anti-German measures. However, this Triple Entente gradually became a channel for responding to concerns about German policy and initiatives. Germany's dash for diplomatic freedom from Bismarck's alliances was leaving it increasingly isolated. It might wish to be at the centre of every European discussion but its neighbours saw its foreign policy as increasingly erratic. The Kaiser blew hot and cold; one minute bullying, the next conciliatory. It was difficult to know who was in charge in Berlin. Individual ministers were appointed by and reported to the Kaiser; there was no cabinet to coordinate government policy. The military reported direct to the Kaiser and were not subject to control by the Reichstag. They followed their own policy. There were continual clashes between the Reichstag and the government.

Germany tried to break out of its diplomatic isolation several times and failed. Conversations between Britain and Germany in 1898 foundered on Germany's reluctance to oppose Russian penetration of Manchuria. Germany tried to break the solidity of the Triple Entente in the first Moroccan crisis of 1905. It then negotiated an understanding with France, envisaging an exchange of territories in the Congo and Cameroon. When this did not last Germany resorted to some gunboat diplomacy in the second Moroccan crisis of 1911, again without success. The royal cousins, the Tsar and the Kaiser, talked together at the Baltic port of Paldiski in 1912 but with no lasting results. That year Haldane, the British Minister of War, met the Germans in Berlin to talk about Germany's naval expansion but no understanding resulted. When Britain was pulling ahead in the naval race the Germans asked for too high a price to cut their programme back, viz. British neutrality in a continental war. The Triple Entente designed to ensure the security of France, Britain and Russia was gradually making Germany feel more insecure.

As the series of Balkan crises became more intense between 1912 and 1914 Germany found itself with only one effective ally, Austria-Hungary. It was tied to a power faced by existential threats from new national movements in Eastern Europe. Faced with the Austrian request for help following the assassination of 28 June Germany decided to test Russian resolve by telling Austria to settle the Serb question once and for all—the so-called "blank cheque". Policy makers in Berlin came to believe that a war in 1914, rather than later, might be to Germany's advantage. By 1917 Russia would have finished its re-armament and built more railways to its western borders. By then France might have remedied its lack of heavy artillery. In three years' time Austria-Hungary might have started to collapse under the weight of competing national aspirations—Czech, Slovak, Hungarian, South Slav and German.

The rush to strike the first blow

Facing enemies to east and west, Germany wanted to get its blows in first. The German military and the Chancellor overrode the Kaiser's desire to pursue British proposals for mediation. German declared war on Russia when the latter refused to cancel its mobilization. Germany also started to move its own troops to the frontiers. The mobilization plans were designed to put the country on a full war footing smoothly and quickly. They were the fruits of a huge bureaucratic exercise. Once the process had started it was difficult to cancel. Germany also demanded that France surrender two key fortresses in eastern France—Toul and Verdun—if it wanted to stay out of a European war. France refused and started its mobilization on 1 August. Germany declared war on France.

The rigidity of German military planning was the final nail in the coffin of peace. Germany issued an ultimatum to Belgium on 2 August to allow the passage of German troops through its territory or it would be considered an enemy. The Belgians were only given twelve hours to reply. Belgium's decision to resist was greatly admired and Germany's bullying widely condemned abroad. Germany's action endowed the Entente with an aura of moral superiority which its own actions so far had not justified. If German forces had simply entered Belgium unannounced the reaction might not have been so fierce. German troops crossed the frontier on 3 August. If Germany had waited for the full concentration of its forces before doing so it would have been more difficult for Grey, the British Foreign Secretary, to make the arguments for intervention. As a footnote it is worth mentioning that Germany's Triple Alliance partner Italy decided to remain neutral, eventually coming in on the Allied side in 1915.

British imperial concerns and their consequences

It is possible, then, to imagine what German soldiers felt as they marched towards Belgium in August 1914: demand for respect, belief in German superiority, but fear for the future and a feeling that their country was under threat on all sides. What of Britain? Until the very end of the nineteenth century it had pursued a policy of splendid isolation. Free of continental entanglements Britain could expand its international trade and defend the empire which grew in the wake of commerce. What dragged it back to more active involvement in European power politics was concern for the future of that empire. Britain had had to face down French attempts to gain a foothold on the Nile at Fashoda in 1898. It was losing market share to German manufactures and saw Germany as a major commercial competitor. The British government was also concerned by growing German colonial possessions in Africa and by that country's interference in relations with China. This concern came to a head during the Boer War of 1899-1902 when Germany's sympathies were clearly with the Boers. Of most direct concern to the British, however, was the expansion of the Russian empire. This was the era of the Great Game, the period of covert conflict all the way from the eastern Mediterranean through Central Asia to Manchuria. Preserving imperial peace was the main motive behind the Entente Cordiale of 1904 with France as well as the Convention with Russia in 1907, which dealt with a number of potential flash-points from the Ottoman Empire through Persia and Afghanistan to Tibet and the Far East. Unfortunately, to maintain these understandings, Britain inevitably became dragged into purely continental affairs. When Lloyd George went to see the Liberal elder statesman Lord Rosebery after the conclusion of the Entente Cordiale between Britain and France, he professed himself pleased that quarrels with France had ceased. Lord Rosebery replied, "You are all wrong. It means war with Germany in the end!"[49] His fears may have been exaggerated but he was right to warn of the danger.

The Entente Cordiale was not a defensive alliance. Rather it was an agreement to cooperate, to consult. Yet in the course of the years which followed the French and the British developed the habit of discussing with each other any important issues which arose for either side. Friendships were formed and a degree of trust developed. Conversations took place between military and naval chiefs in response to perceived threats to both parties. After the Anglo-Russian Convention of 1907 military and naval talks followed between Britain and Russia.

Germany and the balance of power in Europe

As the twentieth century dawned, concern about German policy became important in British official thinking alongside the emphasis on imperial interests. Admiral Tirpitz's programme to create a powerful German fleet was worrying. For Britain a large German fleet in the North Sea was potentially a serious threat. Britain imported much of its food; the North Sea and the Atlantic sea lanes were its lifelines. It seems that Tirpitz miscalculated. The British responded by outbuilding the Germans to maintain their superiority over any other two powers combined: the so-called two power standard. Public opinion and the newspapers supported this response. By 1912 the British knew they were comfortably ahead in the naval race. Yet there is no doubt that the German programme soured the attitude of the Foreign Office and public opinion towards Germany. Hostility to Germany, its bullying and bluster, became part of the official attitude. Gradually the idea that Germany was a threat to the balance of power in Europe took hold.

Grey's balancing act

These twin concerns for the security of the empire and the balance of power in Europe guided British actions during the Balkan wars of 1912-13, as the Ottoman Empire in Europe entered the last phase of its collapse. What direct interest did Britain have in the Balkans? Why support Russia in its desire to emancipate the South Slavs? Sir Edward Grey seems to have taken the view that opposing Russia in the Balkans might drive her into Germany's arms. He accepted the possibility of a Balkan trigger for Britain's military involvement on the continent. During the final crisis in July 1914 Grey was as worried initially about Russian expansion as he was about Germany. He felt that the best way to contain Russia was by maintaining the framework of the Triple Entente, hence his reluctance to question the Russian version of events in Sarajevo. If Britain stayed out of the Great War, he thought, a victory for either side could be disastrous for the security of the British Empire.

To pursue his policy Grey had to balance the anti-interventionist views of many of his Liberal colleagues with the informal promises he had made to his Entente partners. In public he maintained that he had made no binding commitments, which was technically true. In private he consulted closely with France and sanctioned joint military plans which contained morally binding commitments. On 24 July when the British Cabinet discussed the crisis in the Balkans for the first time public opinion and parliament were not pressing for intervention. The majority of the Cabinet were against it. They approved Grey's proposal for the four powers not directly involved (Britain, France, Germany and Italy) to mediate in the dispute between Austria-Hungary and Serbia.

Belgian neutrality

The sequence of events which led to war finished in London. Grey had implied that Britain could enter the war if France and Germany were in conflict. Yet a majority of the Cabinet were opposed to intervention when they met on 29 July. They discussed the neutrality of Belgium and decided it should be protected by all the signatories of the treaty of 1839 and not by Britain alone. Some thought that if Germany only advanced through the south-east corner of Belgium, this would not be a *casus belli*. It was agreed, however, that the fleet should be put on a war footing. The days which followed caused the French Ambassador to Britain, Paul Cambon, more than a little anxiety as Grey sought to balance his own interventionist position with the views of his colleagues. On 1 August Cambon was distraught when he believed Britain would leave France in the lurch. He pointed out that, in accordance with their joint naval plans, France had sent its Atlantic fleet to the Mediterranean. If Britain did not join them in opposing Germany then the French coastline would be exposed to German naval attack.

The Conservative opposition now made it clear that it would support decisive action by Britain. On 2 August the Cabinet finally came down on the side of intervention if certain circumstances occurred—either a German bombardment of the French coast or a substantial violation of Belgian neutrality. A factor which swayed the Cabinet was the fear that, if this proposal was not approved, Grey and Prime Minister Herbert Asquith would resign and the Liberal government might break up in disarray. David Lloyd George had been the leader of the non-intervention majority and his personal decision to support an ultimatum to Germany carried considerable weight. Lloyd George also had some sympathy for a small country like Serbia being bullied by its larger neighbours.

It was the brutality of Germany's twelve-hour ultimatum for free passage for German troops through Belgium which forced Britain to act. On 4 August the British Cabinet learnt that the German Army had crossed the Belgian frontier. The Cabinet issued its ultimatum to Germany to withdraw from Belgian territory immediately. When no reply was received by the deadline of 11 pm on 4 August Britain declared war on Germany.

None of the men who went to war in 1914 had any idea of the horrors they would unleash. The fire power of modern weapons was unknown to all but a few, unlike today. Few of those men could imagine the impact of industrialized warfare on the peoples and nations of Europe.

2: THE BATTLE OF THE FRONTIERS
8-23 AUGUST 1914

War plans

The scale of the movement of men and *matériel* was unprecedented. The mobilized strengths of France and Germany were roughly equivalent at four million men each. In the west and excluding men left at the depots 1,108 French battalions faced 1,077 German. Discussions between the French and British General Staffs envisaged the British Army taking up a position on the left of the French line opposite the Belgian frontier. Accordingly the British Cabinet authorized the despatch of a British Expeditionary Force to France. This added 48 battalions to the Allied strength at the outset of the war and more arrived later. Once Germany had invaded Belgium the Belgian Army cooperated with the Allies and this added 120 battalions to the total opposing Germany in the west.[1]

The General Staffs moved their armies forward according to their preconceived war plans. The Germans had long planned for a war on two fronts against France and possibly Britain in the west and Russia in the east. They had also decided that the best strategy was to attack France first before dealing with Russia. Russia, they assumed, would be slower to mobilize and therefore posed a less immediate threat. The plan was developed by the Chief of General Staff Count Alfred von Schlieffen who was in post between 1891 and 1906, but subsequently modified by von Moltke who commanded the German Armies in 1914. The Schlieffen Plan aimed to destroy the French Army and force its surrender within forty days by repeating the encirclement of the French Armies of 1870 on a grander scale.

The main feature of the plan was the creation of a right wing much more powerful than the centre and left. This right wing would swing through neutral Belgium and west of Paris, eventually trapping the French against the German left wing in Lorraine. In their thinking the Germans drew parallels with Hannibal's legendary victory at Cannae, when he crushed the Roman legions between the two powerful wings of his army. Von Schlieffen's valedictory advice was to keep the right wing strong with the last German soldier brushing the Channel with his sleeve. The violation of Belgian neutrality was essential to create enough space for the huge German Army to advance.

Von Moltke, nephew of the victor in 1870, made two important modifications to the plan. Firstly, he decided not to move any German troops through southern Holland near Maastricht as originally envisaged. He thought it advantageous to keep Holland out of the conflict. This meant that many German troops would have to funnel through a nine-kilometre gap around Liège. Capturing the ring of forts around that city quickly was essential in order to meet the forty-day timetable for victory. Secondly, von Moltke planned for more powerful forces in Lorraine than von Schlieffen. This was believed by some to weaken the Schlieffen plan fatally.

Seven German Armies concentrated on their country's western frontier, from Belgium to the south of Alsace. The First, Second and Third Armies were to swing through Belgium and the Fourth and Fifth through Luxembourg, while the remainder concentrated on France's eastern frontier.

The French war plans went through a number of modifications in the years before the war. The latest version, known as Plan XVII, was drawn up by Joffre after his appointment as Chief of Staff in 1911. Identified with the supposed doctrine of *attaque à outrance*, attack to the limit, it was much criticized after 1914 because of the disastrous losses the French Army sustained in the Battle of the Frontiers between 20 and 23 August. In fact, Plan XVII was not a plan of attack but a plan for mobilization and concentration of the French Armies. Joffre made it clear that he intended to go into battle with all his forces and wanted to take the initiative from the start, but that he could not decide on the details of an offensive a long time in advance.[2]

Five French Armies plus various detachments were to cover the Ardennes, Lorraine and Alsace. The Fifth French Army on the left was positioned to counter a German thrust east of the Meuse. The 100,000-strong British Expeditionary Force would operate on the left flank of the Fifth Army. A previous Chief of Staff had considered a plan to advance into Belgium to face the Germans, but this had been discarded to avoid British opposition. Why did the French leave Belgium unprotected at the outset of war, and more than this allow most of their northern frontier to remain uncovered? In the General Staff's view the Germans would not have sufficient troops to undertake a wider swing through central Belgium. This judgement resulted from an assumption that they would not use their reserve divisions in the front line at the start of the war. The French generals had a very low opinion of their own reserves and assumed the German equivalents were equally badly trained and led. As we will see this judgement was wide of the mark.[3]

The concentration of both armies was completed by 18 August, although this time the French mobilization proceeded as flawlessly as the German. Only twenty trains were late out of a total of 4,278 used.[4]

The march to the frontiers

The Belgian Army actively opposed German forces as they crossed the frontier

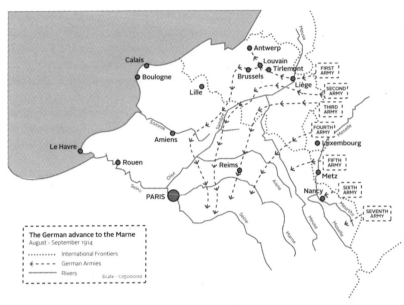

The German advance to the Marne
August - September 1914

.... International Frontiers
← - - - -   German Armies
─────── Rivers   Scale - 1:2500000

on 4 August. The Germans found it more difficult than expected to reduce the massive forts around Liège. They had to bring up their 420 mm cannon known as Big Bertha to finish the job. Now two days behind schedule the First and Second German Armies poured across Belgium.

*

Ignorant of all this, André Benoit marched off from Soissons with the rest of his company on 11 August. Most of the troops were sent in trains to reach the frontiers, but evidently the General Staff felt these reservists could proceed at a more leisurely pace. By 19 August they had covered about eighty kilometres to reach the country near Vervins. André noted that the men lacked discipline and some of them could not keep up on the open road. Two days of exercises and another two days' rest without marching followed, during which André had time to do his washing, play bridge, eat a good dinner and do a spot of guard duty. His friend Lieutenant Armand Lefebvre accompanied him to mass. On 18 August Lefebvre organized a special dinner for his own birthday, which included champagne, chicken, rabbit, fillet of beef and fine wines offered by the local notary. The meal was rounded off with a bottle of Pernod from which the cook had already taken several swigs. André was responsible for distributing raw meat to the men for them to cook on their fires. Some always complained they had too much fat or bone.[5]

Meanwhile his comrades in the British Expeditionary Force were arriving in France, crossing the Channel from Southampton to Le Havre. The peak time for crossing was between 15 and 17 August. After settling in camps around the town, the Tommies took the trains via Rouen and Amiens towards the Belgian frontier. All of them noted the friendliness of the locals who showered them with flowers, cigarettes and chocolate. Frank Richards mentioned the availability of "fillies and booze" in Rouen.

> On arrival at a new station we pre-War soldiers always made enquiries as to what sort of place it was for booze and fillies. If both were in abundance it was a glorious place from our point of view. We soon found out that we had nothing to grumble about as regards Rouen. Each man had been issued with a pamphlet signed by Lord Kitchener warning him about the dangers of French wine and women; they may as well have not been issued for all the notice we took of them.[6]

The first days of the war had an air of unreality, like the phoney war of 1939-40. Brunel de Pérard recalls the evening of a very hot day at Raillicourt on 10 August: "It's evening and the atmosphere is cool and peaceful. Resting on my back, I see above me a deep blue sky, streaked with wisps of white wool. I cannot imagine that I am going to run any kind of danger. That sky promises a world beyond, a future. It seems as if this war is the subject of the last class at my lycée, at my university, in books, in life. It is a bit like my past journey to England with

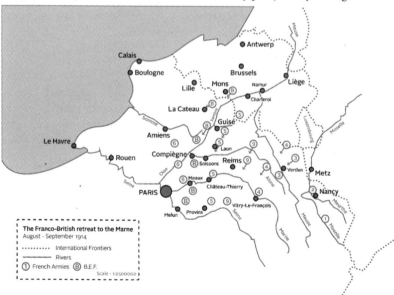

The Franco-British retreat to the Marne
August - September 1914
.... International Frontiers
———— Rivers
① French Armies Ⓑ B.E.F.
Scale - 1:2500000

Guy, a mine full of memories and anecdotes. I will be proud of having fought in this war."[7]

Early clashes on the eastern frontier

The first serious clashes occurred in Alsace near the Swiss frontier. The annexation of Alsace and eastern Lorraine by Germany was not considered a *casus belli* in 1914, but once war broke out the recovery of these lost provinces became a definite objective. From the crest of the Vosges Mountains French troops could see the fertile plain of Alsace below. Today it still looks tantalizingly close. The industrial city of Mulhouse was always more pro-French than anywhere else in Alsace. On 8 August elements of the First French Army rushed downhill to claim their prize. Repulsed by the Germans they entered Mulhouse briefly for a second time on 19 August.

Joffre wanted his army to keep German troops well occupied in Alsace so that he could launch a major attack in Lorraine. He assumed, again wrongly, that the German forces in this area were concentrated behind the ring of forts around Metz, still visible today. He therefore decided to attack to the south and the Second Army advanced towards German positions in the village of Morhange. Inadequate reconnaissance and an underestimation of German strength led to devastating results. French troops attacked uphill in open country on 20 August and many were killed. They lie now in a peaceful cemetery at the bottom of the hill where they fell. The casualties included the Second Army commander Castelnau's own son. The French retreated to protect the major city of Nancy. This was the first disaster of the Battle of the Frontiers.

*

Meanwhile the leisurely pace of André's northern progress continued. One of the soldiers even had time to compose an ode in honour of the captain. Passing Hirson on 21 August they noticed that deep trenches had been dug and large trees cut down to improve the field of fire. They thought this was all ridiculous because they would not be needed when the company occupied Germany. As André admitted, they had not the slightest notion what was going on.[8]

Disaster in the Ardennes

Joffre agreed to the Fifth Army commander Lanrezac's proposal to move forward to the River Sambre between Charleroi and Namur to counter the threat posed by the German advance into Belgium and liaise with Belgian forces. 1st Corps crossed into Belgium on 13 August. On 15 August some German advance

A column of French infantry from the Fifth Army passing the 43rd Artillery Regiment collecting fresh supplies on the road from Chimay to Rance in Belgium, 17 August 1914. (Historial de la Grande Guerre - Péronne (Somme) et © Yazid Medmoun)

units were already at Dinant in the Belgian Ardennes. Forces from 1st Corps got involved in fighting with the German Third Army around Dinant on that day. Étienne Derville with the 33rd Infantry Regiment records that his unit lost 450 men killed or wounded.[9] Yet the commander-in-chief was not convinced that the Germans would make a major thrust west of the Meuse. It is difficult to understand this misapprehension in the era of satellite technology. In 1914, however, aerial reconnaissance was in its infancy. The cavalry were supposed to bring in intelligence as well as acting as a screen for the infantry, but they were stretched. Joffre was the victim of his own assumptions about the front line potential of the German reserves.

He was still determined to attack the Germans further east, this time in the densely wooded Ardennes east of the Meuse. Apart from any other objective he wanted to protect France's vital iron and steel industry near the German border in Lorraine. He thought the German Army must be weak in the centre because of growing evidence of stronger deployment on its wings. He did not realize that as the Germans moved across Belgium, more troops would arrive at the hub of their position in Luxembourg.

We have already considered the French belief in the virtues of the offensive at a tactical level. The offensive was also seen as a strategic option. Joffre decided to launch major attacks in the Battle of the Frontiers in the Ardennes and Alsace-Lorraine because the alternatives—an attack through Belgium or a defensive strategy—seemed unpalatable. Violating Belgian neutrality would prejudice British support. Letting the enemy come to the French would be bad for morale and unacceptable to the politicians. Offence was more likely to unite the French than defence.[10]

On 21 August Joffre ordered the French Third and Fourth Armies to attack north-east towards Luxembourg and south-eastern Belgium. Their reconnaissance was poor and instead of a light screen of German troops they ran into several corps of the German Fourth and Fifth Armies, moving across the line of the French advance. The Germans spotted French movements just in time and hastily improvised positions to meet their assault with heavy artillery in support.

On 22 August Pierre Ruffey's Third Army advanced through heavy fog towards Longwy and its steel furnaces. Once the mist lifted German heavy howitzers decimated the French 75 mm field guns which had been placed forward. French bayonet attacks ran into machine gun positions. Panic ensued and one division broke and fled. Another French division was similarly destroyed near Virton. The slaughter was appalling.

Commandant Alphonse Grasset of the 103rd Infantry Regiment gave a graphic description of the fighting at Ethe, as his men stumbled into the Germans in the fog.[11]

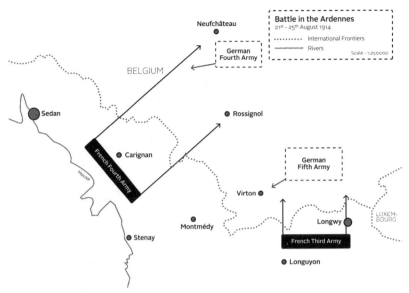

The number of wounded is stunning. Some manage to stand upright in the hail of bullets, covered in blood, sometimes completely hideous. They run without any aim, their arms stretched out, their eyes fixed on the ground. They spin round often mown down by more bullets and then they stop and full heavily to the ground. Harrowing cries, pathetic shouts and frightful moans are all mixed up with the shrieking of machine gun fire; the fierce rattle of death tells you that otherwise healthy and strong bodies refuse to give up on life.[12]

The advance of Langle de Cary's Fourth Army met a similar fate. The worst was to come at Rossignol, south of Neufchâteau. The 3rd Colonial Division attacked a German corps in waves over a front of 600 metres. No fewer than 11,000 men were mown down by artillery and machine gun fire. At the end of the day the division had ceased to exist as a fighting unit. Langle de Cary wrote to Joffre: "On the whole results hardly satisfactory"—one of the great understatements in the history of warfare.[13]

In fact the loss of 20,000 men on that day was as high as the British suffered on the first day of the Somme.[14] Together with casualties elsewhere the total for the French Army on 22 August was 27,000.[15] The colonial troops often ended up taking the worst punishment as they did at Charleroi. There were gaps in the German line which the French could have exploited, but the High Command failed to do so.

*

I have to confess to a bit of cheating! Before setting out to walk the retreat to the Marne I hired a car, brought along an old friend for company and spent four days on a pastime increasingly popular with middle-aged men, touring battlefields: an excuse for male comradeship, if in more comfortable circumstances, beer, generous portions of food, and a contest to work the Sat Nav and read a map dotted with manuscript arrows of military manoeuvres.

It was swelteringly hot in front of the casino hotel below the towering ramparts of Namur's fortress on the confluence of the Meuse and the Sambre rivers. We ignored the crowd of washed out young men having a smoke between sessions at the roulette tables, the flashing lights at the entrance to the hall of chance, the onyx elephants and potted palms. A gentle stroll around the towers and squares of the old town seemed more to our taste, even if we had to brave the cacophony of an August funfair on the way. In today's multinational Europe it ended with an enormous Greek dish of souvlakia, chips, taramasalata and just about every other speciality imaginable. The choice of eating places in Namur seemed distinctly limited. We were quite happy to reminisce and plan our tour.

Next day we weaved our way back and forth across the Sambre canal, seeing whether the Sat Nav would be thrown by the most obscure settlement or narrow street. Pont-au-Loup no problem, but watch out for speedy Belgian drivers whilst listening to the calming tones of the Tom Tom! Don't be put off by the potholes, let alone by the fast moving interchanges in cavernous, ill-lit tunnels around Charleroi. We were so busy we hardly had time for more than a ham roll grabbed from the breakfast buffet and wolfed down in a car park. The first night we stayed in a haven of peace south of the Sambre: a chateau with an enormous parterre, a splattering fountain, a damp *orangerie* with a marble fireplace and views of distant woods. It was difficult to drag ourselves away from breakfast in the sun amidst a riot of clematis and geraniums. After visiting two ashrams in India, *madame* taught meditation in this quiet corner. Perhaps my Type A personality would have benefitted from a longer stay.

We headed south to Chimay, ostensibly to trace the path of the French advance and retreat in 1914, but in reality to taste the monastery's famous beer. In a bed and breakfast cluttered with knick-knacks a Flemish-speaking Belgian couple spoke to us in halting English but admitted their French was non-existent. We understood a little of this divided country over breakfast. "We don't speak their language and they don't speak ours," they said. Back up the meandering gorge of the Meuse to see where 1st Corps contained German thrusts across the river, we came upon the bridge at Dinant decorated with multi-coloured saxophones for the jazz festival. It seemed a weird setting for young Charles de

Dinant: the Collegiate Church of Our Lady and the citadel. (Terry Cudbird)

Gaulle's first taste of battle on 15 August. He was wounded here and sent out of the line to recover.

There were few signs of the fighting which raged for three days between Namur and Charleroi from 21 to 23 August 1914. By the morning of 21 August the French Fifth Army had established its outposts along the Sambre between Floriffoux, just east of Namur, and Marchienne-au-Pont on the western outskirts of Charleroi. The river, which has the regular banks of a canal, marks the northern boundary of an open agricultural plateau stretching sixty kilometres south to the French border. The hills on the south bank sometimes rise steeply from the meadows below, but nowhere is the slope fierce enough to deter a determined assault. To walk down the escarpment from the wheat fields above is to enter a different world, and the French soldiers of 1914 would have felt the same.

Above, villages of mellow buildings, grey stone churches, monasteries and chateaux nestle comfortably into the folds of a landscape broken up by sprigs of woodland. Below is a ribbon of factories, workshops and terraced brick houses either side of the canal and surrounding roads. This is the *borinage*, in 1914 the beating heart of Belgium's industrial wealth and now a decaying sink of dereliction and decline. Barges still unload raw materials at the glass factory at Ham-sur-Sambre and the market at Auvelais is bustling. Elsewhere, weeds sprout through cracked tarmac, railings rust, paint flakes and broken glass crackles underfoot. Pollution streaks the patterned stone and brick of churches and town halls, monuments of one of the biggest iron and steel basins of pre-1914 Europe. The wooded banks of the Sambre near Namur give way to box girder bridges, factory chimneys, pylons, slag heaps and curling concrete helter-skelters carrying traffic away as fast as possible. The presence of raw materials imposed brick, steel and smoke on this formerly sylvan landscape, but now the vegetation is starting to swallow them up again. In Le Châtelet a few drunken, homeless or limping elderly individuals with unhealthy complexions testified to the social problems of industrial Wallonia.

*

General Charles Lanrezac was perhaps the most intellectually gifted commander in the French Army. A former director of studies at the École Supérieure de Guerre, he had a reputation as a strategist. Joffre considered him perhaps his most able general when he appointed him to command the Fifth Army. Edward Spears, the British liaison officer with Fifth Army HQ, was an acute observer of human character. When he met Lanrezac for the first time he noted that:

> The Army Commander was a big flabby man with an emphatic corporation. His moustache had more grey than white in it, as had his hair. His face was weather-beaten and dark, and his cheeks and lower lip hung rather loosely. He was looking upward, his head tilted forward, and appeared to be in a bad temper. My impression was one of relief when I found Muller's lion did not devour me. His Chief of Staff's manner conveyed that the General was a man whom it might be difficult to approach.[16]

When Lanrezac met Sir John French, British commander-in-chief, on 17 August, Spears noted the former's swarthy complexion revealing his creole origins (he was born in Guadeloupe).[17] He also referred to his pessimism.[18] This characteristic, allied to a tendency to hesitate when forced to take a decision, started to become apparent in the early days of the war and became more pronounced as the campaign developed.[19] Spears believed these traits affected Lanrezac's relationship with the British and with Joffre, as we will see.

Lanrezac had hectored Joffre about the growing threat of German forces west of the Meuse. Joffre had allowed him to move forward to the canal, but to what end? He did not dare expose his flanks with a further advance, so he ordered his men to take up positions along the southern edge of the Sambre valley and wait for the German assault.

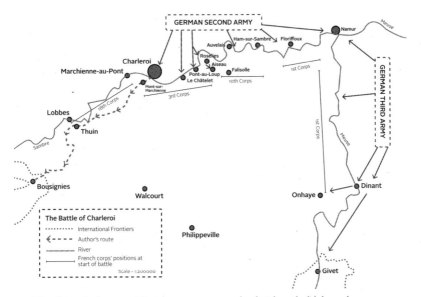

The Battle of Charleroi

International Frontiers
Author's route
River
French corps' positions at
start of battle
Scale - 1:200000

The first clashes on 21 August came at the bridges held by advance posts of the 3rd and 10th Corps at Roselies, Pont-au-Loup and Le Châtelet in the centre of the French front. It was difficult to find these bridges among the close-built streets of towns which turn their backs on the canal and its crossings. The meanders of the river and the contours of the ground make this area a labyrinth where it is easy to get lost, as Lanrezac admitted in his memoirs.[20] Eventually the Germans forced their way over and fierce fighting developed at the foot of the southern hills. Judging by the state of the buildings, there were houses on the slopes in 1914. This made it difficult for troops to find clear fields of fire. Foolhardy French counter-attacks by massed infantry against German positions among the buildings led to many unnecessary deaths. German heavy artillery was able to fire on French troops from north of the Sambre, where it was shielded from French counter-battery fire

Sergeant Albert Omnès in 10th Corps got into the thick of the fighting on 22 August. Early in the morning he came down to the level ground near the Sambre below Falisolle. Suddenly bullets started flying and the first casualties occurred.

We arrive at the eastern boundary of a wood. There's only a field of oats between us and the Germans… The Germans are well dug in with machine guns and my section suffers further losses. Captain Champion standing upright with bullets whistling round him, lights his pipe, talks to a colleague and orders a rush forward in the oat field. The bullets rain down on us and the rush forward costs us dear. One soldier is blinded by a bullet in the eyes. In all I lose nine men. Then the lieutenant suggests a flanking movement. One of my trainee corporals is dragging himself along and begs to be put out of his misery... Through the lieutenant's glasses I look at the company of skirmishers ahead. In fact these men are all dead, lying in lines marking each rush forward which was stopped by machine guns.

After this experience the regiment reformed and decided to retreat back up the hill. Omnès' company lost 76 men out of 250.[21]

Poorly trained and badly led regiments lost thousands of men. In some cases officers up to divisional level could not be found when asked for further orders. The realities of modern warfare destroyed their composure in hours. With the benefit of hindsight Lanrezac wrote in 1920 that it was lack of experience that defeated the French at Charleroi, not German numerical superiority. Indeed the French Fifth Army enjoyed a slight superiority in numbers at the start of the battle.[22] The French infantry launching itself downhill into the maze of the Sambre valley without much artillery support suffered heavy losses. The 3rd and 10th Corps did not dig trenches to help resist German attacks. With a few exceptions the French soldiers and officers fought bravely but without skill. Lanrezac had favoured a defensive posture on top of the hill but he failed to impose his strategy on his commanders.[23] The Fifth Army lost between 6,000 and 7,000 men killed at Charleroi. On the 22nd two battalions involved in a downhill attack lost seventy per cent of their strength and a different single battalion thirty per cent.[24] The results of the carnage can be seen in the military cemetery at Aiseau, rose-bedded ossuaries and white crosses marking the graves of 5,000 soldiers from the 3rd and 10th Corps alone, protected by a mantle of trees. The Islamic inscriptions on some graves bear witness to the bravery of North African troops. The crackle of rifle fire disturbed the peace of the place. Allowing a shooting club to operate next door seemed singularly inappropriate.

Gradually the Germans forced the French back onto the plateau above the valley. By the end of 22 August the French had had to retreat several kilometres but their position was not hopeless. They had not been routed. Edward Spears describes the retreating French battalions in these terms: "hardly any officers, the men in disorder, terrible worn expressions on their faces, exhaustion dragging at their heels and weighing down their tired feet so that they caught on every stone in the roadway, but something driving them on. Was it fear? I do not think so—just the desire to find a place of rest, away from those infernal shells. These men were not beaten, they were worn out."[25] Moreover the 1st Corps in the east had not been heavily engaged and the 18th Corps opposite Charleroi was only just coming into action.

The French plan on the 23rd was for the 1st Corps, well led by Franchet d'Esperey, to intervene decisively in support of the 10th Corps on its left. At this point the effect of the German deployment in Belgium started to tell. Lanrezac faced not only von Bülow's Second Army attacking his front across the Sambre, but also Max von Hausen's Third Army intervening on his right flank from the Meuse. The Germans started to penetrate well behind French lines up the narrow wooded valley at Onhaye not far from Dinant, opposed only by a few reservists. Franchet abandoned the frontal attack to send troops to stiffen resistance on his flank. General Mangin with two battalions of infantry and cavalry swept the Germans back towards the Meuse.

On the afternoon of the 23rd Lanrezac received the alarming intelligence concerning the total rout of the French Armies in the Ardennes to the east, which left his right flank exposed. The Germans had occupied Namur and effective liaison with Belgian forces was no longer possible. He also knew that the British were struggling against the weight of von Kluck's First Army at Mons and might well have to retreat. The 18th Corps on the left had already fallen back to the hilltop town of Thuin, although some of its troops stubbornly held on to the river crossing at Lobbes nearby. Lanrezac was haunted by the memory of Sedan, only seventy kilometres away, where in 1870 the French Emperor Napoleon III was taken prisoner. He ordered a move south out of Belgium.

The Battle of Charleroi became a defeat best forgotten, but it was an encounter of enormous significance for the future. Charleroi was the baptism of fire for the Fifth Army. At the end of three days' fighting they had learnt how the firepower of modern weapons had changed the nature of warfare. They had discovered not only the devastating effect of artillery and machine guns on massed infantry but also the impact of these weapons on the command structure of an army. Unlike in Napoleonic times a senior officer could no longer direct a battle from his horse on a hill top, overlooking his men on the battlefield. Troops had to operate in dispersed formations, and commanders behind the front line relied on communications systems to give orders. Unfortunately, at this stage in the war, field telephones were in their infancy and personal couriers did not always get through. This situation threw more responsibility onto the shoulders of junior officers leading troops at the front. Charleroi and the other battles on the frontiers had also shown that many generals could not cope with the reality of the new warfare. Joffre replaced one-third of the generals in the French army during the two weeks which followed. The battle of Charerloi also foreshadowed another feature of twentieth-century warfare: the involvement of civilians. Claims of German atrocities against civilians such as rape, looting, using non-combatants as human shields and taking and shooting hostages have been substantiated by historians. But there there was also disorder among the ranks of the French Army in the days which followed Charleroi.[26]

*

Meanwhile André Benoit's reserve unit spent that fateful Sunday of 23 August in a heightened state of alert just inside the French border east of Maubeuge. Early in the morning they heard the sound of cannon fire. André remarks naively that they began to think their victorious march forward might encounter some difficulties. He had to execute his first manoeuvre in the war, deploying his section either side of a road. Three German planes flew overhead. At Bousignies, only two kilometres from the Belgian frontier, he saw local people fleeing the fighting for the first time. His illusions were shattered. They were dressed in their Sunday best and carried a few personal possessions. The women, in floods of tears, cradled their children in their arms. At night André's unit bivouacked in a barn and a stable, taking care not to light a fire outside. More distraught civilians followed a retreating column of artillery, their belongings piled up in farm carts.[27]

The Battle of Mons

Early on the morning of Sunday 23 August, with church bells ringing, the Germans had started to engage the British Expeditionary Force at Mons. Today the town is less than half an hour's drive away from Charleroi by motorway, but in 1914 the line of communication between the British and the French was very thin. Mons was much more like a typical Belgian tourist town than Charleroi: solid Flemish houses of red brick with stepped or scrolled gables, a Gothic town hall with the elegant Renaissance House of the Golden Fleece alongside, an enormous square full of cafés. Maybe this is why the site of the battle is given more publicity than at Charleroi. The tourist office immediately produced a map and leaflet. Maybe also the British are prouder of a heroic defence against the odds. The French saw Charleroi as a defeat that resulted in German occupation of seventeen per cent of their country.

The terrain at Mons is in some ways very similar to Charleroi and in certain respects very different. The Mons-Condé canal runs east-west in a straight line for 26 kilometres. It is on average twenty metres wide and there are eighteen bridges along its length. Like the French at Charleroi the British front line was mostly behind the canal, although their forces were well positioned and ready to defend the crossings in force. The canal was not a barrier to the attacking troops despite a gallant defence. The British were fighting in a similar industrial region, with populated streets, mine workings, slag heaps and factories covering the landscape. The Tommies could not entrench as well as they would have liked,

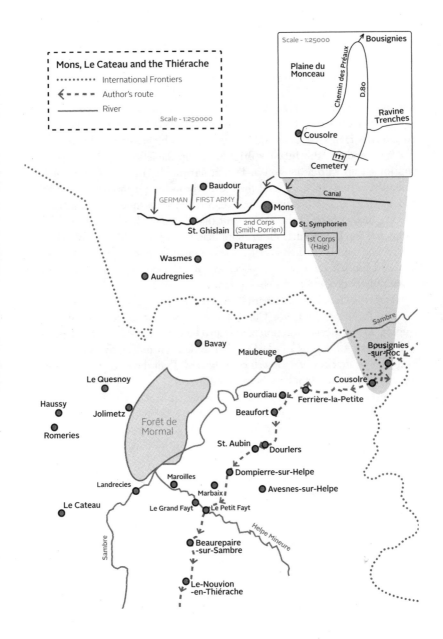

fields of fire were restricted and the artillery found it difficult to manoeuvre. The confused street fighting which developed here had no parallel in the French action at Charleroi. Some three kilometres behind the British was the town of Mons itself and other urban areas further to the west. The northward curve of the canal east of the town formed a dangerous salient for British troops to defend. There were no hills behind the British lines and the bulk of their units were posted on the flat ground near the canal. Sir Horace Smith-Dorrien's 2nd Corps covered the long front along the canal and bore the brunt of the fighting. Sir Douglas Haig's 1st Corps was on the right on higher ground behind Mons. The independent 19th Infantry Brigade was on the left of the British position and joined up with a division of French territorials. The British 5th Division defended most of the canal and the 3rd Division was positioned around Mons and in the dangerous salient. Smith-Dorrien had planned a second line of defence further back in the likely event that the thirty-kilometre front west of Mons was too long to defend for more than a few hours. Mons was really 2nd Corps' and Smith-Dorrien's battle. The commander-in-chief, Sir John French, absented himself on a tour of inspection at Valenciennes during the day, an extraordinary decision in the circumstances.

It was the German 9th and 3rd Corps in von Kluck's First Army who opened the attack on the 23rd, 9th Corps advancing on the salient and 3rd Corps coming up to the central section of the canal between St. Ghislain and Jemappes. The German 4th Corps attacked the British left but only early in the evening. Von Kluck's attacks were not well co-ordinated. If all three corps had advanced together the result might have been very different.

The force which the Germans confronted that day was full of seasoned professional soldiers, if more than half had recently been called back to duty from the Reserve. The rapidity and accuracy of their rifle fire had a devastating effect on German massed attacks, although the British in turn were impressed by the quality of German artillery.

From 9 am the German 9th Corps pressed home its attacks on the salient. The Middlesex, Royal Fusiliers and Royal Irish battalions broke up these attacks with machine gun and rifle fire. The Germans started to infiltrate around the flanks of the Middlesex in small parties and confused fighting followed. The German 3rd Corps had even more difficulty further west along the canal, fighting the Royal Scots, Northumberland and Royal West Kent battalions. The latter scored a notable success against the Brandenburg Grenadiers.

Harry Beaumont, a reservist in the Royal West Kent Regiment, gives a graphic account of what the action that day was like. Life started calmly on that Sunday morning in Mons. Local people brought their children to meet the British troops and others were seen on their way to mass. He continues: "The cattle were still grazing quietly on the scorched pastures, and the worshippers were now returning from mass, gaily chatting to one another as they walked up the long white dusty road stretching like a ribbon into the distance, when all of a sudden the tranquillity of the scene was broken by the short sharp bark of field guns, followed by shells screaming overhead and bursting in all directions. The villagers rushed to their homes in panic, slammed their doors, fastened their shutters, and were seen no more."[28] His company was ordered to advance along the canal to St. Ghislain, west of Mons. At the canal they moved around the front of a slag heap to see the enemy infantry advancing in massed formation with their front rank firing from the hip and showering the top of the slag heap with bullets. On entering St. Ghislain they found much damage to buildings caused by German gunfire, but tired and weary with their heavy packs they were grateful for gifts of wine, food and cigarettes passed out of cottage doors.

Even further west The King's Own Borderers and the East Surrey regiments repulsed more German attacks. All in all the marksmen and machine gunners in the "Old Contemptibles" had had a good morning. Two British divisions had held off four German divisions with only eight out of the 24 battalions in the 2nd Corps engaged.

The crux of the battle of Mons was the struggle in the salient. At noon the Royal Scots and Gordon Highlanders pushed back a German attack on their positions on higher ground south-east of the town. By now, however, the Germans were across the canal in force and the position of the 4th Middlesex Battalion in the salient became critical. The Royal Irish had great difficulty coming to their rescue. The British artillery was unable to help in the enclosed ground. The Middlesex and Royal Irish gradually withdrew protected to some extent by the Gordons on their right. The Royal Fusiliers had already started to pull back. Two members of this battalion won VCs. Lieutenant Maurice Dease was killed commanding the machine gun section at the southern end of the railway bridge over the canal, at the western end of the salient. Private Sidney Godley, in the same section, covered the retreat of his colleagues alone before getting to hospital severely wounded.

Once the British troops in the salient withdrew the others along the canal started a piecemeal retreat. At the same time engineers blew some of the bridges. Harry Beaumont's battalion had taken up positions in a glass factory on the far bank of the canal and fired on the Germans all afternoon as they tried to advance across flat open ground. At nightfall they retreated to an embankment behind and discovered the Germans were moving up their guns and transport. The enemy was so close that they could hear them talking and see them lighting camp fires, not suspecting that British troops were nearby. In the dark the battalion gave them fifteen rounds from their Lee Enfield bolt action rifles,

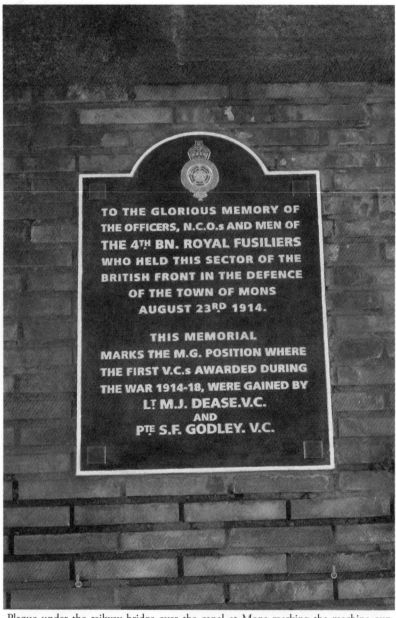

TO THE GLORIOUS MEMORY OF
THE OFFICERS, N.C.O.s AND MEN OF
THE 4TH BN. ROYAL FUSILIERS
WHO HELD THIS SECTOR OF THE
BRITISH FRONT IN THE DEFENCE
OF THE TOWN OF MONS
AUGUST 23RD 1914.

THIS MEMORIAL
MARKS THE M.G. POSITION WHERE
THE FIRST V.C.s AWARDED DURING
THE WAR 1914-18, WERE GAINED BY
LT M.J. DEASE.V.C.
AND
PTE S.F. GODLEY. V.C.

Plaque under the railway bridge over the canal at Mons marking the machine gun position where the first VCs of the Great War were gained by Lt. Maurice Dease and Private Sidney Godley, 4th Battalion, Royal Fusiliers. (Terry Cudbird) the so-called "mad minute" on account of the rapidity of the British infantry's volleys. The German fires died out quickly amid screams from those who had been hit. About midnight Beaumont's battalion received orders to retire across the canal and an hour later a general retreat began with the blowing-up of the St. Ghislain Bridge. Harry's colleagues thought that they had held the Germans and could not understand why they were retreating.[29]

The Germans launched one final attack south-east of Mons at Bois la Haut but the Gordon Highlanders, the Royal Scots and the Irish Rifles broke it up. After this the Germans sounded a cease fire for the night. It remained for the British to extricate their rearguards. Gradually 2nd Corps re-grouped in Smith-Dorrien's chosen position three kilometres to the south.

The BEF lost approximately 1,600 at Mons killed, wounded and missing in action. The 4th Middlesex Battalion and the 2nd Royal Irish sustained 400 losses in the first case and 300 in the second.[30]

When the extent of the French withdrawal after Charleroi became clear Sir John French ordered a general retreat of the whole army. There is no doubt that Sir John felt that Lanrezac had betrayed him, because the latter had decided to withdraw for his own reasons while the British were still heavily engaged.

The French had now lost the Battle of the Frontiers. In Alsace their attacks had been repulsed. They were falling back on Nancy in Lorraine after the disaster at Morhange. Heavy losses in the Ardennes had the same effect. The general retreat of the Allied armies had begun. Soldiers and junior officers did not know why they were falling back. They were given no briefing on the overall situation and therefore could not grasp the threat posed by the German move in strength through Belgium. Some of them, particularly in the British Army, believed they had the measure of the Germans. None knew how long the retreat would last, not even Joffre. However, he was still in control. Orders from his HQ told each army its line of march each day. He was in touch with all his generals and the British, holding his forces together, transmitting intelligence about German movements and working out how he could marshal his forces to strike back. France's survival depended on the eventual success of his plans.

3: THE RETREAT BEGINS
23-25 AUGUST 1914

The Fifth Army escapes from Belgium

Lanrezac's order was dry and to the point: "The Fifth Army will set off before daybreak, retreating during the 24th to a line stretching from Givet in the east to Maubeuge in the west." He noted laconically that many of them would have a tough march through forests west of the Meuse, "a difficult region with very few roads running north-south".[1] He might have added that the winding road in the Meuse gorge would slow them down too. Their task would be made more difficult by the number of refugees on the roads. Edward Spears described the grey mass pouring past at Philippeville in Belgium on 23 August: " I can still see a couple of young girls, sisters perhaps, helping each other, hardly able to drag themselves along, the blood from their torn feet oozing through their low silk shoes: a very sick woman, who looked as if she was dying, balanced somehow on a perambulator; a very old man in a wheelbarrow, pushed by his sturdy daughter; a very old, very respectable couple, who for years had probably done no more than walk arm in arm round a small garden, now, still arm in arm, were helping each other in utter bewilderment of mind and exhaustion of body down the long meaningless road."[2]

Étienne Derville describes very well the confused retreat of the 1st Corps on crowded roads near the Meuse:

> I have never seen such a blockage. Regiments of artillery and infantry, supply convoys, vehicles from headquarters, Belgian soldiers and above all groups of refugees on foot or in vehicles move forward on a narrow road, side by side. As a result they get entangled, overtake each other, keep stopping, shove and jostle and end up in the ditches.[3]

*

On Sunday 4 August 2013 I set off from Charleroi Sud station to walk the retreat, 99 years after Britain declared war on Germany. The contrast with events in 1914 could not have been more striking. I crossed the Sambre and sauntered around the old town in the sunshine, where a market was in full swing. Stalls full of potted plants brought colour to the central square, squashed between a massive late nineteenth-century town hall and a stolid baroque church. Crowds of Belgians, intent on a bargain or buying their Sunday lunch, brushed against the walking poles protruding from my rucksack, not noticing a stranger with

Typical terraced houses in the industrial area of Charleroi with an old iron smelting furnace in the background. (Terry Cudbird)

different things on his mind. After a brief excursion via Princess Astrid's park I returned to the station through arcades of boarded up shops. The sources of Charleroi's former prosperity have long since dried up.

The way south started at the back of the station under the concrete pillars of intersecting freeways, reminiscent of an American industrial city. A rusting iron furnace owned by Lakshmi Mittal protruded on the western skyline. I tripped on the broken pavements outside high, red- brick terraced houses with solid mouldings, built in the era when Belgian steel fuelled the conquest of the Congo. Later, twentieth-century housing and concrete shopping centres replaced the brick as I climbed the hill of Mont-sur-Marchienne where the 3rd Corps had sought refuge as the Germans pressed forward from the Sambre. After scrambling under another motorway viaduct and skirting a cemetery I arrived in the suburban haven of Eden Park: calm tree-lined streets, substantial villas and the purring of lawn mowers.

Sundays are similar over much of our western world. I said good morning to men washing cars and ladies trimming flowers. Lower in the town a dishevelled young man grunted a greeting from his front step bathed in sunlight. Prim, permed matrons gripped the arms of their pale husbands in pressed shirts and beige crimplene slacks.

It was a miracle of modern cartography that I found the path between two houses and through a damp wood to a beer garden on the meandering Sambre. To be truthful, dog walkers on the path prepared me for the crowds of people enjoying themselves outside a local café. I knew I would not get a meal that evening so like the soldiers of 1914 I ate well when I could; in this case *tartare de saumon* and *pavé de boeuf* washed down by Chimay blue beer. The ample girth of some of my lunch companions in the restaurant did not suggest an active life: large napkins protected the Sunday clothes of gnome-like men with heavy jowls and short necks. On a hot afternoon I later regretted the second beer; not a good habit when walking long distances. I resolved to mend my ways. Hardly noticing the graceful tracery of the ruined Abbey of Aulne I staggered on to crick my neck staring up at the massive tower in Thuin, with its belfry surveying the deep valley of the Sambre below. Apparently Victor Hugo came here on a visit in 1861. While in exile during the Second Empire Thuin was about as close to France as he could get.

At Thuin I picked up the line of retreat of the 18th Corps on the left wing of Lanrezac's army as it streamed up onto the open agricultural plateau which led to the French border. A restored Belgian farmhouse provided a comfortable shelter for the night: beams, bricks and dark furniture. *Monsieur* insisted on showing me his collection of First World War books. Haggard faces in crumpled uniforms peered out of the pages of a French illustrated magazine, *Le Miroir*, which was popular at the time. I was to discover that many people wanted to share their families' memories of the Great War.

Next day a path through fields of ripe drooping corn brought me to a main road near the French border. I turned off down a country lane lined with hedges and somewhere I crossed into France. There was nothing to tell me where, except perhaps a subtle change in the landscape from a level plateau to small valleys. Hedges and woods replaced the open fields of Belgium. As I approached Bousignies-sur-Roc to join the route followed by André Benoit I noted the presence of maize, a modern crop for cattle feed and unlikely to have grown here a hundred years ago. The church of grey stone and red brick had been much restored since André's time. Artificial flowers garlanded the Virgin inside and Joan of Arc clasped her right hand to her breastplate while her left grasped the flag of royal France, golden fleur-de-lys on a white background. The faithful had thought it appropriate to decorate her pedestal with white, blue and red flowers. The *école communale*, with the antique medallion of a girl's head over the door, would have stood opposite the church in 1914 as it does today.

Lanrezac's memoirs note that on the 24th the French rearguards dealt easily with the pursing German troops who did not push their attacks home.[4] André's

Statue of Joan of Arc in the church of Ste-Aldegonde at Bousignies-sur-Roc, Nord. (Terry Cudbird)

remarks and those of a number of other witnesses in the Fifth Army seem to contradict this view, however. The role of the Reserve Divisions, of which André's unit formed part, was to ensure continuity between the French front and the British. On Monday 24 August André's day started with his company deploying in a field and digging holes for protection. He wrote a letter to his family and placed it in his map case just in case the worst happened. He wrote: "The battle raged in the direction of Thuin... we heard firing and the deeper sound of cannons and saw smoke from the shell bursts. A farm started to burn, obscuring some of the panorama, and further away hayricks caught alight. My men looked at this theatrical spectacle without realizing how serious it was."[5]

After lunch outside the church I crossed a mill stream to climb onto the Plaine du Monceau, which André mentions, between Bousignies and Cousolre. Looking back from a track called the Chemin des Préaux my view towards Belgium was obscured by woods in the distance. I assume they were less extensive in 1914. He says that his unit's next task was to occupy trenches around a crossroads and along a ravine. I found the crossroads easily enough near Cousolre cemetery where André had lunch, but where was the ravine? On the map a small road led off the *départementale* by a wood. Here the contour lines were close together. I walked downhill to a farm and, looking back at the bottom, could see an overgrown field with steep slopes on either side. I guessed that André's trenches would have been on the southern slope facing north towards the German advance. During a dinner of bread and jam in Cousolre they met soldiers from the 18th Corps who groaned about the hardships of the battle they had just experienced. André's company had to guard the rear of their units, so it was back to the trenches where they huddled in the cold until midnight. Then André roused the men by poking them with his sword and they marched back through the deserted streets of Cousolre. The military authorities had already evacuated the place and his company rested in a field to the south. The grass was damp with dew and he awoke at dawn, stiff and cold.[6]

Sergeant Omnès in the 10th Corps describes a day's hard fighting on 24 August. Overnight his unit had to hold a position facing a wood occupied by Germans, who could not see them hidden in a fold in the ground. Due to the carefree attitude of the French, he remarks ironically, they could not keep quiet. When the day dawned the Germans opened fire. His battalion was left to face the advance of the Prussian guard alone. "The giants ran at us firing from 200 metres away." Several of his colleagues were killed. Omnès picked himself up and ran. Under fire he and a few others eventually reached a farm. The wounded were evacuated by all available means including cycles, cavalry horses and farm carts. "This evening colleagues talk of retreating to the frontier of France... Our fine dream has not lasted long!" In the night they reached Chimay. He bought two pounds of Belgian tobacco because it was cheap. They snatched a meal but could only stop an hour because the Germans were hard on their heels.[7]

On the morning of the 24th Captain Julien La Chaussée in the 3rd Corps was fired on by enemy machine guns. His soldiers urged him to get down like them: "'Think of your wife and your children,' they cried."[8] La Chaussée describes how he kept his men in a shallow valley where they enjoyed some protection. Despite this, some were killed and others lying flat found the rucksacks protecting their heads shot through with bullets. Eventually they were able to retreat to Walcourt and take a short rest. The officers' forced smiles and the men's singing covered up a profound sense of unease. "What is going to become of France?" he wrote.[9] Meanwhile his comrade in the same corps, Brunel de Pérard, just mentions hard marching without any contact with the enemy. However, as a *conducteur de caissons*, Brunel was not right in the firing line.

Étienne Derville recalls the hard retreat of 1st Corps which started with a five- to six-hour march at night and men fighting over water at a fountain. The long stages continued in the heat and these were made worse by having to compete for road space with the artillery. "We marched for whole days alongside the artillery. They occupied the middle of the road way and blinded us with the dust they raised."[10]

The officers arranged for the men's packs to be carried on vehicles but this practice encouraged thieving.

> But this was always done without any sense of order because the officers could not be bothered. The result was a complete mix up of several hundred sacks. Unscrupulous men took their neighbour's sack or stole linen and provisions from it. The wounded were pushed onto the same wagons. They opened the sacks and put their hands on emergency rations which then had to be replaced.[11]

It was, however, an organized retreat from a military point of view, well conducted by Franchet d'Esperey. The Germans rarely caused Derville's regiment any trouble even when they acted as rearguard covering the retreat, as they did frequently.[12]

André roused his men on the 25th and after a few kilometres they passed one of the outlying forts of Maubeuge where soldiers were cutting down trees to create a clear field of fire. Vehicles carrying the wounded passed his unit and he was upset by seeing stretchers spattered with blood for the first time. Then it started to rain hard. The men covered themselves with sheaves of straw to keep dry. Boxes of the much maligned conserved meat were distributed (so-called monkey boxes, like the British tins of bully beef) and they pressed on. Along the narrow slippery roads André's men found abandoned packs and looted them for food. As night fell they reached St. Aubin, a village where pigs were bred. The bivouac smelt strongly.[13]

*

I sympathized with André's plight. When I walked from Cousolre to St. Aubin it rained without interruption all day, sometimes very heavily. Mist shrouded the succession of small villages with their low, brick-built farmhouses. Water dripped from woods and hedgerows, roads were muddy and the cattle looked particularly mournful. At the end of the walk I approached a stream and slithered along a boggy path covered in saturated leaves. The clothes in my rucksack were very damp. I turned my room for the night into a Chinese laundry.

The day had started well with a coffee at Cousolre and a friendly chat with stall owners setting up for the market. A swarthy man with black curly hair was teasing the café owner because he came from the Ardennes rather than being a son of the Nord. "Look at the untidy way he keeps this place," he said to his companions. He told me that you could still visit some of the outlying forts around Maubeuge. This interested me because of the reference in André's diary. I found one fortification covered in dense trees and undergrowth near the village of Ferrière-la-Petite. I could just make out its shape, the mounds created by the earthworks and the brickwork holding up an entrance to the rear. A local farmer in a tractor stopped to talk, clearly somewhat bemused by a hiker pointing a camera at soaking trees in the pouring rain. Yes, he confirmed, this was a Maubeuge fort but not the only one.

Before starting at Cousolre I had taken a day off to visit Maubeuge which played a crucial part in the events of August-September 1914. The Marquis de Vauban constructed one of his great northern fortresses for Louis XIV here. The military engineer Raymond Séré de Rivières added the outer ring of forts as an additional protection after the Franco-Prussian War. In 1914 the garrison held out against the German advance for two crucial weeks between 24 August and 7 September and thus ensured that one German Army Corps did not reach the Battle of the Marne in time to make a difference. In May 1940 the Germans destroyed ninety per cent of the town. Only a few of the old buildings survive including the Porte de Mons built by Vauban, the humble Béguinage where Christian sisters lived a life of poverty and service to others, the eighteenth-century convent of Ste. Aldegonde (now a lycée), the Arsenal and the chapel of the Black Sisters. The massive earthworks, ditches and lakes constructed by Vauban are still intact, surrounded on one side by white blocks of flats built during reconstruction in the 1960s. Most of the new town architecture seems strangely dated now and lacking in style: the concrete mairie, the oblong porthole windows above the shops and the tower of the new church which looks as if it should belong to a fire station with its small squares of obscured glass.

After making out another Maubeuge fort on the horizon, the fort of Bourdiau, I hurried south along the *Vieux Grand Chemin* from Beaufort to Dourlers. Here a British cemetery shelters the bodies of soldiers killed in the last week of the war as well as Germans. One was nineteen years old; some of the Germans are unknown. When I eventually arrived at my B&B I could not find the key which *madame* had promised to leave outside under a pebble until she arrived home later in the evening. A kindly neighbour phoned her son who made Maroilles cheese in a farm nearby. He let me in so I could have a cold shower and eat the meagre supper I had carried with me: slices of cold ham and cheese, eight endive leaves, a tomato and an apple. When madame eventually arrived this was supplemented by more cheese and a beer. She and her husband had recently converted a barn and a chapel into this spacious retirement home and left their son to do the hard work on the farm. She gave me an interesting piece of information confirming one aspect of André's diary. She had started farming in the village in 1968 when there was still one man rearing pigs. Now cows had replaced these animals completely.

The retreat from Mons begins

Lanrezac noted in his diary that on 25 August elements of the 1st British Corps came up against General Mardochée Valabrègue's Reserve Divisions in the area of the River Sambre. This caused conflict, fatigue and delays for both armies.[14] Sir John French decided to retreat from Mons on the evening of 23 August at the same time as the French Fifth Army was beginning to pull back from the hills south of Charleroi. By the morning of the 24th some British units were on their way towards Bavay, north of the forest of Mormal. The Germans did not give Haig's 1st Corps much trouble. Instead they turned their attention to the 2nd Corps which at dawn on the 24th was spread out about five kilometres south-west of Mons, having retreated from the canal. Von Kluck thought the British would retire towards the Channel ports and sent a whole cavalry corps south-west to cut off that route of escape. Meanwhile he intended to drive the British Army towards the great fortress of Maubeuge where they could be bottled up and eliminated. On this assumption an attack on the 2nd Corps well to the west of Maubeuge seemed an obvious course of action.

Smith-Dorrien commanding the 2nd Corps was faced with a logistical nightmare. His infantry and artillery would take up a considerable amount of road space on their own. For example, one infantry brigade would stretch for five kilometres in line of march. But first he had to get the heavy transport off the roads, currently behind the army on the assumption of a further advance. Every witness to the retreat on the 24th refers to the chaos on the roads made worse by the number of civilian refugees fleeing the fighting.

The German artillery started shelling the retreating British at dawn. In an action at closer quarters around Wasmes Harry Beaumont was injured. Miraculously the Belgians discovered him first rather than the German military. In common with a number of others he was given medical treatment secretly and then spirited out of Belgium to neutral Holland and home.[15] There was severe fighting around Audregnies, still in Belgium. The artillery duel developed into an encounter fight involving a suicidal cavalry charge by the 9th Lancers and the 4th Dragoon Guards across totally unsuitable terrain; railway lines, signal wires and ballast pits blocking the way: 234 men were killed or wounded. The 1st Battalion of the Cheshire Regiment did not receive an order to retire and lost three-quarters of its men.

The 2nd Battalion, Duke of Wellington's Regiment, also came in for some rough treatment at Wasmes on 24 August. The German shells started raining down at 11.30 am and their infantry attacked at 1 pm. It seems that the order to the Wellingtons to retire did not get through. The diary of Private Harrop provides a vivid illustration of the action during which half his platoon was lost. They guarded a bridge over the canal at Mons until it was destroyed. Then they grabbed some food in a pub until the roof was shot off, forcing them to bolt out of the back door straight into machine gun fire. Six men were lost rushing to cover behind a pile of railway sleepers. More were killed crawling uphill to some trenches. After rushing through the town they crept on all fours across a turnip and cabbage field and took shelter with a detachment of the Manchesters behind a slag heap. The intensity of the German shell fire did not make this position very comfortable. All was not lost, however. A friendly butcher offered Harrop and his comrades some pork and a brigadier topped this with a glass of champagne. Half an hour after midnight Harrop found his regiment again and had his first rest in twenty-four hours, along with the comfort of a cup of tea and a baked potato. The battalion had lost 400 men.[16] In all the 2nd Corps lost 2,600 officers and men on the 24th of whom two-thirds came from the 5th Division on the left flank. Those who survived had an exhausting march. K.F.B. Tower, a subaltern in the 4th Battalion, Royal Fusiliers, saw men who had dropped to sleep on the road.[17] In the end the two divisions of 2nd Corps reached Bavay as the German pursuit slackened off.

The 1st Corps might have had an easier day but the soldiers were still exhausted after a long march in the heat. Everyone was suffering from lack of sleep and food. The lucky ones were handed bully beef and ate it as they marched, throwing away the cans in the ditch. Some managed to snatch a short rest like A.V. Spencer, a lieutenant in the Oxfordshire and Buckinghamshire

Light Infantry, who dossed down in the square at Paturages in the middle of the night.[18] Many suffered from severe sores on their feet made worse by cobbled roads and also threw away bits of kit they thought were useless.[19] Quite a few men got lost on the way. Most of these were either shot or captured but a handful escaped through Belgium like Harry Beaumont. The officers and men were also disheartened because of the prevailing uncertainty as Major Lord Bernard Gordon-Lennox of the Grenadier Guards remarked: "Owing to the absolute secrecy which pervaded everything, no one knew what was going on anywhere: this has been maintained up to date and is most disheartening. No one knows what one is driving at, where anyone is, what we have got against us, or anything at all, and what is told us generally turns out to be entirely wrong."[20]

At Bavay, French decided to split the British Expeditionary Force, with the 2nd Corps moving on roads to the west of the Forest of Mormal and the 1st Corps to the east. This decision was based on studying maps which appeared not to show any roads running north-south through the forest. It is strange that the cavalry were not sent ahead to reconnoitre. There is at least one road through the forest starting due south of Bavay, which I walked on during an earlier trek through northern France. Haig was supposed to ensure that his corps re-joined the 2nd Corps at Le Cateau, but events took a different turn. The 1st Corps got off to a late start on the 25th and was delayed by refugees and by having to share roads with two French Reserve Divisions and André Sordet's cavalry. Major George Darell Jeffreys of the Grenadiers, known as "Ma Jeffreys", wrote: "A very hot day again and a very trying march, owing to constant blocks and delays. Many refugees now on the roads, causing blockages and confusion. They were a pitiable sight—all ages and sexes, some in carts, many on foot. Some of the latter pushing barrows and hand-carts, piled up with bedding and belongings: a good many with little carts pulled by dogs. Another cause of blocks and delay is 'double-banking', i.e. troops coming up alongside those in front of them, so that two columns are abreast. This generally means that no one can move either way. The Artillery constantly did this and no one stopped them."[21]

Frederic Coleman, an American volunteer driver with GHQ, picked out some different details in the same general mêlée of confusion: "Many refugees mingled with the columns of troops along the road. A cartload made up of two or three families from Maubeuge told us frightened tales of German atrocities. Touring cars loaded with French staff officers hooted madly in an endeavour to pass the lines of big wagons on the narrow road. Family wagonettes filled with well-dressed people were in the line. Now and then a lady of well-to-do appearance passed, walking behind a carriage loaded with goods and chattels. At one point the road was blocked with a lorry containing printing stores, with all the presses and other accessories of a headquarters staff office... Wonder, despair, patience, pain, apathy—the drifting faces [of the refugees] made a heart-breaking picture."[22]

The 6th Brigade had designated Maroilles as a supply point so its men were not best pleased to find the French 53rd and 69th Reserve Divisions in the town. This was not the only encounter between the French and British on the evening of the 25th. The 1st Battalion, Northamptonshire Regiment, lost their billets to some French territorials in Monceau and had to march on to Marbaix east of Maroilles.[23]

Haig ordered a halt at Landrecies on the Sambre-Oise canal where he was surprised by a German attack. After panic and confused fighting in the streets the Coldstream and Grenadier Guards held the attackers off and by dawn on the 26th the British had gone. Haig felt unwell and seems to have exaggerated the threat his corps faced. In any event he relocated his HQ to Le Grand Fayt to the east and the line of the 1st Corps' march took them nowhere near Le Cateau. In the meantime some of his men successfully prevented the Germans from taking the important bridge over the Sambre at Maroilles, more famous nowadays for the eponymous cheese. Corporal Bernard John Denore of the 1st Royal Berkshire Regiment said that the Germans attacked at 9 pm and that about 45 members of his company were killed. "A voice called out in English, 'has anybody got a map?' and when our C.O. stood up with his map, a German walked up, and shot him with a revolver. The German was killed by a bayonet stab from a private."[24]

To the west of the forest von Kluck recalled his cavalry and tried again to outflank the British on their left. A series of actions to hold the Germans off resulted in 450 casualties, fewer than the day before. The congestion on the roads continued and to cap all their difficulties the 2nd Corps had to march through a thunderstorm in the early evening. The men arrived at Le Cateau wet, hungry and very tired with the Germans on their heels. James Lochhead Jack, a young subaltern in the 1st Cameronians (Scottish Rifles) and later a general, recorded in his diary: "Between 7 and 11 pm the soaked and hungry battalions stagger into the square… it is heartrending to witness the exhaustion of all ranks after their march of almost 23 miles in steam-heat and heavily loaded, besides going into action about Romeries and Haussy in support of the cavalry. The men have scarcely been off their feet for three days besides having had no more than snatches of sleep or scraps of food because of transport delays through road-blocks. The last battalion to report, the Welch Fusiliers, drop down on the cobbled square saying they can go no further…"[25] At least the arrival of fresh troops from Britain in the shape of the 4th Division gave them heart.[26]

The German advance

There is no doubt that the Germans opposing the British had found their hard-fought advance tough. Before the engagement at Mons they had marched for two weeks across Belgium and it was a long slog. Lieutenant Ernst Rosenhainer describes his own march to Namur with von Hausen's Third Army in these terms: "the hot, blistering sun made our march across the mountains quite an ordeal. A number of men dropped from exhaustion, especially since many of the reservists were no longer accustomed to such long marches."[27] Walter Bloem, a lieutenant in the Brandenburg Grenadiers, mentions the hostility the Germans met in Wallonia and their surprise at being fired on by civilians from the houses. He talks about the villages burnt by German troops as a reprisal and the taking of civilian hostages, both of which he seems to regard as justifiable behaviour. They also became involved in engagements with scattered units of the Belgian Army. Fritz Nagel records how jumpy the German troops became. Like Bloem he passed through Tirlemont burning so fiercely that he thought they would be consumed by the fires they themselves had started. Next day, on the way to Brussels, Louvain was in flames. Interestingly enough, Bloem felt their reception by the Flemish-speaking population was much friendlier.[28]

When the Brandenburgers ran unexpectedly into the British at Mons they found to their surprise that they were up against much tougher opposition.

German troops advancing through Belgium, August 1914. (Library of Congress, Washington DC)

They admired the professional loop-holing of buildings to provide cover for machine guns and artillery, the fire power of the infantry and their ability to disengage from an action. In a fire fight on meadows north of the canal at St. Ghislain many of Bloem's comrades were killed or wounded. While following the retreating British on 24 August their corps commander stopped to tell them they had won a magnificent victory. This was his slightly dazed reaction:

> We all looked at each other slightly disconcerted, almost shamefaced, mingled [*sic*] with our feelings of great elation. What! Was that called a victory? Had we really won a big, important victory? Undoubtedly we had advanced ten miles southwards since our midday meal yesterday in Baudour, and the enemy who had tried to stop us had gone... but otherwise the only impressions that remained in our dizzy brains were streams of blood, of pale-faced corpses, of confused chaos, of aimless firing, of houses in smoke and flame, of ruins, of sopping clothes, of feverish thirst, of limbs exhausted. So that was victory. Amazing! And yet it must be, the general had said so.[29]

Once they passed the French frontier on the 25th the going became easier. They did not meet the British and found the agricultural countryside eerily deserted. "The enemy had vanished. The traces of a hasty departure, though not of a disorderly rout, were everywhere apparent; broken-down cars, burnt supplies, and so on, but no rifles or equipment lying about."[30] That evening they reached their billets in the village of Jolimetz near Le Quesnoy and west of the forest of Mormal. At the same time the 2nd British Corps was entering Le Cateau and the 1st Corps Landrecies about twelve kilometres away. Bloem and his fellow officers slept in a magnificent private house with a cellar which was "princely in its capacity." He says that they would have preferred to give an official requisition and pay for what they took but there was no one about. "It was with a sense of compulsory ownership that we sat down to dinner that evening round the Louis Seize dining table of our private house, and it was not often that such luxury came our way; for we drank the most exquisite Burgundy out of rich gilt tankards and then champagne from crystal wineglasses. Thank you, Mr. So-and-so of Jolimetz! We then slept in the softest, most comfortable beds for an all too short night."[31] Such cellars were to prove a fatal attraction for the German soldiers as they marched to the Marne.

The retreat of the French Third and Fourth Armies in the Ardennes

While André's allies were starting the general retreat with great difficulty his fellow countrymen in the Ardennes were reeling from their very costly encounter with the Germans. Jean Galtier-Boissière, later a writer and left-wing pacifist, wrote a novel *La fleur au fusil* about his experiences as a soldier in the Great War starting with the Ardennes campaign. The narrator is with the Third Army near Longuyon on 24 August, flat on the ground near a ridge with bullets and shells whistling around him. Then his unit advances in rushes towards an invisible enemy through a hail of fire. "At a signal from the adjutant we get up, jump forward, run straight ahead weighed down by the pack, encumbered with the cartridges, the eating can and the satchel which jumps about at our sides. Then we throw ourselves flat on the ground, gasping for breath; my money belt falls down between my legs. Another pain in the ass! Some men trip up in the rush; others are hit in the head as they get up. No one pays any attention to his neighbour whoever he is. We only have one thought; to advance." His neighbour says to him: "They are mowing us down with their machine guns," and then, a moment later, is dead.[32] The word he uses for mowing, *faucher*, is apt because it describes reaping with a scythe. The men fell dead in immaculate rows piled on top of each other.

And then comes the reality of retreat. Paul Lintier, a law student at Lyon, is caught up in the fighting near Virton, serving with the 44th Regiment of Artillery. He describes the moment of retreat like a torrent:

> And, tossed about from right to left like bits of cork in the swirl of a current, dragged this way and that in the eddies, sometimes pushed into the ditch, and sometimes carried off their feet by the torrent, the tattered remnants of troops surged down the road. Wounded, limping, many without rifle or pack, they made slow progress. Some made an effort to climb up on our gun carriages, and either hoisted themselves on to the ammunition wagons or let themselves be dragged along like automata.

He was particularly affected by the sight of the wounded: "there was already something skull-like about their faces; the eyes, wide open and bright with fever, stared fixedly from out of their sunken sockets as though at something we could not see."[33]

Galtier-Boissière starts to analyze the feelings of the soldiers being forced to retreat, having shortly before whipped themselves into a frenzy for the attack and quite convinced that no force could resist them. Once defeat was certain it was impossible to stop them fleeing.

> But all the isolated groups of soldiers, all those who have survived the first waves of the assault, who just a short while ago were clinging to the crest of the hillside a few paces from the enemy, when they see the reinforcements give way understand—and with what anguish—that they are being abandoned. They see that their officers have been killed. Just

now these enthusiastic soldiers, united in a common wish, were part of a wave bearing down irresistibly on the enemy. But, at the first order to fall back, their equilibrium is interrupted: each unit, weakened, decimated, deprived of its leader, falls apart. The skirmishers who climbed heroically to the assault under a hail of machine gun fire now run to the rear and become again ordinary men, thrown into a terrible cataclysm. After having stupidly risked his skin each soldier takes control of himself and wants to survive at any price.[34]

Once out of the danger zone he breathes a great sigh of relief. But then he sees the wounded staggering past and asks the difficult question. How did this happen? He describes "a flood of men with haggard eyes, covered in sweat and dust, their uniforms in tatters. Some soldiers have lost their hats, their pack and their equipment and have just hung on to their rifle. The wounded, staggering, hopping on one leg, cling to their comrades... the sudden reversal of fortunes is stupefying. In the battle the French Army made a magnificent effort. How have we been defeated?"[35]

Marc Bloch was at the rear of Ruffey's Third Army at the Belgian border near Montmédy. On 23 August he saw the first wounded. He felt he was at the rear of a great battle and, he thought, a great victory. He continued in his diary two days later; "On the morning of the 25th we beat a retreat, and I realized that the hope expressed in the lines I have just quoted was misplaced. This immensely bitter disappointment, the stifling heat, the difficulties of marching along a road encumbered with artillery and convoys, and finally, the dysentery with which I was stricken the night before make 25 August live in my memory as one of the most painful days I have known. Shall I ever forget the two cups of hot coffee that a peasant woman gave me in a village near Han-les-Juvigny, where we happened to stop that day?" He contracted dysentery after drinking water from a stream.[36]

According to Alphonse Grasset, the misery of the experience of the retreat was compounded by German atrocities committed in the aftermath of the Battle of Ethe. The Germans shot sixty Red Cross workers, wounded French soldiers, prisoners and local people because they had been left behind after the French departed and were accused of being troops avoiding surrender or partisans.[37]

These passages sum up more eloquently than any other the disillusionment of defeat. What is remarkable about the retreat which followed is that it did not turn into a rout. Some units fled in the Ardennes and some men dropped out later, but the French Army as a whole did not fall apart. Joffre remained calm and unflappable in the crisis, which gave great reassurance to those serving under him. He ordered the French Armies to pull back and adjusted the balance of forces along the line as circumstances dictated. The commanders tried to keep in step with each other so that flanks were not exposed to enemy attack and gaps between units minimized. The soldiers for their part knew that their country had been invaded and that they had to resist as best they could. There was no alternative. Lintier felt the loss of France was too terrible to contemplate. He quoted some lines from the sixteenth-century poet Du Bellay: "Alas! When will I see the smoke rising from my chimney in my village and in what season? Will I see again the back of my poor house, which is to me a province and a whole lot more?"[38] Perhaps this typical French attachment to the land from which they came kept the troops going as they marched south, in some cases trying to catch up their regimental comrades.

The resilience of both the French and British troops in adversity was remarkable. Later the Germans demonstrated the same ability to keep going as they moved back from the Marne. This resilience showed that the conflict was unlikely to finish quickly. In a telling passage in his book Paul Lintier discusses how troops gradually conquered fear and learnt how to be courageous in coping with the conditions they faced. "Before the war," he wrote, "I used to wonder how it was that old men nearing the extreme limits of existence could continue to live undisturbed in the imminent shadow of death. But now I understand. For us the risk of death has become an element of daily life with which one coolly reckons, which no longer astonishes, and terrifies less."[39]

We must now leave the Ardennes and rejoin André in his pig sty in St. Aubin.

4: LE CATEAU TO GUISE
26-29 AUGUST 1914

Into the Thiérache

On the morning of Wednesday 26 August André Benoit set off south-west through the countryside of the Thiérache. Unknown to him, Lanrezac had already ordered the Reserve Divisions to retreat alongside the 18th Corps behind the great forest at Le Nouvion-en-Thiérache, liaising with the right wing of the British Expeditionary Force. Apart from one incident André's progress was relatively untroubled over the next three days. As Lanrezac noted in his account, the rearguards of the Fifth Army easily contained the advance units of the German Army.[1]

The 1:25000 map looked like an impenetrable maze, a mass of irregular small fields separated by hedgerows and streams. It told me, and no doubt André as well, that I was entering very different country as I followed his route. Geologically the Thiérache is a zone of transition, where silt begins to cover the declining rocks of the Ardennes massif. Stretching south-west from the Belgian border to the valley of the Oise it is low-lying and damp. Around St. Aubin water squelched under my boots. The landscape near Le Petit Fayt, where I bought some bread and cheese, was fairly typical. Shaded by ash trees I stretched out among the few remaining yellow and purple wild flowers on the bank of a sluggish stream called the Helpe Mineure. Water lilies formed a platform at either edge, a haven for insects and a shelter for fish. A black coot scuttled between the leaves, screeching what sounded like a distress call. Predatory otters create their burrows in these banks. In the willow-lined meadow opposite, Friesian cows cropped the lush grass embedded in soft red-brown soil. In 1914 the mixed subsistence agriculture was beginning to change. Now this is almost exclusively cattle country producing milk and rich cheeses like Maroilles, noted for its strong earthy smell. Fields of wheat covered small plateaus of higher land away from the rivers, but very few.

Turning round I could just make out the spire of the village church built of the small red bricks typical of this area. They were also used in the construction of houses, occasionally supplemented by stone and wooden beams. I found several barrack-like farmhouses with heavy brick mouldings built between 1880 and 1914. Often their height was disproportionate to their width. Lower cottages with small dormer windows were more common. Understandably many of the wattle and thatched cottages of André's day were destroyed in the fighting between 1914 and 1918.

There were other signs of the enormous changes witnessed by this region during the twentieth century. Restored houses and modern bungalows with manicured gardens lined the lane approaching Le Petit Fayt. The local milk processing plant or *laiterie* had long since closed down. In the main street through Beaurepaire-sur-Sambre there were *À vendre* boards outside two dilapidated old houses and a shuttered café. The rural depopulation which started in André's day has accelerated since 1945. Country areas like the Thiérache in northern France have suffered because better employment opportunities in Paris or the industrial basin around Lille are not far away. Workers commuting to local towns want new accommodation. Outsiders looking for second or retirement homes prefer to gentrify old houses. Lack of trade forces small local industries, shops and bars to close. The population is ageing, hence the need for a brand new *hôpital pour les personnes agées dépendantes* at Le Nouvion. The magnificent expanse of deciduous woodland behind it once belonged to Henri Comte d'Orléans, one of the families who used to occupy the throne of France. Now his chateau is closed up and the forest belongs to a syndicate of hunters from Belgium which denies access to locals.

At one crossroads after another I discovered a small shrine or cross. On the main road above my B&B at St. Aubin stood a neat, brick-built shrine to the Virgin Mary and all the saints, admirably restored following a public appeal in July 2013. On the other side of the road was a chapel. Later, near Le Petit Fayt I noticed a small grey cylinder of stone on the verge. A hollowed-out space at the top, designed to house a statue of the Virgin, was now empty. One hundred years ago Catholic religious observance was higher than average in this region of northern France. Shrines and crosses created a sacred landscape and religious processions from one to another were a part of everyday life. It is more than likely that many of the soldiers in the Fifth Army stopped by them and prayed for protection.

After fifteen kilometres André's regiment halted for a rest. He could hear the sound of cannon from the forest of Mormal where the British were fighting. Next he noticed smoke drifting above a wooded hill four kilometres to the west. He was ordered to deploy his men on either side of the road and to fire on enemy cavalry expected to appear around a bend only two hundred metres away. Suddenly some troops arrived, but they were French not German. There was relief all round. His men relaxed by pretending to stage a bull fight with cows in the fields. Shortly afterwards he was marching down the hill into Le Petit Fayt and the cannon fire seemed to be getting much nearer. He could see flames only a kilometre away. The cows started to run around as if possessed by spirits. Again he was ordered to deploy his men and a number of shells landed very close.[2]

The British fight for their lives at Le Cateau

What was the reason for all this excitement? We left Haig and the British 1st Corps retiring south from the area around Landrecies on the morning of 26 August. When leaving Le Grand Fayt early in the morning Haig ordered the

Connaught Rangers to act as rearguard. They arrived at Le Grand Fayt at around 3 pm, only two kilometres west of André's position, having been held up by a large detachment of French territorials. At first all seemed quiet but not long afterwards the Germans launched an attack. A fierce action ensued and the Connaughts lost 280 men. Some were taken prisoner but others escaped including a group who joined a French unit in a night march to Le Nouvion. André, remember, was proceeding in that direction too.[3]

Given the timing it is likely that the first cannon fire André heard that day came from Le Cateau some twenty kilometres away where the men of Smith-Dorrien's 2nd Corps were fighting for their lives against superior German forces. Smith-Dorrien had decided to make a stand rather than retire because his men were too disorganized to get away in time. His fear was that the retreat could turn into a rout and his aim to administer a stopping blow to the Germans which would slow down their pursuit of the BEF. After fighting he planned to withdraw again.

The British took up positions south of Le Cateau. The 5th Division on the right occupied higher ground either side of the straight Roman road south to St. Quentin, with their right flank facing east towards the valley of the River Selle. A sunken lane ran diagonally south-west from Le Cateau town across the division's position. On a knoll to the south of the lane were the Suffolks, supported by the King's Own Yorkshire Light Infantry (KOYLI) and later by the Manchesters, together with batteries of the Royal Field Artillery. The Germans were able to concentrate unobserved in Le Cateau and then filter onto the battlefield down the sunken lane and the east-west road to Cambrai further north, protected to some extent by two cuttings. Like all the British units, the 3rd Division occupied hastily dug trenches further west and parallel to the Cambrai road, near the villages of Beaumont and Audencourt and the small lace-making town of Caudry. The position of the 4th Division on the left, again south of the Cambrai road, featured a quarry, the Warnelle ravine and three more settlements: Ligny, Haucourt and Esnes. The cavalry and the 19th Brigade as a reserve were located behind the infantry positions but the artillery batteries were situated in forward positions, often on exposed open spurs. The British front was about sixteen kilometres long and Smith-Dorrien had forty battalions to defend it together with eighty machine guns and 246 artillery pieces.

The weakness of the British position was its exposed right flank. Although Haig could hear the sound of firing from Le Cateau he made no attempt to come to 2nd Corps' aid. Even one infantry brigade would have greatly strengthened 2nd Corps' right. Instead he decided that the higher priority was to preserve 1st Corps intact, and in this he was supported by Sir John French who detested Smith-Dorrien personally and later criticized his handling of the battle. Smith-Dorrien had had to take the decision to fight on his own and on the 26th Sir John was not present near Le Cateau. The only help he gave 2nd Corps was to persuade Joffre to send Sordet's cavalry to assist the British left. The sharp crack of the French 75 mm guns was a great reassurance to Smith-Dorrien during the afternoon.

With room to manoeuvre, Le Cateau was more of a gunner's battle than Mons. It was also in some ways an old-fashioned fight between opposing masses of infantry close-up, with horse-drawn guns in the front line and horses also used for transport and as mounts for senior officers. The most reliable means of communication was also to send a man on horseback.

The British were lucky in that von Kluck was unable to bring all his forces to bear at the start of the battle but fed them into the action progressively during the day. He aimed to attack the British flanks, hoping to precipitate a collapse in the centre as well. The Germans opened the battle with an intense artillery barrage, particularly on the 5th Division. The Suffolks on their knoll had to endure this with very little opportunity to respond. Some of the British gun batteries were destroyed. At the same time the German 4th Corps started to creep along the Selle valley, threatening the British flank. Here they met stiff resistance from the Duke of Cornwall's Light Infantry, the East Surreys and the 3rd Cavalry Brigade. At around 10 am this German corps, which had already occupied Le Cateau, launched massed infantry attacks. The KOYLI saw the German infantry advancing in four waves fifty metres apart across open ground, but the 5th Division halted them with continued firing from those batteries which had not been destroyed, as well as from rifles and machine guns. The Manchesters and the Argyll and Sutherland Highlanders were sent up to the front line from the reserve but had great difficulty reaching their positions in the face of very heavy incoming fire. The German infantry was filtering forward in small parties up the Selle valley and along the sunken lane. The machine guns they brought with them swept the forward British trenches. The situation at noon was critical for the 5th Division but it was still holding on.

In the centre the Germans made no serious attacks before noon, but at 2 pm the fighting became more intense when von Kluck brought up fresh infantry and started shelling Caudry. On the left the Royal Lancasters were surprised in the open by German machine guns and artillery and lost 400 men very quickly. Two companies of the Warwickshires were ordered to counter-attack from Harcourt in a suicidal charge up a bullet-swept hill in order to cover the retirement of the Royal Lancasters behind the Warnelle ravine. This impossible attack made a deep impression on the young Lieutenant Bernard Montgomery who took part. The need for careful preparation to avoid unnecessary loss of life stayed with him for the remainder of his career. He tripped over the scabbard of his sword which may have saved his life.[4] The 4th Division pulled back in the face of the German bombardment but stopped any further advance by their opponents.

After noon Smith-Dorrien agreed that the situation of the 5th Division was so critical that it should start to withdraw, caught as it was by double enfilading fire. This was easier said than done when his troops were so heavily engaged. The British artillerymen displayed great heroism in trying to bring their guns away under intense German bombardment. Three VCs were awarded. Many were killed or wounded and some guns had to be left behind, although they were rendered unusable. The British artillery was sited too far forward and took terrible punishment during the day, particularly on the right where 25 guns were lost. Later in the war the British learnt how to protect their batteries by concealing them well behind the front line. The 2nd Suffolks, the 2nd KOYLI and the 2nd Argyll and Sutherland Highlanders sacrificed themselves so that their colleagues could retire. At roll-call next morning only 111 men and two officers of the Suffolks' 2nd Battalion reported. Some 500 officers and men were taken prisoner, and 80 officers and men were killed on the knoll.[5] The numbers killed among the KOYLI were even higher, probably because their position was more exposed to German machine gun fire from the Cambrai road cutting.[6] By 6 pm the 5th Division had broken contact with the enemy, who had proved themselves too exhausted to drive their flank attack into the retreating British columns.

In the centre the retirement was easier although the artillery suffered further losses. The 1st Gordon Highlanders and a party of the Royal Scots fought on after 6 pm to cover the retreat, marching off after midnight before subsequently being made prisoners. The 4th Division on the left fought two divisions of German cavalry to a standstill. The 1st Rifle Brigade suffered 35 per cent casualties in and around Ligny. Then the German 4th Reserve Corps started attacking in strength at 4 pm. The British infantry dispersed in retreat, assisted by Sordet's cavalry, and a few guns were abandoned.[7] In all the British 2nd Corps lost 7,812 men killed, wounded or taken prisoner and 38 guns.

The battle of Le Cateau had an important effect on the decisions of the generals not at the scene. Von Kluck was convinced that he had been fighting the whole of the British Expeditionary Force and treated the retreating British with more circumspection than he might have done. He effectively gave them twelve hours' start to get away. However, Sir John French seemed to believe that the 2nd Corps had virtually ceased to exist as an effective fighting force. His staff shared this view and it was passed on to his French allies. This was to have far reaching implications for the conduct of the retreat, as we shall see. André Benoit and his colleagues were to feel its effects three days later.

Retreat to the Oise

It was dark by the time André's unit regrouped after its involvement in the British action at Le Grand Fayt. Now they had to march seventeen kilometres to their billets in the hamlet of La Petite Rue, five kilometres south of Le Nouvion. It was a frustrating night. Other regiments and vehicles got mixed up with the 267th Reserve Regiment and it started to rain. Worst of all, the officers had no maps of the area because the General Staff had thought they would be advancing to Germany, not retreating. They did not know the way and stopped every twenty metres. If a halt lasted too long some men would drop off to sleep in the ditch and not get up again. "We will snuff it one way or another," they complained. This went on all night. It was so dark that André bumped into a horse. His friend Lefebvre shone his electric lamp on the road, revealing more men sleeping. It was a relief when they got to La Petite Rue at daybreak.[8] The regimental journal notes that many of the men were overcome with fatigue, because they had been marching since 3 am and could not find any room in the vehicles. As a result they got lost in the forest of Le Nouvion. It also noted that the march had to be accelerated because of the German pursuit.[9]

*

My walk into Le Nouvion was not without its adventures. I climbed around the edge of a quarry not indicated on the map. This involved clinging to a fence, tramping through thistles and dodging pick-up trucks. Nearer Le Nouvion a quiet green lane ended in barbed wire and impenetrable brambles. I had to retrace my steps and tramp down the main road, avoiding rush hour traffic. Le Nouvion has probably not changed much since 1914. A long single street with few shops but an imposing town hall, it is just a small centre for local services: population 2,807, unemployment 19.2 per cent. The historian Ernest Lavisse came from here. His historical works and widely-used teachers' manuals influenced the ideas of André's generation about the France for which they fought and died. A speech he gave at the school in Le Nouvion in 1907 says much about the division between this remote countryside and the capital. He talked about how his audience would no longer be provincial peasants ("little inhabitants of the forests and pastures of the Thiérache, whose minds are quick and practical, who are quarrelsome by nature") but citizens of the fatherland, of France. It seems very condescending today.[10]

Hot and soaked in sweat after a tiring day I was luckier than André with my billet. The hotel in Le Nouvion provided not only a comfortable bed and a hot shower but also an excellent menu consisting of rabbit terrine, steak covered in Maroilles cheese and tart washed down with glasses of *rosé* and Médoc. Next morning, fresh and relaxed, I walked down the wide forest road past Henri d'Orléans' chateau to meet André again in La Petite Rue where he was trying to find some rest.

André wrote that everyone seemed completely worn out. Soldiers were

St-Denis, Le-Nouvion-en-Thiérache, c 1914.

Church of St-Denis and Town Hall, Le-Nouvion-en-Thiérache, 2013 (Terry Cudbird)

sleeping all over the place: on the pavements and the steps of houses. Some were just milling around exhausted in the middle of the road. One weeping captain had lost all but six of the men in his company. When André was told he had to move off again in ten minutes he found an *estaminet* and sunk several anisettes, before filling up his thermos flask with Cointreau.[11] He did not do as well as Sergeant Omnès in the 10th Corps, who was taking champagne from the cellars of a chateau at the same time as well as a fine pair of leather hunting boots. He also loaded up a cart with enough bread for the regiment, helping himself to clean linen and leaving his dirty underwear in a cupboard for the Germans. My colleagues were always crafty, he wrote.[12]

It was not difficult to imagine the scene André describes. La Petite Rue is still a small hamlet, with old and new houses lining a single street. Most of the buildings date from before 1914, humble terraced cottages built of weathered brick with tiny attic windows. I searched for signs of the *estaminet* and found one possible candidate: a small house with a window facing the street which had clearly at one time been larger. Maybe it was used to sell drinks to the passing troops. An old factory with a chimney was a reminder of the dispersed industrial sites in the countryside in 1914.

The next problem for André was to get out of the village. Measures had been taken against enemy cavalry reported to be nearby. Engineers had blocked the roads and hedges with carts and barbed wire. Broken glass covered the surface to deter horses. Outside the village there was a line of refugees with their wagons loaded with furniture, children and hay for the horses, as well as cows attached behind.[13]

André continued in the direction of the Oise valley, but we don't know exactly which route he followed. I walked on to Esquéhéries two kilometres away which had a *salle des fêtes* with a splendid art deco lyre on the gable. The fortified church typical of the Thiérache was unusual in that four towers protected it, two at either end. But of most interest to me was the *estaminet*, Chez Évelyne, which was still open for customers. The modest building was almost an exact replica of the cottages in La Petite Rue. A heavy shower which lasted half an hour encouraged me inside.

I found Évelyne behind a small bar. She was a birdlike old lady who must have been over eighty. Talking to her I gradually entered the lost world of France's rural past. For 2.50 euros she served me an espresso along with her special anisette from Marseille, which she said tasted much better than the well-known brands. She was the last in a long line of innkeepers on the site, going back over two hundred years she claimed. At one time there had been lots of little *estaminets* in the surrounding villages; not any more.

She wagged a bony finger at me as she described the decline of village life in the Aisne. In short, people were much less sociable than they used to be and she

Café Chez Évelyne, Esquéhéries, a surviving example of the many cafés or *estaminets* which André would have encountered in 1914. (Terry Cudbird)

was lonely. There was not the same spirit. "Aide-toi et le ciel t'aidera," but don't depend on others. A heart attack had felled her husband. One of her sons had been killed in an accident and the other had died of disease. Without a family, she said, you were nothing.

The rain driving past the window added to the gloom in the bar, briefly lifted when a younger woman came in to say hello. Évelyne made a great fuss of her poodle called Oscar. While she was preoccupied I started to piece together the picture she was painting of life in Esquéhéries. There was a school and a church, but the priest did not visit very often and could not say mass every week. Most of the small farms had disappeared. The few large operators left had got rich on the back of EU subsidies; money grubbers all of them. Look at the price of grain! They grabbed every sou they could, even enclosing the wide verges on the *chemins vicinaux* which were not rightfully theirs. When she said this Évelyne stared straight at me through her thin spectacle frames as if I were guilty of such greed too.

Her social critique included all rich people. We, "les petits gens", paid the taxes to make the rich fatter. Politicians! She could scarcely utter the word. The French only had themselves to blame. The Germans ran Europe; they were more disciplined. "Les petits français" were very "comme ci, comme ça." After this formidable blast of French rhetoric I needed some more fresh air.

Fortunately the rain had stopped. A gentle stroll brought me to the village of Leschelles with its immaculately restored brickwork and elegant eighteenth-century chateau, complete with wrought-iron grille and parterre festooned with marigolds. I emerged guiltily from the private hunting wood behind the chateau to find an ideal picnic spot on the edge of fields bursting with ripe wheat. A wide vista stretched as far as a wind farm on the plateau south of the Oise. I was leaving the closed world of the Thiérache behind. The river itself became clearly visible from the terrace outside the battered church in Chigny. A series of ponds stretched across a marsh and it was difficult to distinguish the course of the river itself among the trees. Behind me was a neat village green surrounded by sculpted chestnut trees and an old house of brick, stone and beams, my next comfortable stop for a night. André claims he was so tired when he reached the Oise that he fell asleep on top of a harrow.[14]

Another old lady greeted me with a kind smile which suggested she was more at peace with the world than Évelyne. The heavy old furniture and wooden floors gleamed with polish. A picture of the Sacred Heart, images of the Virgin Mary and a *prie-dieu* in my bedroom suggested Catholic devotion. The simple but nourishing supper included home-made tarts and puréed gooseberries with Friday's fish. *Madame* and her sister, who lived next door, painted a similar picture of the area to Évelyne's. They had lived in the locality for a long time and yes, the region had lost a lot of people. Now there were only three farms in the village, many fewer than before. The *fromagerie* was now a *salle des fêtes*. They remembered when many women from the village worked there. All the artisans had left, there was little for the young to do and a lot of second homes. The Dutch seemed to enjoy the contrast with the crowded Netherlands. I observed a notice outside the *mairie* saying that a Dutchman had agreed to rent the local communal woodland for a number of private shooting parties each year. You had to drive all the way to Le Nouvion or Guise to shop, and if the accident and emergency department was closed there was no alternative to calling the *sapeurs-pompiers*. The elderly priest had to cover forty small churches so they did not see him very often. Once a young priest had arrived from Africa, but went back home because the cultural adjustment was too great. A community of younger priests near Le Nouvion helped out occasionally. The sisters went to mass regularly at a nunnery which also ran a very good school. This was only possible as long as they had a car.

The transformation of villages from vibrant self-sufficient communities to total dependence on the towns started before the Great War and accelerated after 1945. The reduction in the number of farms and the closure of thousands of small-scale factories and associated services, particularly in the textile industry, drastically reduced social contact between neighbours and the spirit of *entr'aide* or helping each other. Two figures demonstrate the enormity of the change in the twentieth century. In 1901 there were 43,000 workers in the textile industry of the Aisne, which accounted for 39 per cent of all industrial employment. However, all these jobs have disappeared. In 1892 the average farm size was 2.54 hectares and 27,900 people worked as day labourers on the land.[15] It was the coming of the railways which ushered in the era of factory farming for a national market instead of small-scale agriculture for local consumption. If you look at a railway map of northern France in 1914 the network is very dense. The myriad lines which transported the troops to the front helped destroy the society from which many of them came.

Just before reaching Chigny I stopped in another small settlement to look at the war memorial, erected after 1918 and commemorating local boys *morts pour la France*. Many of these soldiers came from such isolated communities, yet they, like their comrades from the large towns, did their duty. Their grieving relatives were willing to describe this sacrifice as made for France. "Died for France" is not a very Anglo-Saxon turn of phrase. We rarely say that our soldiers died for Britain. "La France" is not just a country but also a set of values; a certain idea of France, as de Gaulle once said, which was hotly discussed politically but which in 1914 transcended class, political and religious barriers. *Mort pour la France* was a credo that, whatever happened, France and its Republic must be kept alive. This phrase was so universal in France after 1918 that it perpetuated the memory of the war and the sacrifices made. Once *madame* in Chigny found out why I was there she immediately said: "my grandfather fought at Verdun. He was one of three brothers. One of them died in that battle."

The idea of France as a country to which all its inhabitants belonged only came to be universally accepted in the generation before 1914. Up until around 1890 the concept would not have meant a great deal to the majority of the rural population, particularly south of a line from Geneva to the mouth of the Loire. Most peasants regarded people who came from more than a few kilometres away as foreigners and no concern of theirs. Even as late as 1906 some 36 per cent of army recruits "were unaware that France was vanquished in 1870 and barely half knew of the annexation of Alsace-Lorraine".[16] They spoke different tongues and had different customs: religious feasts, social celebrations, oral traditions, music and dances, and ways of doing business. Universal education, military service and national politics gradually reduced this diversity, but for some of the soldiers of 1914, particularly those from the south, the veneer of French civilization was still only skin deep. *Mort pour la France* did more than anything else perhaps to create a truly national consciousness.

*

Once André had woken up from his sleep on a harrow he set off along the Oise valley, which he describes as pretty and green. The regiment halted in a vast orchard near the river at Romery, where the 1911 *mairie* still stands today. He felt too tired to eat and longed to take his boots off and have a nap. His men went scrounging and came back with bottles and some chickens, which they said they had been given. It does not sound as if he believed them.[17]

Looking across the valley from the hill at Chigny I was surprised by the steepness of the escarpment beyond the southern bank. It was clear why Lanrezac selected the plateau above as a defensive position. This was the second major river barrier which I had to cross: the Sambre and now the Oise; later the Aisne, the Marne and the Petit and Grand Morins. I continued along the ridge before dropping down to the valley floor at Le Brûlé. This was easier said than done as my chosen route ran into dense undergrowth and the back garden of a chateau, from which I had to beat a hasty retreat. Le Brûlé had ten massive farmhouses, side on to the street, all of which looked as if they had seen better days. If the number of farms has reduced then presumably fewer such buildings are needed for their original purpose.

The road to Proisy on the south bank of the Oise went past a large embankment and a set of hydraulic gates. These defences against flooding were constructed after widespread water damage in 1993, rated as a serious risk every thirty years. In 1914 the river was not confined neatly within its banks as it is today. No doubt the water meadows about two kilometres wide were covered regularly. A former railway line at the side of the valley provided an easy footpath. Now covered in grass and lined with trees, it is known as the *axe vert* or green axis and plays a useful part in attracting tourists. From Romery I climbed the hill, with André, to the small settlement of Wiège-Faty where he stayed the night of 27 August.

Wiège-Faty is on the edge of a vast undulating plateau of wheat fields, which stretches from the Oise to La Fère and the Forêt de St. Gobain, thirty kilometres to the south. Some small woods dot the edge of the valley, but wherever you look west and south the ground is completely naked, as if stripped bare. Wiège itself is not much of a village; just a scattered settlement around a crossroads and a chateau. Remarkably I was able to reconstruct all the comings and goings André describes in his diary.

All but a few inhabitants had left the village. The regiment gathered in a large farm which was unoccupied. Here André had dinner with his fellow officers. They had found some tasty morsels and several bottles of fine wine in the cellars which they were not prepared to leave for the connoisseurs from across the Rhine. Everyone became fairly drunk, ironic when the captain had just been addressing his men on the danger of imbibing on a route march. Poor André was so tired that he could not enjoy what was on offer. I was sure that the farm was in fact the chateau, whose grand gatehouse and roof I could see from the road. Some dilapidated farm buildings adjoined it. The courtyard was full of rubbish and guarded by two Alsatians.

André had to man a police post and deal with minor disciplinary offences. He put up some tables in the school, a two-storey brick building which I found opposite the chateau and next to the church. The priest lent him three candles. His presbytery still stands nearby. My most curious discovery, however, was the outhouse used to store the village fire pumps, where André says he installed the men of his section. Looking across from the school, now shared with the *mairie*, I could see this building set into the wall of the chateau on the other side of the road. Now partly ruined, it consisted of four rooms like the inside of an air raid shelter, their windows surmounted by green vitreous tiles. The legend *ompes à incendie* occupied a plinth over the main door. The missing "P" must have dropped off in the last one hundred years. In between dealing with cases of drunkenness and an accidental firearms injury André tried to snatch some sleep. His feet were very painful and he rubbed them with formol or formaldehyde, a common remedy used by the infantry on this long march.[18]

Pompes à Incendie shelter, Wiège-Faty. (Terry Cudbird)

The great British escape after Le Cateau

While André and his regiment were crossing the Oise east of Guise, the British were streaming along the roads to Guise itself and the textile town of St. Quentin further west. They were incredibly lucky. Von Kluck swung his forces south-west once again as he had done after Mons. Faulty intelligence suggested that the British bases were still at Calais and that he could cut their supply lines. As a result the British Expeditionary Force proceeded without major interference from the Germans. On the whole the mounted troops who followed them kept a respectful distance after the mauling they had received. Both corps commanders took advantage of the situation, urging their men southwards as fast as possible. By dawn on 28 August the 2nd Corps had reached the Somme, 55 kilometres from Le Cateau. The 1st Corps marched well south of Guise in the same time.[19]

Had the German First Army pursued the 2nd Corps relentlessly in the hours after Le Cateau the result could have been entirely different. At first the British retreat was disorganized to put it mildly. This was the view of K.F.B. Tower of the 4th Battalion Royal Fusiliers who wrote later: "The scene on the road baffles any description I can give of it. It was a veritable rout, men, horses, guns, refugees and wagons struggling along in disorder to get away at all costs."[20] Individual groups of survivors marched south without knowing whether their comrades were dead or alive. Some of them had become separated from their units in the fighting. Others fell out on the march because they could not keep up.

It took a lot of work by staff officers and others to sort them back into regiments again. They made a start at St. Quentin on the morning of 27 August, standing by crossroads and directing lost soldiers to their units. Major Tom Bridges of the Dragoon Guards was shocked to see two or three hundred men lying around the Place. Even worse, their commanding officers had assured the *maire* that they would surrender to avoid the town being bombarded by the Germans. Bridges countermanded this order and told the men to get moving. The commanding officers were later cashiered.[21]

Frank Richards of the Royal Welch Fusiliers described how he became separated from his regiment when he went to wake up some men in a hayrick. They tried to catch up but took the wrong turning at a crossroads. He and a disparate group of men wandered south for days, living on anything they could forage. They got involved in some fighting, cadged a lift from ladies in a carriage and shared a meal with gypsies in a wood. Eventually they reached a railhead where an officer directed them onto a train to take them to the British base at Le Mans.[22] During the first five days of the retreat between 2,500 and 3,000 men suffering from bad feet and exhaustion were sent to Le Mans for recuperation.[23]

F. Gaunt, a private in the 4th Battalion Royal Fusiliers, had a similar experience.

"I fell out, owing to my feet being all blistered, so I followed up behind the best way I could. I lost my regiment for three days." A staff officer sent him in the wrong direction, but he helped carry some ammunition to a firing line before he found his regiment again.[24] The most famous straggler in the left wing of the British Expeditionary Force was Bernard Montgomery. He was part of a group which got left behind when the retreat began. For three days they marched behind the German cavalry screen and their main columns, moving by night and hiding by day. This was dangerous as the Germans started to shoot stragglers as spies if they did not surrender immediately. "Monty" paid tribute to Major A.J. Poole without whom he would never have got back to his battalion.[25]

Although the retreat was easier for the 1st Corps, because they had not been involved in the fighting at Le Cateau, its soldiers still found the going tough. On the 26th itself they had sustained casualties of 1,200 due to exhaustion and crippled feet.[26] H.J. Rowthorn, a private with the Northamptonshire Regiment, dropped behind because of the state of his feet, and his mate was taken prisoner by the German cavalry. A group of Hussars helped him out with a decent meal and eventually he found his regiment again at La Fère, about sixty kilometres from Le Cateau.[27]

What made the retreat so hard, particularly for the unfit reservists? First of all the soldiers had to march for a long period, day and night, with virtually no sleep. Lance-Corporal Arthur Cook of the 1st Somerset Light Infantry saw his lieutenant stretched out on a horse's back fast asleep without falling off.[28] James Jack wrote that "the chargers bore equipment or exhausted soldiers, and towed a man hanging on to the stirrup on either flank. Transport vehicles gave similar assistance."[29] Lieutenant Cedric Brereton of the 68th Battery of the Royal Horse Artillery described how they helped the infantry during the retreat on 27 August to Voyennes on the Somme: "As our Infantry were quite done, we were to commandeer carts and horse them with horses out of our teams, and put as many Infantrymen as possible on our wagons and limbers. This was an awful march, not more than 2 horses in any team, about 6 Infantrymen on each limber or wagon body, and everybody going to sleep and falling off limbers and horses the whole time. Halts, of which there were many, were perfect hell, because it was almost impossible to start off again."[30]

Some exhausted soldiers started seeing things. Frank Richard's mate Billy Stevens said: "'There's a fine castle there, see?' pointing to one side of the road. But there was nothing there. Very nearly everyone were seeing things, we were all so dead beat."[31] The exhausted Gaunt recalled a strange occurrence as he lay on his back half-dozing. "I… saw in the sky a curious effect, which looked like a number of spirits or angel forms… Later on I mentioned it to others, and they said they had seen the same appearance."[32] Maybe in this state soldiers saw the Angels of Mons; spirit forms which some claimed protected them during the battle.

Long marches are likely to cause blisters even with the most comfortable modern boots. In 1914 the soldiers wore leather boots held together with nails which often pierced the skin and caused great pain. Some removed their boots, preferring to make slippers out of their puttees. Rowthorn said that the nails were sticking into his feet. "My socks were all holes where the nails had torn them and my feet were bleeding so I bound the putties round them and threw the boots over the hedge, and when I started walking again it seemed lovely. The only thing now was they would keep slipping off the toes. Time after time I would keep pulling them up again but within a few yards they would be off again; so in the end I left them off. It wasn't very nice, but better than the nails." Later the Medical Officer sorted him out with some Condes fluid, bandages and a pair of gym slippers.[33] Sergeant Bradlaugh Sanderson of the 2nd King's Royal Rifle Corps tried Vaseline around his socks to ease the discomfort.[34] The problem was made worse by the cobbled roads then prevalent in this part of France.

The German infantry, who had marched without a single rest day since around 10 August, were suffering from sore feet as well.[35] Even General von Kluck was concerned about this possibility.[36] Private Ludwig Renn described the state of his unit at Lugny not far from Vervins in his book of memoirs.

> We had had no bread for days. At midday and in the evening we ate beef, in fat hot gravy. There was no time to prepare vegetables, when we were crawling into some shed every evening in the dark and were wakened in the mornings before sunrise. All one night we remained lying in the road at one place, because they had forgotten to tell us that it was our spell to turn in. That night the moon was shining. It was cold on the stony ground.

The next day he records: "On that day we were even able to wash our feet, which for a fortnight—or even longer—had never been out of our boots."[37]

Later he talks about the hot and sultry weather, the fatigue of the march with lots of stops and starts, the dust and soldiers lying by the road with dirty handkerchiefs over their heads soaked in sweat, unable to go any further.[38]

Nearly all participants mention the suffocating heat on several days. The meteorological records show that from 10 August until the end of the month an anticyclone brought generally fine, hot weather to the northern half of France. The average monthly temperature in August was normal in the east, but up to one degree higher than normal in the north and west. In Paris the temperature was 0.9 degrees above normal and the fine weather continued until 9 September.[39] This weather made thick shirts and uniforms very uncomfortable to wear. According to Bernard Denore, quite a few soldiers threw clothes away, including their greatcoats which could ensure a more comfortable rest at night. Tropical kit might have been more appropriate. Drinking the local water was forbidden,[40] but desperate men ignored this advice even at the risk of bowel problems.[41]

Understandably a lot of men also threw away kit and equipment like entrenching tools because they found them too heavy to carry. Sometimes they were even ordered to throw them away, as Lt. Brereton was on the morning of the 28th.[42] Indeed, General Henry Wilson, Deputy Chief of Staff in GHQ, ordered the destruction of much of 4th Division's kit, although Smith-Dorrien later reversed his subordinate's decision.[43] Unwanted items cluttered the verges of the country roads, including discarded food tins. Frank Richards also mentions the broken down lorries, motor cycles, wagons and dead horses which made it more difficult for the infantry to pass.[44] Walter Bloem of the Brandenburg Grenadiers noted the abandoned private vans and burning supplies. He joked that the flames had cooked thousands of tins of Fray Bentos bully beef which were excellent to eat.[45] It was not only abandoned equipment and the press of their comrades which held up the retreating troops. They also had to contend with civilian refugees. Denore noted on the 28th that it was the variety of vehicles they used which cluttered the roadway.[46]

Food supplies were erratic but not totally lacking. The transport tried to keep up with the men and often left dumps of food at strategic points along the roads. C.E.M. Richards, a subaltern with the East Lancashire Regiment, noted that biscuits, corned beef, cheese, tea and sugar were often left on the side of the road and the men helped themselves. One of his men went to a local shop and bought what he thought was a cake. To his surprise it was a Camembert cheese.[47] Rowthorn recalled two soldiers handing out half a dozen dog biscuits and a tin of bully beef as he marched past without stopping. Opening a tin on the move was a bit tricky.[48]

The generosity of the local people often made up for the food which the army could not supply. Frederic Coleman noted: "The French women were splendidly helpful. Steaming bowls of coffee, little boxes of food, bits of cake, pitchers of tea or jugs of milk, matches, cigarettes, anything they thought would help to cheer or comfort, they brought to the roadside for the Tommies."[49] James Jack agreed: "As to the French peasantry: deeply concerned as they were about their own security, and bitterly disappointed at being left to the enemy's hands, their kindness by deed as well as word all the way from Mons can never be exceeded. At no time did I see on their faces, or hear in their remarks, anything but pity for our men. They stood at their doors with pails of water, sometimes wine, long rolls of bread and butter, fruit, just what they had. We must never forget them."[50] As we have seen, the self-sufficient agricultural society of northern

France in 1914 prized a spirit of *entr'aide* or helping your neighbour. It was this social solidarity perhaps which accounted for the generosity of poor and no doubt frightened peasants towards the British Army.

Apart from tiredness, lack of food and painful feet, the anxiety of not knowing what was going on and why they were retreating affected the soldiers' morale. Bernard Denore complained that his unit beat off German attacks every day and yet they kept retiring. It was, he said, heart-breaking work.[51] Lieutenant Edgington of the Royal Field Artillery pointed to the lack of information: "All ranks are very much depressed owing not only to the fact of us continuously retiring, but at the total absence of any information. We appear to be simply driven blindly back."[52] With these thoughts in their minds, the sheer monotony of marching for many kilometres along dead straight, tree-lined roads across a flat plain tested the men's morale to the limit. Tower of the Royal Fusiliers again: "Nothing could have been finer than the bearing of the men through all this long tedious march, largely on cobblestones over mile after mile of road through endless flat country past hundreds and hundreds of poplar trees acting as sentinels along the line of retreat. We sang, we played mouth organs and penny whistles, to forget tired feet."[53]

Despite everything music, humour and the regimental spirit kept them going. Major Tom Bridges encouraged the soldiers to their feet in St. Quentin by playing *The British Grenadiers and It's a Long Way to Tipperary* with a whistle and a drum.[54] Denore told the story of a soldier called Ginger Gilmore who found a mouth organ and "despite the fact that his feet were bound in blood-soaked rags, he staggered along at the head of the company playing tunes all day. Mostly he played 'The Irish Emigrant,' which is a good marching tune. He reminded me of Captain Oates."[55] Frederic Coleman spent the morning of 27 August in St. Quentin directing the stragglers of the 2nd Corps. He was amazed at their sense of humour in adversity. He met an Irishman in a Scottish regiment who held his right ear between thumb and finger. "'And what do ye think o' that?' he queried. Right through the lobe of his ear, close to his cheek, a Mauser bullet had drilled a clean hole. 'Close that, I'm thinkin',' said the proud owner of the damaged member, 'and I niver knew how close me ear was to me head till that thing came along.'"[56] Rowleston West noted that men who had fallen out by the roadside would get to their feet when some of their comrades came "swinging along in step and making a brave show. The old regimental spirit was strong…"[57]

The British did not have to fight a major action in the days immediately following Le Cateau. Sir John French was determined to keep his men out of harm's way. However, one avoidable tragedy led to the loss of 800 men. On 27 August the Second Munsters were asked to act as the rearguard for the 1st Corps in the area of Étreux. The order for them to retire did not get through.

Surrounded by the Germans, they fought to the last man.[58]

The Battle of Guise

On the evening of 27 August the French Fifth Army occupied positions stretching from Guise in the west to Aubenton, east of Vervins, a distance of 53 kilometres. Meanwhile, von Kluck's First Army was advancing south-westerly and thus presented its flank to the French. The British 1st Corps had reached Guise on the night of the 27th, where it bumped into large numbers of French troops.[59] It was due to proceed immediately further south, with the 2nd Corps much further to the west. Joffre told General Lanrezac that he should take advantage of the German manoeuvre by attacking north-west in the direction of St. Quentin. Joffre saw this as a stopping blow which would allow him time to create a new army in the west for an eventual major counter-offensive.[60] To carry out his superior's wishes Lanrezac would have to rotate the 3rd and 18th Corps through 45 degrees, supported by General Valabrègue's Reserve Divisions on their left. He was reluctant to commit himself to a difficult manoeuvre when he might face renewed pressure from the German Second Army to the north. Joffre insisted, however, and came personally to Lanrezac's HQ on the 28th to make sure the adjustments he wanted were carried out on that day, so that the Fifth Army would be ready to attack on the 29th. Lanrezac knew that if he did not cooperate his job was on the line.

Sir Douglas Haig could see the possibility of attacking the German First Army in the flank and was keen to support the proposed French action. He was overruled by French, who was not prepared to risk any further losses and considered his allies unreliable after being left in the lurch at Mons. Joffre was well aware of French's attitude but still wanted Lanrezac to go ahead on his own. The Fifth Army commander ordered the 3rd and 18th Corps to attack the Germans across the Oise between Origny and Ribemont, south of Guise. He also instructed the Reserve Divisions to cross the river between Moÿ and Vendeuil even further downstream. The 10th Corps were to occupy the high ground south of Guise to deal with any German attack from the north and 1st Corps to form a reserve.

*

When André Benoit set out from Wiège-Faty with his men on 28 August he did not realize that, as part of Valabrègue's Reserve Divisions, he was being manoeuvred into a battle position on the extreme left of the French Army. We do not know from his diary exactly which route he took. It was a long march of around thirty kilometres and when he reached his billets after dark he was exhausted.

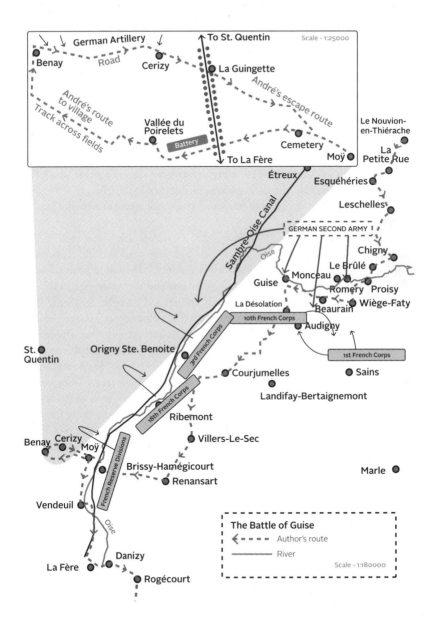

Inset map (Scale - 1:25000):

German Artillery
To St. Quentin
Benay
Road
Cerizy
La Guingette
André's escape route
André's route to village
Track across fields
Vallée du Poirelets
Battery
Le Nouvion-en-Thiérache
Cemetery
Moÿ
La Petite Rue
To La Fère

Main map:

Étreux
Esquéhéries
Leschelles
Sambre-Oise Canal
GERMAN SECOND ARMY
Oise
Chigny
Le Brûlé
Monceau
Guise
Romery
Proisy
La Désolation
Beaurain
Wiège-Faty
10th French Corps
Audigny
3rd French Corps
St. Quentin
Origny Ste. Benoite
1st French Corps
Courjumelles
Sains
Landifay-Bertaignemont
18th French Corps
Ribemont
Benay
Cerizy
Moÿ
Villers-Le-Sec
French Reserve Divisions
Brissy-Hamégicourt
Renansart
Marle
Vendeuil
Oise
Danizy
La Fère
Rogécourt

The Battle of Guise
← - - - - Author's route
——— River
Scale - 1:180000

His unit started by making a short reconnaissance back towards the Oise valley at Monceau. He was not there long before he was ordered to turn about and march south-west. André was lucky because at 1 pm the advancing German Second Army attacked two companies in his regiment at the bridge over the Oise, using artillery and machine guns. According to the regimental journal five officers and sixty men were lost.[61] André marched around twelve kilometres to the main road from Guise to Marle, probably passing through Sains where other elements of the Fifth Army were to take up positions that day. Most likely he met the Marle road just south of Landifay-Bertaig03nemont. There his unit was warned that a German column was approaching. Their artillery set off north to meet the threat and the infantry followed west of the road. He remarks that: "up to the crest of a hill some three kilometres distant we only saw fields which had already been harvested. The dark packets of infantry looked like pawns on an immense chess board."[62] Lines of harvested crops still create exactly the pattern he describes.

Having failed to meet the enemy they retreated south-west again. "We marched and marched," he wrote later, "our legs were tired and the countryside monotonous. We could hear artillery in the distance." They were aiming for the village of Renansart, a long way away. Night came and the moon rose in the sky. They reached the village to find a swarm of soldiers and no room for them. Their billets were another two kilometres further on. The company settled into the long narrow barn of a farm whose inhabitants did not make them welcome. The captain had to roll his sleeves up and make the condensed soup. André was half-conscious with fatigue and dropped off to sleep at the table as the officers dined in a candle-lit room. The captain sent him to sleep on a mattress with his friend Lefebvre.[63]

While André's reserve troops and the four French corps were manoeuvring according to Joffre's plan, the British 1st Corps marched south along the Oise valley below. The gap between Haig's troops and the 2nd Corps was now thirty kilometres. The German cavalry tried to force themselves between the two corps and came up against units of the British cavalry. There was a sharp fight between German Dragoons and the 20th Hussars, 12th Lancers and the Royal Scots Greys around La Guingette, an intersection on the St. Quentin-La Fère road near Moÿ-de-l'Aisne. The Germans retired afterwards.[64] La Guingette was the location of fighting in which André got involved the following day. I found some of the British cavalrymen's graves in the Moÿ cemetery nearby: a captain, sergeant and private from the 12th Lancers, a major from the Royal Scots Greys and a lance-corporal from the 20th Hussars.

I decided to take two days to cover the ground which André crossed in one. On the first I walked over the plateau and then along the *axe vert* from Beaurain to Guise. This gave me an opportunity to explore the town after which the battle is named. On the second I walked south across the agricultural plateau all the way to Renansart, taking in the battlefield of Guise on the way.

The road to Beaurain crosses the northern edge of the plateau. This gently undulating country is completely open, with scattered copses and almost no hedgerows. It is a complete contrast to the verdant profusion of the Thiérache, and crops like oil seed rape, maize, wheat and sugar beet replace cattle. In two days I saw only one small herd of Charolais. The topsoil sits on a bed of solid chalk and frequently streaks of white powder come to the surface. The slope down to the valley floor is fringed with trees. Lanrezac decided to site his troops some way back from this escarpment so that they would enjoy a clear field of fire when the Germans emerged from the Oise valley. He had no intention of contesting the river crossings. The Oise was not a sufficient barrier to make this a credible defensive option. It was also immediately clear that offensive action could be very costly across this open plateau with very little natural cover.

Having descended to the long village street of Beaurain, I re-joined the *axe vert* on the side of the Oise valley and cruised into Guise through a rich tunnel of foliage which screened the view on both sides. From previous visits to the region I had gained the impression that Guise was a depressing town with few signs of development and little hope for the young. While unemployment there is still very high at 24 per cent, the town centre is kept in good repair. Some old, patterned brick houses line a cobbled street to the church and in the main square municipal petunias surround the statue of Camille Desmoulins, hero of the Revolution and local favourite son. Tributaries of the Oise wind their way between the streets. There are two main attractions for visitors. A ruined fortress overlooks the town's 5,000 inhabitants from a limestone outcrop. The keep on a central mound is all that remains of the medieval castle. Vauban revamped the defensive walls and ditches with massive earthworks which are certainly impressive. The network of underground tunnels was supposed to provide protection from bombardment, but the German big guns caused considerable damage during the Battle of Guise. After 1914 the fort became a ruin. Nowadays young volunteers camp in the grounds and learn practical skills restoring the remains and guiding visitors. Two 75 mm field guns from the Great War are a suitable reminder of the conflict. What you will not find in Guise itself is any mention of the battle of 29 August 1914: no plaques, no battlefield tours. The main monument is on the outskirts.

The other attraction is a collection of buildings called the Familistère, all that remains of an unusual nineteenth-century experiment in social engineering. Jean-Baptiste André Godin was a successful industrialist who manufactured metal heating stoves. He wanted to do more than make money, however. His ambition was to create a better environment for industrial workers and to give them more control over their lives. He made his company into a worker-owned cooperative and used his fortune to build apartments for the employees; dwellings which were light and spacious compared with the hovels they had lived in before. Common facilities included a laundry, a swimming pool, a small theatre and a park, all now restored. There used to be a wide range of social events which were also an excuse for dressing up: for example, brass band concerts and festivals of youth. Godin lived on site, albeit in a somewhat larger apartment than his colleagues. The museum explains the experiment as well as containing a collection of his elaborate wrought-iron creations. At the time of the Battle of Guise the Familistère was still a thriving concern, along with the textile factories which provided the town's main employment. The First World War and the depression which followed a decade later put an end to Godin's industrial enterprise. The flats were subsequently refurbished and are now used as social housing.

Guise might have two tourist attractions but it only seemed to have one hotel, recently refurbished by a Moroccan businessman who made an excellent tagine. Many of his ancestors lie in the military graveyard along with their French comrades. Next morning I discovered them for myself.

The monument to the Battle of Guise stands on the main road to Marle. A post-war-style relief sculpture depicts the troops involved as well as the town. The latter includes factory chimneys, a reminder of the industry which was more important then than now. The inscription reads: "To the glory of the Fifth French Army and of its chief General Lanrezac - Battle of Guise 28 and 29 August 1914." These words are ironic because Joffre sacked Lanrezac on 3 September despite his capable conduct of the battle. The commander-in-chief did not consider he had the necessary resilience and drive for the counter-offensive on the Marne.

Climbing further onto the bleak plateau I reached the cemetery aptly named La Désolation. French and German soldiers killed in the battle occupy some of the graves. The cemetery also includes those killed in 1917, 1918 and even 1940. French, Moroccans, Germans, Belgians and British lie together. Roses cover two large ossuaries, a final resting place for those who could not be identified. The fresh wind flapping my jacket was not enough to turn the wind turbines nearby. I climbed to the top of the slope and took in the open view in all directions. The 10th Corps' positions opposite Guise were nearer the edge of the plateau than those of the 1st Corps further east. To my right I could see the village of Audigny across the fields. Some of the hottest fighting took place there.

The story of the Battle of Guise on 29 August is simply told.[65] The French 3rd and 18th Corps, supported by the Reserve Divisions, pushed north-west across the Oise as planned. They made some progress towards St. Quentin, but

Grave of two German soldiers killed on 29 August 1914 during the Battle of Guise, La Désolation. (Terry Cudbird)

a counter-attack by the Germans in that area pushed them back across the river. Meanwhile the German Second Army crossed the Oise at Guise further east and attacked the 10th Corps on the plateau above. The French came under severe pressure and had to yield ground. At this point Lanrezac brought the 1st Corps into play led by Franchet d'Esperey. With flags flying and Franchet's staff leading the men on horseback, the corps manoeuvred between the 10th and 3rd Corps and drove the Germans back down the hill towards Guise.

This limited success came at a cost. Sergeant Omnès describes the severe fighting that the Bretons of his 47th Regiment (10th Corps) experienced around Audigny. They had to attack the Germans in the village, who machine gunned them as soon as they appeared over a crest. The 47th got to the edge of Audigny after great losses. The Germans retired, but then the regiment was exposed to machine gun fire again which ravaged their ranks. Barbed wire impeded them and then the Germans counter-attacked. Omnès was left clutching the regimental flag as they rushed away in disorder. The regimental artillery kept firing as long as they could, but then they had to drag their guns away across a ravine. Several gunners and horses were killed. The scattered elements of the regiment rallied around the flag with the wounded and counted their losses. Omnès talked to one of his fellow sergeants who survived three bullets in his chest. Others spoke about Germans they had killed. Later fresh troops replaced them in the front line.[66]

Captain La Chaussée describes the resilience needed to endure enemy shelling near Landifay for a whole afternoon. "I found it difficult to make the men stay in position because it is hard to lie flat on the ground waiting for death which comes close at every moment."[67] Yet the men cheered up when they saw the 1st Corps with its general staff coming from the rear with *La Marseillaise* playing. They wanted to advance again against the fleeing Germans.[68] At the end of the battle there was nothing to eat. The men went off to forage while La Chaussée slept. Someone had given him a shot of alcohol which tasted like a "corrosive".[69] Brunel de Pérard describes the carnage near Landifay in a slightly macabre passage comparing dead bodies to waxworks in the Musée Grévin in Paris. Maybe this was his way with dealing with the horror of death: to liken his experience to something contrived and therefore unreal.[70]

*

I crossed the plateau on a series of *chemins d'exploitation*; tracks marked on the 1:25000 maps between different areas of crops which are not delineated by hedges. These *chemins* belong to the farmers and there is no right of way across them. Occasionally they came to an end unexpectedly and I had to walk along the edge of a field, taking care not to trample on crops. None of the workers I saw appeared to mind. The featureless, undulating landscape seemed to go on and on. I sympathized with André's word "*monotone*". It reminded me of the stretch of down land between Marlborough and Devizes at home, completely naked like a desert. Without a map and a compass it would have been easy to get lost because there are so few features to help orientate the lonely walker. Around lunchtime I was glad to see the hamlet of Courjumelles.

Although they had threshing machines in André's day the wheat itself was reaped by hand. Now industrial farming has taken over. I saw large numbers of combine harvesters, lights flashing, stripping fields in hours and blowing the grain into huge trailers towed alongside. Trucks dumped this grain on the concrete base of a large enclosure at Courjumelles while a bulldozer pushed it into a neat cone. Modern agriculture uses a lot of capital and little labour. Before 1914 extra labourers could be hired very cheaply for the harvest. In the year of the war itself, old men, boys and women had to complete what their men at the front could not do.

After lunch I swung west to see the valley of the Oise from a hill above Ribemont. The towers of the beet sugar refining plant at Origny-Ste.-Benoite broke through the bed of trees in the river valley. The sugar beet industry started

Harvest in progress near Courjumelles, Oise *département*, August 2013. (Terry Cudbird)

when Napoleon wanted to make France less dependent on sugar from the West Indies, supplies of which were affected by the British naval blockade at that time. It was important economically pre-1914 and still is today, although EU protection was removed in 2006 and prices reduced. In 1914 there were many small sugar factories but now production is concentrated into a few sites. It was in this area that the 18th and 3rd Corps launched themselves across the river and onto the plateau on the far side.

Continuing south my track ran alongside a commercial apple and pear orchard for at least a kilometre. Many soldiers' diaries mention camping near apple orchards or taking apples from farms to supplement their meagre rations. During my walk so far I had not seen any orchards at all; only the occasional tree in a private garden. No doubt growing apples, like many other crops, has been concentrated into much larger units in one hundred years.

Villers-Le-Sec was the only proper village I came across the whole day. It seemed a forlorn place, with one or two old houses in poor repair alongside functional modern constructions. There was a church and a bus service but no shop. A large placard said "No to wind farms!" but I counted thirteen turbines south of the village. From a vantage point close by the panorama stretched to all points of the compass. In the distance to the south-east I could see the towers of Laon cathedral on its long escarpment. Lanrezac controlled the battle from there, a formidable task over such a wide area without the aid of modern communications. No doubt it was made more difficult with Joffre literally looking over his shoulder. Due south were the beginnings of the Forêt de St. Gobain, masking the heights of the Aisne, the next barrier on the long march to the Marne.

When I reached Renansart I had some idea why André had found this march so exhausting. Tractors and trailers clattered up and down the main street in a hurry to get the harvest finished before the weather changed. I left André to his mattress and took myself off to a nearby hotel.

Lanrezac knew that the Reserve Divisions had limited experience and offensive capability. He could not feel a lot of confidence in them, but he had no choice. The British would not help. Lanrezac was aware that André's units had arrived at Renansart during the night and were very tired. They would not be able to start their offensive as early as he would have liked. Valabrègue's chief of staff had warned him.[71] André was roused at 2 am on 29 August when he would have preferred to go on sleeping. As I followed his route west down the hill towards the Oise valley I looked around for his farm. We cannot be certain where he slept, but there is a Ferme des Moulins over a kilometre from the village and it had a large old barn built of brick. Understandably André was not on top form. He had marched one hundred kilometres in the previous 72 hours and slept for only three. His section felt more cheerful when the sun rose. To wake up they wiped their beards with the leaves of sugar beet plants moist with dew. A crop of sugar beet with large green leaves was growing just below the farm as I stopped to stare at the view of the Oise and the plateau beyond that André would have seen one hundred years ago. Only some power lines, wind turbines and the *autoroute* in the distance spoilt the illusion.

Like André I passed through Brissy-Hamégicourt, but I had time to drink a coffee in a café not far from the Oise. A sociable proprietor told me how much he liked London, but that a French teacher friend of his found the rents near his school in the Home Counties very high. He then leapt out of the window to have a smoke, jumping back again when another customer arrived. His observance of the relatively new no smoking law was impressive. The road across the Oise canal and the river itself negotiated a maze of marshes, overgrown vegetation, woods and water meadows. At the other side was the village of Moÿ, which André marched through. A placard warned of the dangers of drinking the water after a flood, advice which would have been readily understood in 1914. André reported that Moÿ was a stylish little town, unlike the poor villages he had marched through in the previous few days. Old pictures show more single-storey brick cottages than exist today. Now it gives the impression of a substantial settlement with a number of shops and also a secondary school or *collège*. The houses are well kept and the design of some of the older ones original. André's description of Moÿ as "*coquet*", translated as stylish, seems justified.

The regimental journal records that two battalions were ordered north-west from Moÿ in the direction of Urvillers.[72] Having crossed the main road from St. Quentin to La Fère, I spent some time walking around the *chemins d'exploitation* towards Benay, which is south of Urvillers, trying to match André's record of events with what I could see on the ground. He wrote that cartridges were distributed and that his section, along with another, was ordered to protect the artillery.[73] The battery was stationed in a "*repli du terrain*" or fold in the ground, a little distance beyond the main road and facing north-west. He took up a position to the left of the battery. Only 32 men remained in his section out of a full complement of 96. The rest had either dropped out on the road, been injured or were simply shirkers. To the right he could see scattered woods around the village of Benay but otherwise only fields. Nothing happened during the next two hours. They nibbled some bread and apples but felt uncomfortable in the heat. From the north came the sound of rifle fire and cannon.

The first mystery to solve was the location of this "*repli du terrain*". Having examined various possibilities I settled on a depression marked on the map as the Vallée des Poirelets. It was a fairly pronounced feature, a sheltered hollow backed by trees and undergrowth and invisible from the north-west. A line of cannon could only have been drawn up facing in that direction. André's section further to the left would have faced uphill, with the old village of Benay and its church about thirty degrees to the right. The area around the village still has a few copses.

The captain of the battery decided to change position to Benay by taking the road, presumably the current D72 from La Guingette to Benay through Cerizy. This was the spot where the British cavalry had fought the day before. André led his section across the wheat fields to the village. They arrived there first and had time to relieve their thirst and fill their flasks. I suspect that the route they took was very close to a *chemin d'exploitation* which I followed uphill alongside fields of harvested wheat covering most of the area. My *chemin* came out at the cemetery just below the village. It seems entirely likely that the infantry got there first because later on it took me longer to walk the road route.

The fighting started in the village. A French officer on horseback shouted to André to get his men together because two companies of German infantry had arrived on the other side. He grouped his men near the battery which had just reached the village. A company of French cavalry appeared on foot and shots were exchanged. The bullets went over André's section's heads. The battery captain was asked to support the cavalry with cannon fire, but he said that enemy bullets flying past the horses' ears frightened them and made such action impossible. He wanted to return to his original position and André had to follow. Benay is not a big village and would have been even smaller in 1914, consisting probably of a few old houses around the church. If the Germans entered the village from the far side they could not have been more than three hundred metres away. It is surprising that casualties were not higher.

André was lucky to escape along the road to La Guingette, a distance of some 2½ kilometres, and from there back towards Moÿ. He led his section in single file in the ditch by the side of the road. Bullets whistled across it and he wished they could have moved faster, but he had to keep in step with the artillery. Some large German shells, probably from their howitzers, landed in the fields to the left about three hundred metres away, throwing up showers of black dust. The ditch cannot have afforded much protection. The modern road is under a metre above the fields. The firing in Benay became more intense and wounded men started to stream across the fields and along the road. André's battery stopped and fired a few salvos.

Then events took a turn for the worse. André saw four grey objects on a crest about fifteen hundred metres away. He says "in front of us" but I think he was referring to the skyline of the hill to his left, not the main road straight ahead. The Germans would have been attacking from that direction. Two shells burst in the air fifty metres away. He realized in a flash that the grey objects were a German battery getting into position. One of his experienced career sergeants named Walter shouted, "that's for us!" and a moment later two more shells exploded on the road right where they were. One of André's corporals was killed outright and several men were wounded. They rolled on the ground squirming and screaming. Walter yelled; "We can't stay here!" A hayrick stood fifty metres ahead and a hundred metres beyond that was the main road. In one rush they reached the hayrick. Then one after another they threw themselves across the road and into the ditch on the far side. Shells followed them as they ran. The ditch was not very deep but at least it afforded some protection if they lay flat. German shells rained down on the road, which at this point runs along a crest between two lines of trees. It was no different in 1914. André remarks that the shell bursts passed over them like the sound of broken bottles. The author of the regimental journal noted laconically that the German artillery bombardment caused a precipitate retirement.[74]

Suddenly all was calm. Scrambling out of the ditch André stood up behind one of the big trees and saw that Walter had led some of his men off to the south. He gathered the remains of his section: twelve men of whom some were wounded. One had a bullet in his stomach, another one in his thigh and another one in his heel. They set off towards Moÿ and on the road he entrusted the wounded to a passing ambulance. According to the regimental journal, many wounded had to be left in Moÿ and were no doubt taken prisoner by the Germans. Now André only had eight men left, having started the action with thirty-two. This was the

Road from St. Quentin to La Fère near La Guingette, where André Benoit evaded German shells on 29 August 1914 during the Battle of Guise. (Terry Cudbird)

end of the Battle of Guise for André.[75]

*

Lanrezac could have exploited his 1st Corps commander Franchet d'Esperey's success. For example, the German Second Army's left wing had been weakened in the fighting and was fifty kilometres from the next German army in the line. Lanrezac still had uncommitted forces in that area. Yet at the end of 29 August he considered that his Fifth Army was in a perilous position. His left flank was exposed to the German First Army overlapping it. The British afforded no protection on that side. To the east General Langle de Cary's Fourth Army had had to retreat to Rethel on the Aisne and the gap between Fourth and Fifth Armies was now thirty kilometres. At 8 am on the 30th Lanrezac received General Headquarters' order to retreat to Laon. Despite the tiredness of his troops he gave his own order to retire. In any case a renewed offensive by the German Second Army on the 30th was pushing him back. The British had already marched through La Fère to the south of the plateau. Lanrezac instructed an active regiment to reinforce Valabrègue's Reserve Divisions because he realized they were less reliable than his main army corps. These divisions were to occupy the north of the Forêt de St. Gobain, with a rearguard at La Fère. We will shortly follow André in this direction.[76]

Continued retreat from the Ardennes and offensive in Lorraine

All the French and German Armies were interdependent. One could not move without considering the movements of the others. The French Fourth Army had recovered some of its composure after the disaster in the Ardennes. Starting from a line running through Sedan and Montmédy it retreated towards the Aisne between Rethel and Grandpré, at the northern end of the great forest of the Argonne. First, however, it had to organize the crossing of the River Meuse.

Lieutenant Robert Deville in the Army's artillery had witnessed the action in Belgium, when the Germans had the better positions and the French had to attack them. The German heavy artillery got the better of the duel between gunners and the French artillery suffered appalling losses.[77] The day of 26 August found him shepherding the Army's precious 75 mm calibre field artillery across the Meuse at Stenay, south of Sedan. On the 27th he witnessed a successful delaying attack against a few Germans who had already crossed the Meuse.[78] On the other hand, Private Antoine Guasson, a socialist cabinet maker from Tulle in the Corrèze serving in the Fourth Army, records a sense of panic as the Germans crossed this important river in the same region. Two colonels drew their revolvers to force fleeing troops back into combat.

The mêlée was frightful: cries, shouts, wounded men running, an officer with his sabre singing and spinning round where he stood, absolutely mad. The Germans came at us from all quarters. They overlapped our flanks and we could not hold on any longer. We had to retreat. The order was given to retire and a stampede started. The Germans jumped on us and there was hand to hand fighting. Bayonets and the butts of rifles came into play while the artillery fell silent. I threw away my rucksack and jumped into a hollow way followed by some of my comrades. Our flight was frenzied.[79]

The Fourth Army did fight some effective rearguard actions. For example, Pierre Dubois' 9th Corps distinguished itself in one such fight around Signy l'Abbaye south-west of Charleville-Mézières. Yet despite these efforts the retreat went on. They were all ready to drop. Deville was so exhausted that he went to sleep riding his horse and did not hear his colonel's greeting. Why, he asked, had they given up the defence of the Meuse and retreated this far? His account is not without a sense of humour, however. At Grandpré they found lodging in a friendly house. The owner let them use his vegetable garden and Deville decided to try his hand at preparing food. He discovered an excellent melon but unfortunately it made everyone ill, except him. After that he abandoned cooking.[80] Guasson and his comrades raided a local shop for cigarettes, Pernod and biscuits. The owner gave up trying to serve them and let them help themselves. Eventually they made it to Grandpré too.[81]

Further east with the Third Army Marc Bloch rhapsodized about the pleasures of sleeping in woods in the open air. "The leafy branches of the shelter filter any raw edge from the night air, and their barely perceptible fragrance lightly perfumes the fresh breezes that occasionally caress the sleeper's face." A delay in moving on, however, meant that the enemy nearly caught them. In a long forced march they saw more miserable refugees and Bloch recalls the feeling of bitterness that they could not protect these "pathetic figures... wrenched from their homes, disoriented, dazed and bullied by the gendarmes". One night Bloch and his comrades slept in a stable while the refugees rested outside with their carts in the rain, the women holding their babies in their arms. The next morning they watched "the smoke from burning villages rise into a shrapnel-speckled sky".[82]

The floods of refugees seem to have made a similar impression on the tired soldiers in all sectors. Maurice Genevoix, second lieutenant in the 106th Infantry Regiment, Third Army, and later a famous writer, brings to life in graphic detail a convoy of fleeing civilians on 26 August north of Verdun: "Midday. At the bottom of the slope some vehicles passed on the road, thin mangy horses dragging big carts with four wheels. Basket-work panniers, bundles and cages with rabbits were piled up any old how; on top were mattresses, pillows and faded red eiderdowns in heaps. The women sat up top, with straight backs, pathetic, their hands hanging down and an absent look in their eyes. They seemed to be numbed by a nightmare which had no end. Here and there in this lamentable pile of bric-à-brac the heads of kids emerged, with golden tousled hair and snotty noses. Some cows followed behind the carts, with their tethers around their necks, bellowing. Gawky lads with wide hands and huge feet, a whip in their fists, pushed them forward with blows to their shanks."[83]

Some of the refugees were scared because they had heard so many stories of German atrocities. Paul Lintier, the artilleryman in the eastern sector, recorded the following conversation with an old man. "'What is the use of staying?' asked an old man querulously. 'They'll burn everything just the same, and I'd rather find myself ruined and roofless here, but free, than back yonder where I should be in the hands of the Germans. Besides, I've my daughter-in-law to think of— the wife of my son, who is a gunner like you. She's with child—seven months gone—and when she heard the guns begin yesterday the pains came on. At first I thought she was going to be confined; but it passed off. But I thought we had better leave at once. These beasts of Germans, who violate and disembowel women... who knows whether they would have respected her condition?'"[84]

Meanwhile, further east in Lorraine, events were beginning to favour Joffre's plans for an eventual count-offensive. After the earlier disaster at Morhange the

Refugees during the retreat in a typical cart. (Library of Congress, Washington DC)

French Second Army retired behind the River Meurthe to protect Nancy, with its left wing resting on the Grand Couronné, the arc of hills which dominates the city. The German Sixth and Seventh Armies obtained additional men from Moltke and advanced west through a gap between the Vosges Mountains and the fortress of Toul known as the Trouée des Charmes. General Vicomte Édouard de Curières de Castelnau, known as *le capucin botté* (the booted friar) because of his devout Catholicism, was in command of the Second Army. He was able to launch a devastating flank attack against the advancing Germans. The French were operating from well-fortified positions and by 28 August they had checked the German thrust. The Germans poured troops against these strong French lines in Lorraine but without success.

Joffre had now learnt that he could keep the Lorraine front secure with fewer men. He was free to redeploy some of his forces there to create the new Sixth Army on von Kluck's right flank. He moved 23 divisions by rail from his right to his centre or left. Between 27 August and 2 September an average of 32 trains sped westwards every 24 hours. As a result, the 24 divisions on the German right eventually faced 41 Allied divisions, not eighteen.[85]

One of the units he was able to re-deploy was the 19th Company of the 276th Infantry Regiment, in which the prominent writer Charles Péguy was a reserve lieutenant. On 28 August they boarded a train at Lérouville near Commercy and a day later arrived at Tricot, south of Montdider in the Oise *département*. The journeys took much longer than they would today. The soldiers travelled in the second class passenger carriages of the time. There were seats at least, even if they were less well upholstered than those in a modern train. On the 30th Péguy's company were involved in fighting near Tricot before continuing the retreat in the west as part of the new Sixth Army. We will hear more about Péguy before the end of the retreat.[86] Now, however, we must return to the French Fifth Army trying to escape from the clutches of its enemy after the Battle of Guise.

5: ACROSS THE AISNE TO THE MARNE
30 AUGUST-2 SEPTEMBER 1914

André recovers from the fight

On the evening of 29 August André Benoit was marching downhill towards Moÿ on the River Oise along with other groups of men from different regiments. He met two officers from the 254th Regiment. They had been ordered to fall back but did not know where to go. No one had a map. André abandoned his idea of going to Moÿ, where in any case there was a huge traffic jam of regimental vehicles and men retiring back to Renansart.[1] He suggested following the Oise on the west bank until they found a bridge further downstream. Setting out across the marshy fields surrounding the river they discovered a bridge at Vendeuil two kilometres further on.

I followed André through woods and meadows, more organized I suspect than in 1914. Charolais cattle grazed in the fields. The evening sun glinted on the bark of elegant stands of silver birch. I tried to imagine André and his men hurrying along, wondering whether the Germans would catch them. They must have asked themselves questions like: will I survive all this? How is this retreat going to end?

Vendeuil is a small town on the river with a grandiose *mairie* and a massive church, the latter clearly reconstructed after the Great War. On 29 August 1914 confusion reigned in its streets. Soldiers were rushing along not knowing where to go. Wounded men filled large carts. At a crossroads a colonel was gesticulating, attempting to give orders. André approached him to put his few men under his command. A captain remarked: "Go your own way. You can see he has gone mad!" Like André I crossed the channel of the Oise by a weir and then passed a large lake where young men were fishing against a backdrop of deep green trees. Lilies covered much of the water's surface and a multitude of flies tempted the fish.

André then took the road on the east bank towards La Fère. He records going into a little farm with his companions because they were hungry. Two women gave them a large loaf and some milk before departing with their bundles of clothes. A flood of men and vehicles was streaming down the same road. André thought La Fère would be chaotic, so he took a little side road to a village called Rogécourt. There he found a café and bought some bottles of beer for his men who did not want anything more. They slept in a hayloft and he stretched out on a mattress in the billiard room, having ordered reveille at 4 am.

I decided to take a more peaceful route to La Fère along the towpath on the west bank of the Sambre-Oise canal, a motorway of water cutting straight through the marshy river valley and its meandering stream. Industrial barges lined the banks. Near La Fère two were waiting to be loaded with gravel. A large Belgian vessel just squeezed past a drawbridge on its way north. At one point the canal crossed the sleepy Oise below on a small aqueduct. A stone recorded the construction dates: 1837-38. The original purpose of the canal was to transport coal from the Belgian pits near Charleroi to Paris. Its successful opening was a triumph for James de Rothschild working in partnership with Belgian bankers.

La Fère was an important military town in 1914. Now it seemed a place without much life—few shops, no decent café, no square, cramped streets. One worker in five is out of a job; not a unique situation in the Aisne where unemployment is the third highest of any *département* in France. Five water channels ran between the houses, some of them full of rubbish. I found a bar to have a drink, a quiet place with an Australian flag and an old-fashioned toilet which flooded the floor. While *monsieur* dispensed Foster's lager, *madame* looked disconsolately out of the window in skin tight denims and platform shoes, puffing a cigarette. The eastern suburb of Danizy contained a mixture of nineteenth-century villas and social housing. I picked up André's road from Vendeuil and turned right towards Rogécourt. Immediately the countryside appeared again: maize, wheat stubble and ahead the Forêt de St. Gobain. Rogécourt was another village deserted during the daytime. New houses surrounded the older properties along the road. I found two candidates for the hayloft in which André's men slept and several possible *estaminets*. One of the barns bore the date 1846.

During the night André woke up with a start several times after hearing troops passing on the road. Apparently they had been brought across from Alsace. After six hours' sleep the section all felt a lot better. André washed and ordered a huge bacon omelette. They consumed it at a table in the courtyard with bread and as much beer as everyone wanted, finishing with cigars all round. His little troop felt like new men, but now they had to track down the regiment. They were told that they might find them near Renansart. So André set off in that direction with his eight men and twenty stragglers whom he picked up on the way. After twelve kilometres he saw soldiers in a field and recognized his friend Lefebvre through his binoculars. He rushed across to him waving his arms with joy.

The regiment had suffered heavy losses the day before. The major and two captains had been killed. In his battalion two companies had been devastated in fighting at Monceau on the Oise. According to André the losses there had now mounted to 400 out of 500 men. The Germans had put on flat caps to look like the British. The captain of André's company was now in charge of the whole battalion.

After a pause André set off again for Rogécourt and from there to rest with the remainder of the regiment at the sugar factory at Berteaucourt on the main La Fère-Laon road. The men made themselves comfortable but were not allowed to use straw as bedding because of the fire risk. The staircases were very narrow. The cooks had the use of a large kitchen and the employees of the factory made everyone very welcome. After dinner André once again shared a proper bed with his mate Lefebvre. The next morning they had time to take it easy: a wash and brush up followed by lunch and a siesta. At 4 pm they set off to march through the Forêt de St. Gobain.[2]

After leaving Rogécourt I walked up the same main road to find the sugar factory to which André refers. Large trucks and cars sped past at 100 kph and I kept well back on the verge. Three older buildings stood together, one of which was probably the former factory and described as La Fabrique on the map. High with tall windows it was too long to be a private house and unlikely to be a farm because there was no access to the fields at the back. The inhabitants made a living selling strawberries.

Situation of the combatants after Guise

The effect of the battle in which André had just taken part was to slow the overall German advance. The soldiers of the German First Army were exhausted, having already marched three hundred kilometres from their homeland without a rest day. Their supplies constantly lagged behind. As they had already committed their reserves to the front line there was no immediate prospect of reinforcements. Walter Bloem described the state of his Brandenburg Grenadiers:

> Heavens alive, what a sight they were after three weeks of constant marching and fighting! Unshaved, and scarcely washed at all for days, their good-natured faces covered with a scrubby beard, they looked like prehistoric savages. Their coats were covered with dust and spattered with blood from bandaging the wounded, blackened with powder-smoke, and torn threadbare by thorns and barbed-wire.[3]

Even more serious, whole patches of skin on their feet had often been rubbed down to the raw flesh.[4] In these circumstances it is not surprising that they succumbed to the temptation to loot many bottles of wine from cellars, as Gaunt of the Royal Fusiliers remarked.[5]

Von Kluck now directed his army south-east to pursue the retreating French Fifth Army and the British. He had been ordered to close the gap with the Second Army. Bloem understood that they were wheeling south-east and approved of the mission to surround and destroy the enemy.[6] His men marched thirty kilometres on 30 August and a further forty-five kilometres on the 31st in the blazing sun. From Roye much further west they crossed the Oise and made for the forest of Compiègne. By 1 September they were on the Aisne at Attichy, only fifty kilometres from Paris.[7] The result of von Kluck's change of direction was to reduce the threat of his outflanking the British on their left. It also allowed Manoury to build up his Sixth Army undisturbed. The new route took von Kluck east of Paris towards the Marne. Arguably the action at Guise dragged the First Army to the point where Joffre could launch his successful counter-attack eight days later.

Joffre had many worries on his mind. On 30 August he warned the government that it would be prudent to leave Paris. On the same day news of the German victory over the Russians at Tannenberg came through, somewhat mitigated by intelligence that Germany had withdrawn two corps from the Western Front to help its forces in East Prussia. Joffre was concerned to extricate the Fifth Army from its forward position after Guise. On Lanrezac's right he created a new army detachment, later the Ninth Army, under the command of Ferdinand Foch. Its role was to cover the gap between Lanrezac and Langle de Cary on the Meuse. His main worry, however, was whether the British Expeditionary Force would stay in the line. Already it was retreating more quickly than Lanrezac's men, thus uncovering their left flank.

On 29 August the British rested. Some enjoyed better food now that the supply trains had caught up. C.E.M. Richards remembered fifty years later the sheep and chickens with which the mess sergeant supplemented their meals, the bars of *Chocolat Menier* and delicious fruit.[8] But on the 30th their retreat picked up pace again and the gap between the two main army corps was finally closed. It was scorching hot as Intelligence Officer Rowleston West on his motorbike dashed back with Engineer James Pennycuick to blow the bridge at Pontoise-lès-Noyon, an important crossing on the River Oise.[9] Cedric Brereton recalled marching thirty kilometres on 30 August. It was also the first day during the retreat when he could take off his boots.[10] K.F.B. Tower remembered the endless retreat, hungry and footsore, but above all he longed to change his socks.[11] The 1st Corps crossed the Aisne at Soissons on the 30th. Even the Grenadiers were tired after 37 kilometres.[12] The following day the heat was unbearable during another long march and Haig called a halt early.

On 30 August Sir John French announced that he wanted to pull the British Expeditionary Force out of the line for ten days to refit. He had been told not to put his army into a hazardous situation because Britain's reserves of manpower were limited. For Joffre this would mean the end of all his hopes of counter-attacking the German right flank. He appealed to French but to no avail, so he took the only course open to him and went to his political masters. Representations were made to the British Cabinet and Lord Kitchener, Secretary of State for War, was despatched in a destroyer to Paris to meet French at the

GEN. SIR J. FRENCH IN PARIS   3209-10

Field-Marshal Sir John French in his uniform as he might have appeared to Kitchener. (Library of Congress, Washington DC)

British Embassy. Here he appeared in his full field-marshal's uniform, outranking French because he was the senior field-marshal. French was severely put out but did what he was told. The British Expeditionary Force's retreat continued but it stayed in the line.

The Fifth Army escapes the Germans

Lanrezac was under no illusion about the state of the men under his command after the Battle of Guise. Morale was good but the men were tired, their officers well below complement and supplies had been disrupted. Ideally he would have stopped for two days to sort things out but this was totally impossible. They had to keep going.[13] After falling back on the 30th the Army continued its retreat on the 31st to a line either side of Laon.

Between 10 and 11 am on this day Lanrezac received a German communication intercepted by the listening post on the Eiffel Tower. Georg von der Marwitz's Cavalry Corps, accompanied by artillery and infantry in lorries, was crossing the Oise beyond Noyon to sweep round to the village of Vauxaillon, south of the Forêt de St. Gobain, and cut off the retreat of Lanrezac's left wing, threatening his communications and transport. The bulk of the Fifth Army's troops were too exhausted to rush off in that direction. Although the British were relatively near Haig said they could not help. However, Fifth Army HQ managed to commandeer seven trains to take the Brigade d'Afrique under Colonel Simon to Vauxaillon station by 5 pm. Lanrezac also ordered Valabrègue's Reserve Divisions to hurry forward to support Simon, although unfortunately they did not emerge from the forest before nightfall. They were then supposed to advance together to occupy a position dominating the River Aisne to safeguard the passage of troops. Lanrezac said he was lucky in that the Germans did not pursue their advance speedily. When they reached the area of Vauxaillon Simon and his men had already arrived. At this point they left some observers and retraced their steps westward.[14] Some German horses had lost their shoes and suitable nails to re-fix them were not available.[15]

Lanrezac's account simplifies what actually happened during those few frantic hours and does not mention the chaos at the southern end of the forest during the night of the 31st. French and British flyers confirmed the rapid advance by the German cavalry during the 31st. By 5 pm two German cavalry divisions were two kilometres west of Vauxaillon, while the remaining three in the corps had turned south towards the British Expeditionary Force. Some elements were on the Aisne near Soissons. For several hours there was no news from Colonel Simon. The uncertainty was near to causing panic.

At four in the afternoon Valabrègue's staff were setting up his new HQ in Brancourt when someone rushed in shouting "les Boches!" The report was vague

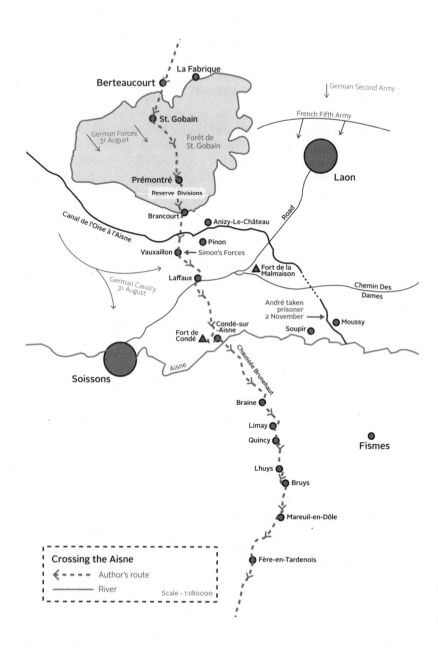

La Fabrique

Berteaucourt

German Second Army

French Fifth Army

St. Gobain

German Forces
31 August

Forêt de
St. Gobain

Laon

Prémontré

Reserve Divisions

Brancourt

Canal de l'Oise à l'Aisne

Anizy-Le-Château

Pinon

Vauxaillon

Simon's Forces

Road

Fort de la
Malmaison

German Cavalry
31 August

Laffaux

Chemin Des
Dames

André taken
prisoner
2 November

Moussy

Condé-sur
-Aisne

Soupir

Fort de Condé

Chaussée Brunehaut

Soissons

Aisne

Braine

Limay

Quincy

Fismes

Lhuys

Bruys

Mareuil-en-Dôle

Fère-en-Tardenois

Crossing the Aisne

Author's route

River

Scale - 1:180000

110

but a substantial force was believed to be nearby. The staff consulted Valabrègue, an experienced general who had been head of the École de Guerre and a *chef de cabinet* to the Minister of War. He was waiting for dinner to be served to him by flustered nuns in the Abbey of Prémontré up the road. Valabrègue decided to send messengers led by a Captain Wemaëre via Anizy-Le-Château to Vauxaillon to get news of Colonel Simon and to instruct him to act as flank guard for all the Reserve Divisions as they passed south later in the night. Valabrègue clearly feared that the bulk of his disorganized forces could be subject to a devastating attack without this protection.

The messengers crept into Vauxaillon in the dark, having been warned by other troops that they were walking into a German trap. By pure chance they bumped into one of Simon's men in the village. He led them a long way up the steep wooded slopes of the valley to a sheltered spot where Simon and his men had taken cover. German forces had shelled them as they got off their trains at Vauxaillon station. Simon had left his artillery at Pinon a short distance away. He was reluctant to carry out Valabrègue's orders because he believed the Germans were blocking the roads south. He eventually agreed, however, to move south and take up the flank guard position at Laffaux at the top of the hill leading down to the River Aisne. As a condition he demanded that the messengers went and retrieved his artillery.

They set off in the middle of the night to find indescribable chaos on the roads. Dense columns of reservists were pouring south. The messengers had to rescue the guns from among this seething mass of men and hurry them to Simon whose advance had been delayed by the chaos. They were clearly worried that a German attack could come at any moment. Captain Wemaëre wrote later: "The spectacle was a sad one. The men were absolutely worn out, some fell and would not or could not get up, packs were thrown away."[16] In the event the attack never came but some of Simon's men got into position to meet it. The German cavalry had missed a unique opportunity.[17]

*

Our story has often shown how the best laid plans of generals went awry because of ignorance of actual conditions at the front line. Officers and men had to adapt to circumstances as they found them. Edward Spears' account is fascinating because, when comparing it with André's diary, it is clear that our reserve second lieutenant was probably in the middle of this mass of reservists but completely oblivious to the potential danger. Many of the places mentioned in the account of the incident provided to Spears by the messengers appear in André's diary. I visited others during my walk. We therefore return to André leaving the sugar factory for the Forêt de St. Gobain to see what happened to him next.

First of all he ran into some Zouaves from Lyon who seemed to be wandering north with virtually no officers. The Zouaves (*zwava* was the name of a Berber tribe) were light infantry from Algeria and Morocco who initially wore a distinctive uniform with billowing trousers. Then André came across a camp of civilians from the Nord fleeing the fighting. It had the atmosphere of a circus, he reported. The regiment bivouacked at the far edge of the forest at 10 pm. It was chilly but the officers dined on a rabbit fricassée in a house nearby. They were just about to bed down on mattresses in the dining room when the order to depart arrived. It was midnight. The march through the night was difficult because the road was full of vehicles and sometimes obstructed by barricades. Without maps they went wrong and sometimes had to retrace their steps. At sunrise they crossed the main road from Laon to Soissons. This is south of the point where Spears locates the chaos of the night before.[18] This is all André says. There is no hint of the mayhem which Spears describes or the poor condition of the reserve troops. Either he missed this episode or his memory was selective when he wrote his account later.

The town of St. Gobain is perched on a steep hill above the trees of the eponymous forest and the plateau where the Battle of Guise took place. The church was different from so many I had seen in the previous week, being built of white stone. The *mairie* is a grand classical building, a little out of scale with the surrounding town. But the chief feature of St. Gobain is the former glass works part of which is used as a depot by the municipality. The story of this factory encapsulates much of the industrial history of modern France. It was founded by Jean-Baptiste Colbert, Louis XIV's Finance Minster, and the state contributed to its capital. It continued as a state company until the early nineteenth century when it became a public limited company. The firm of Saint-Gobain has expanded all over the world, diversifying far beyond its original business of making glass mirrors and other luxury products. The St. Gobain plant was sited in the forest because of the plentiful supply of wood for fuel and also of sand used in glass making. The ferns in the forest were also processed to add colouring to the glass. St. Gobain has not proved to be a successful location in modern times, however. Many such plants dispersed in the countryside have had to close down and relocate nearer their markets and new sources of materials and labour. The St. Gobain plant closed on 1 December 1993.

Adaptability is a key characteristic of successful enterprises in the global economy and *madame* at my B&B believed it is in short supply in France. She owned a florist's business in La Fère and talked over supper about how the Dutch now dominated the international flower market because of their commercial flexibility. Her partner had refurbished an elegant eighteenth-century house, another string to his bow. He divided his time between family affairs in Paris and paving the rear patio, which so far had taken seven years. When I explained the purpose of my walk he immediately told me about his grandfather who was awarded the *médaille militaire* for service at Verdun. The old man had never discussed the horror of war; only the good things like comradeship and the generosity of farmers who gave the troops food.

André does not say how he crossed the forest but I suspect he used one of the country roads. I decided to plunge in among the trees, following a dark and boggy forest path which frequently became indistinct. Four intersections after leaving the road I turned right along a track, weaving my way between the beech trees and eventually ending up in a thicket of brambles. Trusting in the map, I breasted my way through, soon reaching a wider road which was also a *Grande Randonnée* (long-distance footpath). Brambles were not the only hazard. In the warm weather my flesh received the attention of flies which settled for a good blood-sucking session. Perhaps they were attracted by the complete supper I was carrying in a plastic bag suspended from my rucksack. The next B&B at Vauxaillon did not provide meals.

The forest seemed to go on for a long time as I laboured up a slippery slope. A whole regiment could not have passed the way I had come. And then to my surprise I suddenly found I was at the back gate of a large hospital surrounded by a high brick wall and banks of trees. I could not be bothered to go back to find the GR so I walked inside. The site was depressing with many buildings crammed into a very small space. I got lost in a maze of paths and it took several attempts to find the way out. There were few people about and no one challenged me. At last I found myself standing in a massive eighteenth-century courtyard with a formal parterre and a large iron gate to the road. It was then that I discovered I was in a major psychiatric hospital with six hundred beds— run down and claustrophobic. The Direction Générale might have been sited in the elegant former Prémontré abbey at the front but the staff seemed decidedly unhappy. Banners hung everywhere advertising their grievances: in 1848 slavery was abolished but not here! *Indignez-vous* (i.e. get angry, a reference to a book published in 2010 by Stéphane Hessel, a former *résistant* and socialist famous for his stand on human rights. The book was a huge success in France). Exhausted nurses! Patients sacrificed! Dreaming about change leads to revolution! I struggled to imagine how the families of mentally sick patients might have felt entrusting their loved ones to staff who expressed their disaffection so openly and were allowed to do so. The French attitude to authority—sometimes embracing strong leaders but remaining deeply individualistic—is often perplexing to the Anglo-Saxon mind.

This then was the place where General Valabrègue was preparing to eat

The Prémontré Abbey, where General Valabrègue was informed that the Germans were nearby while being served supper by the nuns on 31 August 1914 (now a psychiatric hospital). (Terry Cudbird)

supper when his staff arrived to tell him the Germans were nearby. His HQ at Brancourt was only a short distance away down a narrow valley surrounded by the forest. After resting at the church there I took another path through field and woodland to Vauxaillon. On a crest I got a good view of a sweep of country to east and west. It was through the wooded valleys on the right that the German cavalry units felt their way on the afternoon of 31 August 1914. Once past the Canal de l'Aisne à l'Oise at the end of the wood I strolled to a farm on the edge of the village and found my bed for the night.

My room was very comfortable but I think André would have looked askance at my supper. The microwave spattered the moussaka from the supermarket at St. Gobain everywhere. I retrieved the glutinous mass and tried to eat it but the smell and taste were repulsive. At least André knew what went into the regiment's cooking pot, but we have no idea where half the contents of our food come from. I nibbled some cold pâté and Maroilles cheese instead and watched TV. Vauxaillon seemed to have a profusion of new houses. Next morning I discovered from *madame* that it was a commuter village as Paris was only two hours away by train. The only people around as I walked down the main street were a few elderly residents.

I passed the station where the African brigade left their trains at 5 pm on 31 August 1914 and climbed up to the woods above the village, more or less where the messengers had walked in the night looking for Colonel Simon. Now there is a large war cemetery half way up the slope containing over two thousand graves, mostly of troops killed on the Chemin des Dames in the offensives of 1917.

The plateau of wheat fields at the top of the hill forms one end of the heights above the Aisne which cost so much blood. The front must have been very near here between autumn 1914 and 1918. By 1917 it was a sea of ploughed earth and twisted metal with the occasional ruined building. I turned to cross the Laon-Soissons road by the Laffaux roundabout only to find another monument to the fallen of the Great War. A stone column in the shape of a mortar shell commemorated the contribution of the *crapouillots*, an affectionate term for the artillerymen of the French Army. The trajectory of the shells resembled a toad's (*crapaud*) jump, hence the word for a trench mortar and the nickname for the gunners. From this point I could see all the way to the hills surrounding the River Marne. André must have passed near here on his way down to the River Aisne in the early morning of 1 September.

André recalled that his unit climbed the heights dominated by the Fort de Condé above Condé-sur-Aisne. Then they descended the other side, crossed the Aisne and, after a further eight kilometres, entered the hamlet of Braine. The regiment stopped in a large field and everyone was very thirsty. The captain sent André off on a mission to get something to drink and he came back later with a few bottles. The regiment found billets in Braine. André's company was scattered in seven or eight houses and he found a double bed to share with Lefebvre. He remembers some German planes flying over. A few shots at them made a racket in the streets, and the women were very frightened.

He was then tasked with finding a cart and some horses to carry all the packs for the battalion. First of all he went to a small farm but the farmer's wife sent him packing. He took her to the *mairie* but the mayor upheld her complaint. Then someone suggested trying the sugar factory on the Reims road. He borrowed a soldier's bicycle despite his protests but found nothing of use in the factory. In the end he discovered what he needed on a farm at the other end of Braine: a large cart, two horses and the sixteen-year-old son of the farmer as a driver. The boy was asked to rendezvous outside the captain's house at 11.30 pm precisely. The battalion's officers had a boozy dinner and then slumped on their beds for a couple of hours fully dressed. A glass of rum at 11 pm and they were off. André was relieved not to be carrying his sack which cut his shoulders.[19] I know the feeling!

I visited the restored fort above Condé-sur-Aisne before descending a steep embanked track to the river. Séré de Rivières built this fort between 1877 and 1882 as part of his programme to improve the French defences following the German victory in the war of 1870. It is typical of its period; a pentagon of stone under three metres of turf, containing barrack blocks for 650 men and protection for the big guns. This fortress was declassified in 1912 because it could not stand up to modern artillery. The Germans used it as a hospital during the Great War. I had expected to stand on the top and look right down to the River Aisne. Unfortunately the trees of the forested slopes blocked my view. During lunch I contented myself with a view north across the open country towards the *crapouillots'* monument.

The Aisne itself was a disappointment; a stagnant river through muddy banks amidst overgrown vegetation. On the other side I crossed a plain, passing a number of recreational ponds along the river's banks. The sun bounced off the tarmac road in temperatures hovering around 26 degrees; nothing like the thirty plus some troops had to endure in 1914. Marching at night, as André did frequently, avoided the sun's rays. This practice also concealed troop movements from the enemy and ensured enough road space was available. I was strolling along when suddenly a French couple in a BMW stopped alongside and started firing questions at me. "What are you doing?" They seemed amazed that I had chosen to walk on that road, and even more so when I explained the purpose of my trek. Well oiled after a good lunch, they could not seem to understand that it is possible to set off on foot with a map and navigate your way successfully across the countryside. Maybe the sight of an old Englishman on his own, with a rucksack, walking poles and a plastic bag, was too much for them. The French tend to walk in organized groups along proper footpaths.

A dead straight track across the fields marked as the Chaussée Brunehaut seemed the ideal way to get to Braine. I saw some walkers using it and at first progress was easy. Then the track ran abruptly into a barbed wire fence and continued on the other side along an embankment in the middle of a field. Not to be deterred I walked left along the fence and then hurled myself across a deep ditch before climbing the barbed wire where it was one strand lower. Two more fences and a herd of heifers later I re-joined the track which continued across open farmland to the village. Clearly the Chaussée Brunehaut was not an official footpath, but what was the origin of its curious name I wondered? It appears that there are several Chaussées Brunehaut in northern France and Belgium. They may be of very ancient origin but they were certainly improved by the Romans. Perhaps they were named after a Visigothic princess. At Bavay, through which the British Expeditionary Force passed after Mons, there is a column mentioning the seven *chaussées* which depart from that spot. So much we know, but there are many legends attached to the name Brunehaut.

André described Braine as a hamlet although it had a population of 1,500 in his day. This stayed constant until the growth of the post-1945 era. Now it has 2,162 inhabitants. Estates of new houses surround the old centre which André saw, along with a supermarket, a *collège* and an old people's home. The

Rue St. Yved and the schools, Braine: this street, which leads from the market place to the large church in the background, has hardly changed in a century. (Archives départementales de l'Aisne FRAD00226_00645)

main square has hardly changed in one hundred years, consisting of an imposing *mairie* with a classical pediment, a large open space for markets and a number of eighteenth- and early nineteenth-century houses. One has a courtyard in front with a large gateway. Most are built of stone but one of fifteenth-century origin has a brick façade with ancient beams. Any of them could have been the house occupied by the officers on the night of 1 September. A factory tower in the distance towards Reims belonged to the former sugar factory where André looked for a cart. It used to be a major employer. Before the Great War there were over a hundred such plants in the Aisne and now there are only three. The war devastated much of the growing area for sugar beet and provoked a crisis which led to rationalization of the number of factories.

While André struggled southwards his comrades in the Fifth Army were enduring an equally difficult march. General Lanrezac remarked that they had to march day and night to avoid being outflanked, while fighting rearguard actions at the same time. The heat was oppressive and the conditions worse than before Guise. The road network did not help. The Army was on a line to the north of Laon on 31 August. All the roads south pass through Laon and as a result there was a serious bottleneck in the town. Brunel de Pérard describes an exhausting march on the night of the 31st, moving slowly at two kilometres an hour and stopping every five minutes. He occupied the time by reciting lines from Victor Hugo's *Ruy Blas*. Eventually they passed through the town at dawn.[20]

After that the troops had to traverse a series of narrow, forested plateaus separated by deep valleys running east-west. The few roads crossing these valleys are steep and involve a number of detours. Fortunately there were not many civilian refugees because they had all gone ahead while the Army was fighting at Guise. They were replaced by soldiers who said they were lost or who pretended they were ill. These deserters looked pathetic and over-tired but were very clever at evading the gendarmes. Somehow they managed to stay ahead of the combat troops even though the latter were covering a good deal of ground every day. They lived by pillage and terrified the local population with their tall stories. It took a while for the High Command to impose tough sanctions.[21] At the beginning of September Joffre persuaded the politicians to issue a decree authorizing special military courts which could make a quick judgement to set an example. Generally the commanding officer of a regiment plus two other officers made up the court and a majority decision was enough. Executions were carried out within twenty-four hours. On 7 September seven soldiers in the 327th Reserve Infantry Regiment were executed on the orders of General René Boutegourd for abandoning their positions.[22] His units formed part of the Fifth Army. Perhaps General Christian Sauret, the commander of the 3rd Corps, was lucky to escape with being cashiered. He was found weeping for his men behind a hayrick.[23]

Units kept bumping into each other during night marches thus delaying the retreat. The baggage trains were disorganized and their constant halts obstructed the infantry. Lanrezac admitted that the men had little sleep or regular food: "They put up with tiredness beyond the limits of human endurance."[24] The men kept going admirably but many horses simply gave up. The Army had to abandon vehicles, munitions and even some heavy artillery which could not be dragged up the slopes south of the Marne. Lanrezac underlined the exceptional conditions that the Fifth Army overcame between 30 August and 5 September as it marched two hundred kilometres. Even so, it was still able to fight effectively at the Battle of the Marne.[25]

One must bear in mind that Lanrezac wrote this in 1920. Joffre dismissed him on 3 September before the retreat was complete. No doubt Lanrezac wanted to emphasize the fighting qualities of the Army which he had developed. Yet Spears corroborates his account, also noting the lack of shade from a scorching sun, the dusty and airless valleys and the lack of water.[26] Rouquerol, who was in charge of the 3rd Corps' artillery, echoes what Lanrezac wrote in his own account of the campaign written in 1934: "We wondered how these men could summon up the energy to stand upright and how it was they did not collapse in the ditches."[27] Like others he rode through the night, then dropped off for a nap in an orchard and had to be roused from his slumber. His companions said they did not like to wake him but the rearguard was leaving. The 3rd Corps crossed the Aisne further east than André and on 1 September was at Fismes. On the 2nd Rouquerol got caught up in the biggest military traffic jam he had ever seen lasting several kilometres. It looked like a mass of sheep all trying to push forward in a crush.[28]

Captain La Chaussée tried to get men lying on the banks of a road to get up. Some cried because they did not want to be captured by the enemy. Later he remarked that the most difficult thing for them was to set off after a halt because their legs were numb. "Some of them had to march on the points of their feet and others on their heels. Others shuffled forward like puppets. Many soldiers had bloody feet."[29] There was also no doubt that the Army missed many of the officers and NCOs who had been killed or injured and who would have provided leadership. We have already noted the shortages of officers before the Army mobilized.

Lanrezac was particularly alarmed by the state of the Reserve Divisions of which André's unit formed part. John Terraine has written that after Guise they were little more than a mob.[30] Lanrezac remarks that, according to General Valabrègue, these units were so washed out and demoralized they would run away and throw neighbouring troops into confusion if they became involved in serious fighting. Ideally Lanrezac would have liked to sandwich them between two corps of experienced troops rather than having them on the extreme left wing. Such a manoeuvre, however, was impossible during a rapid retreat. It would have to wait until the whole Fifth Army was safely south of the River Marne.[31]

By the evening of 1 September the Fifth Army had crossed the Aisne safely and on the 2nd the left and centre reached a line through Fère-en-Tardenois, about thirty kilometres south of the river. The right was able to liaise more easily with Foch's troops around Reims. Joffre formed another cavalry division under General Louis Conneau to cover the Fifth Army's left flank as the gap with the British Expeditionary Force widened to forty kilometres. He would operate south of Château-Thierry on the Marne, which the Fifth Army should reach on 3 September.

A further retreat in the east and deadlock in Lorraine

Lanrezac was given some reassurance by a counter-attack launched successfully by the armies to his east on 1 September. The Third and Fourth Armies and Foch's detachment moved against the centre of the German line in the area of Stenay on the Meuse. They were then able to retire again before the Germans could catch them. The pursuers did not capture many guns or take a lot of prisoners. Did this suggest that the French Armies were not defeated as they had hitherto believed?

Antoine Guasson did not see a lot of this action. On 30 August he was at Grandpré like Marc Bloch. The next day he was at Alleux, at the northern extremity of the Argonne forest. Guasson recorded German shelling but Campagne and Ducasse, respectively a captain and a sergeant in the 107th Infantry Regiment, gave the impression of a serious attack resulting in many wounded. On 1 September Guasson's unit was able to leave under a clear sky for a long march in the heat along dusty roads. He remembered with great pleasure being able to rest in a farm for a meal of soup and chips. Unfortunately he had to get moving again before he could eat it. He stuffed some *frites* in his pocket to eat later as his unit carried on in the moonlight. At 2 am he collapsed on a bank by the road having marched 85 kilometres in twenty hours. He had to leave again at 5 am.[32] Guasson was lucky to have a few *frites*. Sergeant Ducasse ate raw potatoes and turnips to keep going. Some of his men slept standing up.[33]

Meanwhile, even further east, the Germans continued to batter at the French lines around Nancy but without success. The fighting here was savage in its intensity. Here is our gendarme, Célestin Brothier, describing the results of the carnage near the Grand Couronné hills on 30 August.

Before the war a magnificent harvest covered this vast battlefield. Now this fine wheat is flat on the ground, rolled on, stamped on, chopped down and totally lost. The straw has been blackened by gunpowder, stained with blood and stuck to the ground by shreds of dead flesh. It is a vast litter of several square kilometres, where hundreds, perhaps thousands of corpses lie, of which some have no head and others no legs; yet others have been torn in half, and the two halves lie two or three metres apart, sometimes joined by a string of entrails. I saw legs and arms thrown a long distance. Brains and flesh cover the green spaces. There is blood everywhere.[34]

One can only wonder how he and a party of ten men coped with the job of burying the dead.

The new Sixth Army in the west

We have noted that Charles Péguy, originally operating in Lorraine, was now on the far west of the French line with Manoury's Army. He was not involved in the direct clashes with the German First Army, for example at Armancourt on 30 August, but he knew they were just behind him. On that day his men were worn out and there was no food. Péguy was in front, leading his men and encouraging them. Each night they got very little sleep; they just had to keep marching. On the 31st they gnawed a few green apples to assuage the pangs of hunger. Some of the men dropped out despite Péguy's exhortations. On 2 September he witnessed the German bombardment of the old cathedral town of Senlis as he fled into the forest of Chantilly. German cavalry captured their baggage but they kept advancing in the dark, with bloody feet and still precious little food. Victor Boudon wrote: "tiredness destroyed our ability to think. We march or rather run like automatons. Hunger tears at our stomachs. The morsel of bread eaten in the morning was the only food we had that day. Lieutenant Péguy kept his position at the front of the company which had become separated from the rest of the battalion. He lit up our route with his lamp."[35] This image of one of France's foremost poets and Catholic writers lighting the way for his men in the darkness was intended to be touching.

Frederic Coleman, the optimistic and humorous American driver, saw some of the Sixth Army's infantry marching near Senlis and gives a different, if rather condescending, impression.

For the first time during the campaign I saw the sturdy little French foot soldiers on the march. With a goodly interval between each company, in loose marching order they scattered all over the road. Their heavy kits included the inevitable tin pots packed on their backs. It seemed cruel to garb a soldier in such clothes on a hot day. I little realized how much

I was to admire them before the end of the campaign. None of us knew what we were yet to owe to the French Army, and in what high regard we were one day to hold it. Near St. Vaast the road wound upwards through the woods. All the way up the ascent we passed the toiling legion in long blue coats over heavy red breeches, pattering along, uncomplaining, always on the move, covering the ground with most wonderful rapidity in what seemed to me a most unorthodox manner of doing so.[36]

The British fight at Néry and Villers-Cotterêts

As August turned into September the British Expeditionary Force sped south through the Compiègne forest and on to the Marne east of Paris. The Germans fired villages as they approached the north of the forest and the flames created an eerie atmosphere between the stands of trees. Local fighting between German advance guards and the British rearguard developed into two more serious actions on 1 September at Néry and Villers-Cotterêts. At Néry German cavalry surprised the British 1st Cavalry Brigade watering their horses and having breakfast. The German gunners wiped out twelve British guns trying desperately to return their fire. Three British artillerymen won VCs. Then the British 4th Cavalry Brigade came on the scene and turned the tables on the Germans. What should have been a defeat for the BEF ended instead with the defeat of the German 4th Cavalry Division. The British lost 135 officers and men. Meanwhile, the infantry of the 2nd Division in Haig's 1st Corps got into difficulties retreating through the forest at Villers-Cotterêts further east. The 4th (Guards) Brigade formed the rearguard and was involved in confused fighting in the woodlands. The commanding officer of the Irish Guards died. Two platoons of the Second Grenadiers were surrounded and killed as they fought to the very end. The 4th Brigade lost over 300 men and the 6th Brigade another 160.[37]

Fifteen of Bernard Denore's company were killed at Villers-Cotterêts. On 2 September his unit marched forty kilometres in the heat along uneven dusty roads full of refugees. There was no more fighting, however, and in the evening they reached Meaux. He even had time to look at the cathedral, which he admitted was beautiful.[38] As von Kluck's First Army continued south-east it left the British left flank alone, although cavalry patrols continued to run into the right and centre. As even this threat melted away the British Tommies seemed in better heart, as a French citizen who saw them pass recorded: "The soldiers, phlegmatic and stolid, march without appearing to hurry themselves; their calm is in striking contrast to the confusion of the refugees… as sportsmen who have just returned from a successful raid, our brave English eat with a good appetite, drink solidly and pay royally those who present their bills… and depart at daybreak, silently like ghosts, on the whistle of the officer in charge."[39]

Von Kluck wheels east of Paris

It was on 1 September that observations by the Royal Flying Corps and information from a map found when a German officer was captured told Joffre that von Kluck was definitely wheeling east of Paris. Manoury's Sixth Army moved to defensive positions east of the French capital as Joffre waited for the right opportunity to launch his counter-stroke. The German First Army commander seems not to have realized that the French troops he encountered at Senlis formed part of the same Army he had met on 29 August further north-west. He was oblivious to the danger of an attack on his right flank, only posting one corps and a cavalry division there. Instead he pushed his men forward against what he thought were the remnants of a defeated force, the French Fifth Army and the British Expeditionary Force. The German attacks in Lorraine were drawing the focus of their line to the east. The High Command therefore wanted von Kluck to close up to von Bülow's Second Army and march in echelon behind it. Von Kluck ignored this request.

As von Kluck drove his men onwards there is no doubt that even his hardened troops, who had marched all the way from Germany, felt the strain. They became even more prone to the solace of wine if some bottles came to hand. Walter Bloem recalls reaching the last ridge before the Marne after forty kilometres of marching in the heat and past the press of refugees. "And then we crossed the Marne. On the far side we halted awaiting the order for billeting. Never shall I forget that evening. The firing to our left had ceased. The sun had sunk into a misty haze of deepest gold. The whole valley, steeped in the perfect stillness of a summer evening, shimmered in the golden light. Could this be war? Could anyone fight here? Impossible. It was peace on earth, the peace that passeth understanding… And tomorrow Bülow would be enveloping the remnants of the French Army opposing him. In a couple of weeks the campaign would be over. Just like a fairy tale!"[40]

Crossing the Marne with André and his comrades

On 2 September André Benoit set out for the River Marne. Leaving Braine at 1 am his unit reached Fère-en-Tardenois as the sun rose. The march was fairly monotonous, but they halted in a riverside orchard at the village of Beuvardes where they enjoyed a snack followed by a siesta. At 6 pm dinner followed in a little house where the cooks had installed the unit's cooking pot. They set off again at 7 pm and it was soon dark. Guards had been posted on the slopes leading down to the Marne to protect their crossing. After the bridge at Mézy they came out on the road between Épernay and Château-Thierry. It was one o'clock in the morning. Two big fires were raging in Château-Thierry and shots were heard. They curled up on bundles of hay by the road, waiting for dawn.[41]

At this point André was only 26 kilometres from his parents' house at Charly-sur-Marne further west along the river. He seems to have liked the family home. Later in his life he would spend time there writing books during school holidays. He also had a married sister. One can imagine that he might have been concerned what would happen to them when the Germans arrived. However, he does not say so. Little did he know that the 3rd Corps of von Kluck's First Army would pass right through Charly on 2 and 3 September.[42]

According to André's account his unit of Valabrègue's Reserve Divisions crossed the bridge at Mézy peacefully enough just after midnight on 3 September. Edward Spears paints an entirely different picture, however, recalling what amounted to a panic later in the night. He relates how on 2 September the Fifth Army moved its HQ to Châtillon-sur-Marne, somewhat to the east of André's position. The molten rays of the sun poured down and the guns boomed. The tired staff of the Fifth Army felt hunted. They knew that they would have to withdraw south of the river during the night. Lanrezac seemed to have reached the end of his tether when he wailed, *Nous sommes foutus! Nous sommes foutus!* (Spears translates this politely as "done for" but today we would say fucked.) He contrasts this scene with the *sang-froid* of the local postmistress who was determined to carry on with her work no matter what.

The plan had been for the Reserve Divisions to cross the river at Château-Thierry as well as at Mézy. Everything depended on elements of Conneau's

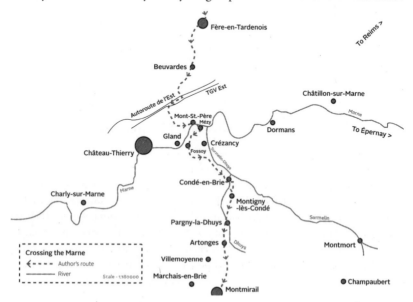

Cavalry Corps getting to Château-Thierry in time to hold the crossing. If the Germans got there first a disaster might follow. The French cavalry despatched to the town seemed to get the mistaken impression that the Germans had occupied it in force, whereas a few cavalry patrols at most had reached the spot. Two French cavalry officers from the HQ of the Reserve Divisions reached Château-Thierry in the evening and managed to organize some French territorial units to occupy the Marne bridge. They exchanged shots with the enemy, who also opened up with a machine gun and artillery for a brief period. These German attacks did not continue and the two officers went in search of General Conneau while the territorials settled down at the bridge. Lanrezac was aware of the situation. At one point he ordered the Reserve Divisions to drive any Germans out of Château-Thierry but then cancelled the order when reports arrived of a German infantry division nearby. (These reports later proved to be false.) Instead he ordered all the Reserve Divisions to cross at Mézy and to form up by 4 am south of the Marne facing west in support of General Conneau's cavalry.[43]

According to Spears, at 6 am on 3 September the Reserve Divisions were still crossing the bridge at Mézy.

> To say they were crossing is an exaggeration. They were stuck. The spectacle was painful; such scenes can only be understood if they have been experienced. The infantry in a solid, struggling mass was literally wedged on the bridge, mixed up with artillery, all pushing wildly to get across. There were so many men in the narrow passage that they could hardly move. To make matters worse, elements of the 4th Cavalry Division, which was supposed to be keeping in touch with the enemy north of the river and protecting the retreat, appeared and joined the rush, to be at once swallowed up by the struggling mob, which was dominated here and there by small groups of horsemen squeezed in with the infantry. No one who has been caught in such a trap can ever forget the growing panic that inevitably seizes one, the feeling that the enemy is at one's heels, the wild desire to get on. General Valabrègue himself and his Chief of Staff stood in the street by the bridge trying to establish some sort of order, to disengage the exits, to get the column to advance. They were to some extent successful, for presently a slight movement was discernible, and then suddenly the whole human torrent swept forward, carrying with it in seemingly inextricable confusion, men, limbers and horsemen.[44]

In view of the disorganization of the Reservists it is entirely understandable that Lanrezac used the opportunity to move the 18th Corps to the left opposite Château-Thierry with some cavalry and to sandwich the Reserve Divisions between them and the 3rd Corps further east.[45] He had long wanted to take this step to ensure that his left flank was stronger to deal with any attack by the German First Army.

*

I followed in André's footsteps on 2 September, stopping in Fère-en-Tardenois on the way to the Marne. On the outskirts of Braine I examined the fine abbey church of St.-Yved. It has a remarkable tympanum over the central doorway, a solid tower above the crossing with a lantern and prominent flying buttresses. Braine was once the seat of the early Merovingian and Carolingian kings, hence the presence of such a substantial church in a small village. A little further on, geraniums decorated a weir over the River Vesle. The church at Limay had an unusual stepped gable on top of the clock tower. Closer inspection, however, revealed a much heavier Gothic building than its elegant medieval sister in Braine. It had been rebuilt after the Great War. Two young men were doing stretches in the square opposite the church. One was an international lawyer from Paris and the other at a business school. They had come down to the country for a meal with friends, a few drinks and some relaxation over the Assumption Day holiday weekend. At Limay we were very much in the Île-de-France around Paris. I mentioned my project and like everyone in the area they immediately asked: "are you going to the Chemin des Dames?"

After Limay I ascended a steep hill onto a series of plateaus separated by wooded valleys. Flax was growing on the first expanse of fields as well as the usual wheat and sugar beet. Linen is made from flax and this used to be a major industry in the Aisne before the Great War. It is a comparatively rare crop these days. Quincy had a very large old farmhouse, more a barrack-like manor which appeared to be unoccupied. A metal grille led to a three-sided courtyard of tall buildings, the rear one topped with a cupola. Weeds were growing out of the mortar and several tiles were missing. The other six houses in the village did not look so dilapidated.

The next plain beyond Quincy's valley was absolutely featureless with wheat fields running to infinity either side of the path. At a crossroads of *chemins d'exploitation* a lone chestnut tree and a box hedge covered a picnic table and seats, providing welcome shade. According to the map a cross once stood here. Once again I was falling under the spell of the mythical emptiness of *la France profonde*. It was impossible to imagine that I was in an area where armies have manoeuvred for hundreds of years, fighting over this fertile soil, the foundation of France's wealth from the Roman Empire onwards. Marching boots would have kicked up the chalky soil which is never very far below the surface.

It was becoming clear that, superficially at least, the countryside through

Welcome shade near Quincy, Aisne (Terry Cudbird)

which André marched has not changed a great deal in a hundred years. Yes, there are new houses in the small villages and towns, new roads and some factories. However, no massive developments have completely obliterated the physical features that André noticed. Conversely, agriculture has changed beyond recognition. Many fewer people work the land and the crops have changed too. Local industries have disappeared, not to be replaced with any major new developments. More people commute to Paris, local shops and bars have closed and villages are quiet during the day. The heart has been ripped out of rural communities in a landscape with an appearance of continuity.

The next two villages were alliteratively named Lhuys and Bruys. At Lhuys small features suggested a degree of individuality—decorative diamonds on old plaster walls, a Romanesque doorway on the church, old stone cottages dated 1879. A farm had become a pony trekking and equestrian centre. Leisure activities in the countryside are replacing farming. Bruys had one large farm like a small fortress: high walls, massive barns, a manor house and a small Gothic chapel all within its precincts. Charolais grazed in the valley, flat-bottomed like a canal barge, with woods guarding its flanks.

A sultry breeze beat across the next plain under a metallic blue sky through which wisps of cumulus twisted at random. The green leaves of the sugar beet provided the only contrast to brown wheaten stubble. The sun beat down with unforgiving hostility and I began to feel distinctly uncomfortable. The sheer brutality of André's march across the northern plains in August is impossible to exaggerate. He must have felt drained looking at a horizon receding mile after mile, a destination never attained, always a chimera. The heat would have bounced off the cobbles, creating a furnace from which it was impossible to escape. Few clouds or trees interrupted the sunshine's downward trajectory. It was a struggle for survival and, if you stopped, the enemy would catch you like a bogey-man in a nightmare. No military retreat on this scale has taken place in modern times, with men marching long distances in the sun.

Shortly after the village of Mareuil-en-Dôle I dived into the cool shade of a forest. The sun felt less threatening when glimpsed on the surface of a shaded pond or dancing across clearings of ferns and bark. Eventually I came out alongside the Château-de-Fère, once a ramshackle house of different periods jumbled up in uncomfortable proximity and now converted into a smart country hotel. I must have found the staff entrance judging by the number of people standing smoking by the door. On the other side of the grounds the romantic ruin of a medieval castle nestled in the trees. Crossing the main road into Fère-en-Tardenois I picked my way through banks of heather on a sandy heath populated by stands of pine and silver birch dropping their leaves. The clatter of goods trains and the rumble of lorries were audible beyond two lakes, although the railway and neighbouring industrial estate were invisible. This was a favourite recreation spot for local families lounging on the grass like the plump bathers in Seurat's *Une Baignade, Asnières*. Obesity was not the problem in André's day it is now. Large stomachs, tattooed arms, tight fitting bikinis around tired flesh, pink streaked hair hanging on heaving shoulders—not a pretty sight. The universally svelte figures of French women compared to their Anglo-Saxon neighbours are another myth.

Fère-en-Tardenois seemed a slightly sad place despite its obvious attractions: the chateau, the grand *mairie* facing a green sward surrounded by sculpted trees, the old market hall open to the world, the turret on the Office de Tourisme. I was the only guest in a cavernous hotel, served by a lady who made it clear that, once I had signed in, she was off and I was on my own. If I forgot the code to the door then I would have to sleep on the street or break my neck climbing a drainpipe. In the morning she gave me breakfast in the panelled salon with its chandeliers and double doors, but I was not to get any ideas about checking out at 11 am. I had to take myself off straight away because she was going to lock up.

She sent me for dinner to Chez Odette, a rough restaurant and bar. The French word *douteux* was the best way of describing it. Dubious, questionable, down at heel, something not quite right; but I could not put my finger on it.

The staff looked either emaciated or overfed and the smell in the bar suggested French anti-smoking laws more honoured in the breach than in the observance. The most acceptable choice seemed to be a *macédoine* of vegetables from a tin, steak with "homemade" but soggy chips and overripe fruit salad. The more appealing items were off the menu. I was not very confident about the quality but the family next door wolfed their food down appreciatively. I looked out at the main street and could not help noticing the faded lettering on the building opposite and the crumbling stone work. Trade could not be easy in a town of three thousand people with 22 per cent unemployment. As soon as I got back to my room my stomach was telling me I had made a mistake; it was completely empty by the morning.

If you are undertaking a long distance walk to a timetable you cannot let such things interrupt onward progress any more than André could. He was struggling against the pace of the advancing Germans; I had to catch the train home from Paris on a certain day. I crossed the headwaters of the Ourcq which later joins the Marne and was the focus of a desperate struggle in the great battle to come. Labouring uphill once again to the plains above, what should I find but wheat and sugar beet?

At Beuvardes the orchard where André halted had been swallowed up by modern development. Only a few straggly fruit trees on the edge of a field survived. A monotonous road stretched over the plain towards a telecommunications tower and the Marne valley. I turned off down a track to hear the rush of traffic on the Autoroute de l'Est and the occasional whoosh of a TGV on the new high-speed line to Strasbourg. The track continued sandwiched between these two express ways, but protected from them by sound-absorbing greenery. There was no possibility of turning either left or right until I came out at a village uncomfortably close to the noise of fast moving vehicles. Even here there were enticing rural pleasures like a fishing pond surrounded by forest and full of pike. Rather than use the road I decided it would be infinitely preferable to find my way along forest tracks and come out above Mont-St.-Père, my destination on the Marne. I was surprised when the black lines on the map led me exactly where I wanted to go. Suddenly there I was overlooking the Marne valley and thinking I had come to heaven, like Walter Bloem. The sun sparkled on the water and highlighted the vineyards lining graceful curving hills, topped in turn with sprouting woodland.

The evening which followed was the highlight of my walking tour. I had tried to book accommodation at the bed and breakfast of Eric and Danièle Debaize at Gland, the village next door to Mont-St.-Père. They replied very charmingly that they were *désolés* but all the rooms were taken for the night I wanted. However, they had read about my previous book on walking around France and wanted to meet me. They arranged to put me up with a friend in Mont-St.-Père and asked if I would like to come to dinner as their guest along with my hostess for the night. After a very English "if it is not too much trouble" I accepted with alacrity.

Francine made me comfortable in her house while talking about our interests—walking of course, skiing, and also riding on her part, although I have never sat on a horse. Then I sank into her car and we drove up the hillside behind us to Eric and Danièle's house. A terrace faced across the vineyards to the Marne below. Eric said that the grapes just below us were grown for Moët et Chandon but a good local grower produced an excellent fruity *rosé* champagne. Could I manage a glass? As if he needed to ask. We nibbled, sipped and absorbed the view before going inside for dinner. Eric thought I was interested in the Second Battle of the Marne which took place around Château-Thierry in 1918. Once I had explained further about 1914 he immediately offered to put me in touch with a friend who was president of a local historical association. An appetizing meal and more champagne followed. We talked a lot about the places we had been in France. I even managed to crack a few jokes in French at which they laughed. At least they seemed to have understood, even if the English sense of humour is slightly different. I thought about André sleeping on the road somewhere below and wondered whether he thought he had come home. He must have had mixed emotions.

6: THE RETREAT'S LAST PHASE
2-6 SEPTEMBER 1914

The British retreat draws to an end

Von Kluck had wasted time on 2 September trying to catch the British Expeditionary Force but now he turned First Army's attention to striking at the left flank of the French Fifth Army. The gap between Fifth Army and the British was now forty kilometres, so the latter could offer no immediate help even though Sir John French had ordered his cavalry to contact Conneau's on the road from Château-Thierry to Meaux. He also told Joffre that he would incline his march south-east to reduce this gap between the Allies.

On 3 September the British troops crossed the Marne. Denore recalled the march that day as the most terrible he ever did: "men were falling down like ninepins. They would fall flat on their faces on the road, while the rest of us staggered round them, as we couldn't lift our feet high enough to step over them, and, as for picking them up, that was impossible, as to bend meant to fall. What happened to them, God only knows." Two men threw themselves in a river to cool off and drowned. "I, like a fool, took my boots off, and found my feet were covered with blood. I could find no sores or cuts, so I thought I must have sweated blood... As I couldn't get my boots on again I cut the sides away, and when we started marching again, my feet hurt like hell."

Denore noted the number of refugees still on the road, as Frederic Coleman did towards Meaux and in Lagny.[1] Coleman wrote: "now and then a quartette of milk-white oxen lumbered along pulling a clumsy wagon crowned with a score of women and children huddled together under a dozen huge black umbrellas, an odd sight indeed."

In the diaries of the Grenadier Guards there is little evidence of similar distress. The distances they were marching at this stage seemed to be shorter although they did notice the heat on 4 September.[2] For Denore that day was as trying as the one before. Two sentries who fell asleep for half an hour were later shot. At dawn on the 5th Denore eventually turned off the road into a farm and had two hours' sleep in a pig sty. He was still able to make an interesting observation about French farms: "I noticed the same thing about that farm that I'd noticed about most French farms. That was, although they seemed more intensively cultivated than English farms, the farm implements were very old-fashioned."

On 5 September some troops who had been held in reserve arrived. They looked clean and tidy compared with the ragged appearance of Denore and his colleagues. "We were filthy, thin and haggard. Most of us had beards; what equipment was left was torn; instead of boots we had puttees, rags, old shoes, field boots—anything and everything wrapped round our feet. Our hats were the same, women's hats, peasants' hats, caps, any old covering, while our trousers were mostly in ribbons. The officers were in a similar condition." But then they had all marched 251 miles in the retreat, as Denore noted.[3] James Jack also mentions the use of unconventional headgear in his notes on 5 September.[4]

Von Kluck chases the French Fifth Army

Units of von Kluck's Army advanced in the direction of Château-Thierry and gave the 18th Corps and Conneau's cavalry a difficult time. The 18th Corps abandoned the high ground west of the valleys of the Dhuys and the Surmelin along which much of the Fifth Army was passing. The Corps commander retracted his left wing to avoid conflict with the enemy. Meanwhile, General Conneau's cavalry took every opportunity to harry the German columns to try and keep them in check.[5] On 4 September Pétain's 6th Division had to fight a rearguard action in the region between Condé-en-Brie and Montmirail.[6] The French troops were very tired and it is significant that Joffre issued a note to the armies on the 3rd ordering that everything must be done to lighten the burden on them: careful preparation of itineraries, wide intervals between parts of a column, transport to carry rucksacks, provision of food depots along the roads and transport of totally exhausted men.[7]

Von Kluck was also driving his men to the limit. In his memoirs, written after the war, he boasted about their achievements.

> Marches, whether of record length or short, had alternated with occasional local rest days and almost incessant fighting under conditions that did every possible credit to the mental capacity and physical endurance of the subordinate leaders and the gallant troops under their command.
>
> The Army was unquestionably capable of carrying out further successful operations, but was not in a position to co-operate in extensive movements of the whole force demanding still greater efforts.
>
> If the marches and battles of the corps and their transport columns and Trains are reviewed, it will be found that they establish a record of achievement which has seldom been obtained in the history of war.[8]

Captain Harry Huebner, also with the First Army, recalls marching in the heat from 6 am to 10 pm on 3 September with only a two-hour rest at lunchtime, but still they could not overtake the enemy. "The strain and exertion which we endured on 3 September were almost beyond human capacity." On the 4th he wrote: "Nothing to eat for three days; abjectly wretched." He realized, though, that the French were suffering too. For example, some of their men were wandering aimlessly between the German columns completely lost until rounded up.[9] On the same day Rouquerol of the French 3rd Corps noted that deserters wandering around were still a problem.[10]

The Germans kept up this pressure on the following two days as Walter Bloem recalls in his diary. Exchanges of fire took place occasionally and there were some casualties, but no decisive engagements. On 4 September he observed that the situation was becoming increasingly unpleasant. The Germans had driven the enemy out of Belgium and a great part of northern France but were getting a long way from home with ever-lengthening lines of communication. More and more enemy were appearing on their front. They were feeling uneasy.[11] "How many miles had I covered the last few days on foot, being so tired that if I got on my horse I fell asleep at once and would have fallen off? How many anxious discussions had I had with Ahlert regarding the company's boots: scarcely a single pair that hadn't a nail sticking through the soles, which were as thin as paper. A few more days on the road and my Grenadiers would be marching barefoot."[12] Sometimes an incident raised a smile. On the evening of 5 September they encountered an angry bullock at a farm but at the same time drank as much Burgundy as they wanted.

There is no doubt that the German First Army was not the fighting force which had crossed the French frontier twelve days before. They too had sustained losses and some units were down to half-strength. All their reserves were already committed. The 2nd Corps had been detached to watch Maubeuge and Antwerp. The nearest railhead was at Chauny, 140 kilometres from their position on 5 September.

South to Montmirail with André

As André's unit marched south from the Marne on 3 September he might have wondered how many more rivers he had to cross. Joffre thought the retreat would have to continue until the right opportunity for a counter-offensive occurred. Contingency planning included crossing the Seine. I knew I had only two and a half days' walking left but André had no such comfort. Moreover, the advance of von Kluck's forces and the continued weakness of the Fifth Army's left wing made his route insecure. His diary betrays a sense of unease.

Early in the morning people coming from Château-Thierry told André that the flames he could see came from two boats carrying petrol. Some said there were few Germans about; others that large numbers were in the town. At about 10 am the Reserve Divisions took up action stations. André's section was either side of the Épernay-Château-Thierry road with another section a little further forward. The latter saw a patrol of five German dragoons appear round a corner two hundred metres away. The men fired and one of the dragoons fell. The others retreated. The men brought back a helmet, a revolver and also binoculars as a present for the colonel because he did not have any. Some shells passed overhead but they did not know where they came from.

About midday André and his section climbed up a steep and difficult path to the south. They came to a bare plateau and saw a line of French skirmishers along an avenue of poplars two hundred metres ahead. There was a good deal of firing with the artillery joining in. They did not see much of the action because it was out of sight on a descending slope. André's men turned left and entered a wood along a narrow path. At that very moment a volley of shells of different calibres fell on the wood. The smaller ones made a clean silvery "zing" sound and burst like broken bottles. The larger ones made a great noise like "crack!" These sounds echoed around the wood. Luckily for them all these shells fell some way to their right, but they did hit some regimental colleagues according to the regimental journal.[13] (Then André brings us down to earth by saying that he had not had lunch so he picked some blackberries.)

They descended to the valley of the River Dhuys which runs into the Marne near Mézy. The regiment gathered in a marshy meadow where they ate bread and sardines to make up for the lunch they had missed. Then they set off for Condé-en-Brie. On the road it was pandemonium: all sorts of regimental vehicles, dragoons, and infantrymen who tried to overtake each other by wandering through the neighbouring fields. The regiment pushed into this muddle.[14] André's description of the retreating army sounds more like Spears' account of the scene at the bridge.

Still tasting the delicious rosé champagne of the night before I set off early from Mont-St.-Père towards the bridge at Mézy. I had nearly thirty kilometres ahead of me to reach Montmirail. A few fishermen had already installed themselves along the wooded banks of the Marne under an overcast sky. A stiff breeze ruffled the verdant water of the otherwise peaceful river. I stopped to admire the impressive Gothic church of Mézy-Moulins which dominates the surrounding fields with its sturdy tower, flying buttresses and elegant rose window. Ahead was the main Épernay-Château-Thierry road which André describes and beyond it rows of vines climbing the chalky escarpment to more woods.

Like André I turned right through a hamlet called Fossoy to find a point where the line of the old road met the modern highway. This, I felt, could well have been the spot where the German dragoons came round the corner. From here a steep track wide enough for a vehicle climbed up through the woods. It would not have been easy for a group of laden infantrymen to follow this route. At one time it was paved with stones but these have long since broken up. Deep in the deciduous wood the surface is rough and slippery. The hazels looked as if

CHATEAU-THIERRY *(Septembre 1914).*
Effet du bombardement.

Part of the Hôtel de l'Éléphant damaged by a shell during the German attack on Château-Thierry and the surrounding area, 3 September 1914. (Archives départementales de l'Aisne FRAD00226_01483)

they would have been coppiced and used for making fences before 1914.

Eventually the track came out on an open agricultural plateau. Ahead was a large *manoir* and farm, which André does not mention, but to the right a line of trees on a crest stood above a pronounced slope dropping towards Château-Thierry. I could see the industrial buildings on the outskirts of the modern conurbation. It was a logical place from which a line of skirmishers could fire at Germans coming from that direction as we know they were. The place fitted André's description exactly. Looking the other way, a different avenue of trees led towards the woods which run along the top of the Dhuys valley. It seems likely that André departed in this direction with the sounds of shell fire ringing in his ears.

I decided to observe the road along the Dhuys valley from a distance by following the line of the GR14 footpath further up the hillside. This makes use of an embankment which runs for several kilometres and covers an aqueduct bringing water to Paris. On the other side of the valley another range of vine-clad hills came to an abrupt end at the town of Condé-en-Brie where André's regiment halted. He knew this whole area well because he spent happy days on holiday in Condé with his friend Comміny, about whom we know nothing apart from this one reference. The traffic jam André saw here was solid. Soldiers were coming out of the notary's house with some bottles and a large jar of prunes in syrup. One after another his mates were putting their hands in and pulling out the delicious prunes streaming with sugary juice. André did the same.

He was then ordered to take the road south by the station in the direction of Montmirail. His section was to ensure that vehicles did not try to run alongside the infantry columns, but although their efforts were in vain the column picked up speed. They felt insecure, thinking of the carnage a burst of artillery fire could cause in the crush on the road. The lines of French dragoons on the hills on both sides did not reduce their fear. At nightfall they arrived at Artonges about ten kilometres from Condé. The regiment bivouacked in a large field near the exit from the village, with their cooking stove in a comfortable house left unoccupied by the inhabitants. They found clean shirts and sheets in the cupboards. Beds were also available. They could only enjoy them for a brief rest until midnight.

Later André found out why they had to leave so quickly. A soldier, whose home was not far away, went on a visit and heard some men speaking German near a little wood. His captain alerted the divisional general who knew the Germans were as far south as the French reserves, if on a parallel route. He gave the order to depart so that the French could get ahead of them.[15]

Condé-en-Brie is an attractive large village of 650 inhabitants with a seventeenth- and eighteenth-century chateau and an old church. Geraniums cascaded over the fountain in the square nearby and the stone bridge across the

Dhuys. An open market hall with refurbished columns stands behind the *mairie*. I climbed to Montigny-les-Condé up one of the hills where the cavalry kept watch on the Reserve Divisions. Opposite was the high ground evacuated by the 18th Corps during the day.

I left the land of champagne grapes behind me to traverse yet again the undulating plains of eastern France; wheat fields, a few meadows, woods dotted along hilltops, quiet villages, water towers and grain silos like the one outside Artonges in the distance. While not as bleak as similar areas elsewhere, the landscape took on a monotonous regularity. After lunch at Pargy I joined the Grande Randonnée du Pays Tour de l'Omois which took me straight to the places mentioned in André's diary on the southern edge of Artonges: a large field next to a farmhouse which in turn stood alongside the chateau marked on the walking map. The path crossed the line of the railway from Artonges to Montmirail which is no longer in use for passenger traffic. A notice on the crossing, however, stated that a company called VFLI had been given permission to run trains along this section, thus ensuring continuity of employment for 26 people at Montmirail repairing locomotives.

The farm which André mentions looked dilapidated, with wrought-iron gates which had seen better days swinging from crumbling breeze block pillars. Old fridges and other rubbish cluttered the farmyard and barns. Yet the other side of this eyesore was a large and imposing chateau with a big parterre. Open windows suggested it was currently occupied as a private dwelling. Was this building too grand to be the comfortable house with the clean linen which André describes? There were no other likely candidates.

Having left Artonges I had six kilometres of hard road walking to reach Montmirail and a comfortable bed for the night. It was difficult dodging the cars in the wind and rain at the end of a long day. At first the road crossed a large forest, but then I was exposed to the full force of the elements on the open plain. Anonymous modern houses and a stark, concrete *maison de retraite* greeted me before I found a faded commercial travellers' hotel near the chateau.

Joffre dismisses Lanrezac

On 3 September Lanrezac transferred his HQ to Sézanne, its last stop during the retreat. While André was enjoying a meal at Artonges Joffre made a visit to Lanrezac for a painful interview. He informed his colleague that he was relieving him of his command because he was tired, hesitant and indecisive. Relations between Joffre and Lanrezac had been strained since the middle of August. Lanrezac had criticized his superior for being slow to realize that German forces in Belgium were more numerous than thought and would outflank the French west of the Meuse. His relations with Sir John French were poor; his decision at Charleroi to retreat before the British made worse by his sarcasm. He had resisted Joffre's wish for a stopping offensive at Guise. Joffre believed Lanrezac had a brilliant mind but not the force of character necessary at this critical juncture to lead his men and dominate events.

It is not surprising that we get a very different impression of what passed between the two men when reading their memoirs written after the event. Joffre describes the interview as brief. Lanrezac accepted the decision as if relieved of a great burden. After a brief moment he told Joffre he was right. Lanrezac's account, on the other hand, states that he argued with Joffre for some time before accepting the inevitable. Spears recollects watching the interview between the two men as they walked outside the HQ building. He says it was not over in a few minutes and the staff had a sixth sense of what was happening. Certainly Lanrezac did not look relieved. No doubt the talk was painful as Joffre had promoted him in the first place and his sacking now reflected poor judgement by the commander-in-chief.[16]

Joffre had already spoken to Franchet d'Esperey, commander of the 1st Corps, and knew he was ready to take over. Franchet was everything Lanrezac was not: resilient, decisive and tough. "General Franchet d'Esperey was short and square. His hair was cut 'en brosse.' Seen from the back, his head reminded one of a howitzer shell. His broad face, with high cheekbones and straight jaw, was a series of parallel lines, straight top to his head, straight eyebrows, straight toothbrush moustache, straight chin. He moved quickly, almost fiercely, bent arms keeping time like those of a runner with the movement of his legs. His dark eyes were piercing, his voice sharp, his diction precise." When he arrived at HQ the next day his presence was like an electric shock. He told his staff officers that the severest penalty, i.e. the firing squad, would be visited on those who did not do their duty—and that included the general staff. Spears remarks that "a certain lieutenant-colonel who had come in for D'Esperey's unfavourable notice looked as if he had fallen down several flights of stairs."[17] When Joffre asked Franchet later whether his Army was ready to attack the answer was yes—without the ifs and buts that Lanrezac would have added.

Joffre decides to counter-attack

By 3 September Joffre had decided that the time for a counter-offensive had arrived. He knew that von Kluck's First Army was strung out over a long front east of Paris. In fact, it stretched in an arc from Esternay via Coulommiers to Meaux, a distance of seventy kilometres. Manoury's Army of 150,000 men had taken up positions east of the capital. It was just a question of exactly how and when Manoury should strike and the Allied armies between the Marne and Verdun turn about and attack the Germans together. On 4 September

Franchet met Wilson, the British Expeditionary Force's Deputy Chief of Staff, and discussed a plan of attack. When Wilson got back to GHQ at Melun near Fontainebleau he found that Galliéni, the Military Governor of Paris, had been and gone, having talked to the Chief of Staff Archibald Murray. The upshot was that Joffre accepted Franchet and Wilson's suggestion that Manoury should attack the flank of German First Army north of the Marne on the River Ourcq, while the French Fifth Army and the British pivoted and opposed the German First and Second Armies facing them. Yet GHQ had already given orders for the British to retreat a further 24 kilometres following the Galliéni-Murray meeting, so they would take longer to reach their place in the line than Joffre would have liked. Foch's newly formed Ninth Army would hold the centre, around the spot where the Marne monument now stands. The remaining French Armies to the east would also hold their positions between Vitry-Le-François and Verdun and east into Lorraine. The attack was to begin on 6 September.[18]

The end of the retreat in the east and the Battle for Nancy

Joffre knew that holding on in the east would not be easy. Between 2 and 5 September the Third and Fourth Armies continued their retreat towards Vitry-le-François and Verdun. The same themes re-occur in the witnesses' diaries: refugees blocking the roads, processions of the wounded, sporadic engagements, dead horses. In this situation there was no clear line between the retreating French and the advancing Germans; units could easily overlap in the same area. Deville described how he got caught between opposing fire at night on the edge of the Argonne forest. He could not go back the way he had come. Nor was it sensible to get lost in the forest at night. He collected a few men together and they crept along the edge of a wood in single file, those with horses having dismounted. Eventually they reached a railway line which guided them back to the French positions after an anxious hour.[19]

On 2 September Guasson found himself retreating towards Suippes, north-east of Châlons and east of Reims. The Germans had just attacked and driven them further back. By now he was battle hardened. He remarks that the sight of a dead soldier had absolutely no effect on him and his comrades. He was more concerned about getting something to eat, even to the extent of chasing chickens around a farmyard. He and his comrade went to look for food, then could not find their regiment and were locked up as deserters. After being released they set off in the direction of Vitry to try and catch up with their comrades. He remembers collapsing in a ditch with fatigue and a trip on a cart with a drunken soldier. They re-joined their regiment on the 5th when Vitry was only eight kilometres away.[20] Captain Louis-Benjamin Campagne in the 107th Infantry Regiment mentions one very practical problem when marching across the chalky country towards Suippes on 2 and 3 September—not a drop of water. Rain drains right through this sort of rock. I have experienced extreme thirst on the chalk plateaus near Grenoble. Campagne had to threaten soldiers with his revolver to keep them moving but he felt sorry for them.[21]

Back in the Argonne again Galtier-Boissière recreates the atmosphere of the small town of Varennes at this time. Louis XVI escaped here in 1791 on his way to the frontier, only to be captured and taken back to Paris. "A lot of the shops and houses are closed. Some remaining civilians interrogate the soldiers, trying to decide whether to flee. The roads are cluttered with artillery, engineers' vehicles and carts full of refugees. The drivers threaten each other, then whip their horses who charge off in a shower of sparks as their shoes strike the cobbles. Crazy peasants run after calves, chickens and goats. In the middle of all this soldiers just manage to filter through. A man whose foot has just been crushed is hopping around looking for his shoe. Elegant officers on horseback shout orders to the vehicles, 'don't cut across the others you drunken louts!' At each street corner generals in sparkling hats look at this frightful crush and give instructions. Some of the shopkeepers make a present of their merchandise to the soldiers rather than see it fall into the enemy's hands. From a second floor window an old woman is emptying the contents of her drawers into the street. Some soldiers besiege the sisters of charity's hospice where they are offering food."[22]

Further east in Lorraine, Joffre had stripped the Second Army around Nancy of many units to build up Manoury's Sixth Army near Paris. The crucial test for this decision came on 3 September when Crown Prince Rupprecht and his Bavarians launched yet another attack. Fighting took place around Épinal on the edge of the Vosges and along the River Meurthe. The main assault, however, was directed at the hills north of Nancy, the Grand Couronné, as well as at the forts to the south-east and north-west. The fighting was particularly brutal with intense shelling by artillery and waves of bayonet charges by German troops desperate to carry the hills to the north. On 5 September the commander of the French Second Army, Castelnau, was thinking of withdrawal. As Joffre was putting the finishing touches to his plans for the counter-attack he had to stiffen Castelnau's resolve. The survival of Nancy hung by a thread.[23]

Joffre visits Sir John French

Joffre wanted to make absolutely sure that Sir John French was personally committed to the planned counter-offensive on the Marne. French had threatened to drop out of the Allied line once before. So the portly Joffre got into his motor car again and drove all the way from Bar-sur-Aube to Melun on 5 September, a distance of 185 kilometres. Held up by a distraught mayor who wanted to know what advice to give civilians in view of the German advance, he only reached the chateau of Vaux-le-Penil at Melun at 2 pm. French was surrounded by his staff and Joffre made a passionate speech:

> As far as the French Army is concerned I have given my orders and, whatever happens, I have decided to throw my last man into the balance to achieve victory and save France, in whose name I come to ask for British help. I cannot doubt that that the British Army will play its part in this supreme struggle. If it stands aside it will be severely judged by history.

Then Joffre recalls in his memoirs[24] that he banged his fist on the table and said, "The honour of England is at stake, Field-Marshal."

Joffre noticed French's face redden and waited during a pregnant pause. He did not quite understand the English of the field-marshal's reply and recalled asking what French had said. It fell to Henry Wilson, the veteran of many Anglo-French staff conferences, to reply: "The marshal says yes." It was pointed out that the British would not be able to start their advance quite as early as Joffre wanted. "It does not matter," replied Joffre, "the Field-Marshal has given his word."

Edward Spears was present and brilliantly captures the drama of this moment. Although the essentials are the same his version differs from Joffre's in one respect. He says that Joffre pleaded rather than suggesting that French might take a dishonourable decision: "c'est la France qui vous supplie" (it is France which begs you). Given the tact with which Joffre had handled French in the past Spears' account seems more appropriate.[25] After the ritual cup of tea Joffre now drove 188 kilometres back to his new HQ at Châtillon-sur-Seine to give his final orders and wait.

The end of the retreat for André

André and his men crossed Montmirail at daybreak and then continued south, often across the fields, until they reached a village called Morsains about ten kilometres away. They stopped in a field eight hundred metres after the village and had a cold meal. André's company was then ordered to return to the village to guard General Valabrègue's HQ in the chateau. Here he found the same crowd as in other places: vehicles, artillery and infantry all milling around, Zouaves and Tirailleurs in small groups. The gendarmes had occupied the school so the company took over the church. About 4 pm everyone saw smoke from shell bursts about three to four kilometres to the north. It was getting nearer. This might have been the rearguard action being fought by Pétain's division referred to above, or possibly the 18th Corps covering its retreat. The HQ was in a state of alert. A convoy of lorries came to pick up the 236th Infantry Regiment (part of

The church at Morsains, Marne, where André Benoit's troops camped. (Terry Cudbird)

the Reserve Divisions) to take them for a rest near Provins (some 45 kilometres to the south). The HQ left the chateau in cars and on horseback. There was almost no one left on the road and night fell.[26]

Montmirail is one of those small French towns (population four thousand) which seems isolated, even though it is only a hundred kilometres from Paris by road. The nearest large town is Reims, over sixty kilometres away. There is no passenger railway service. The rush of modern life has passed it by compared with towns a similar distance from London. I wandered around the market to buy my picnic without being stampeded by a crush of cars and pedestrians. The old centre sits on the wooded southern end of an escarpment sixty metres above a horseshoe valley and dominating another farming plateau. The Petit Morin flows below the chateau and then through a meadow-bottomed chasm towards its junction with the Marne at La Ferté-sous-Jouarre.

Napoleon fought the Prussians and Russians near here in February 1814. His nephew Napoleon III erected a column in 1866 to commemorate the Emperor's brilliant rearguard actions on the main road three kilometres to the west. The French soldiers passing by might have hoped that their retreat would not end the same way as Napoleon's, in defeat and exile. Curiously the monument to the Marne near the station is much less prominent although much of the fighting happened near here.

I climbed down into the valley of the Petit Morin and up again onto the agricultural plateau of maize, wheat and a few meadows for cattle. The sun was gentler than André would have found it at this stage of the retreat. The back road I selected to Morsains was almost devoid of traffic. Two groups of nodding donkeys pumping oil caught my attention however, as well as other installations forming a pipeline network in the area. They looked incongruous in a totally isolated group of wheat fields surrounded by woods. I was very surprised to discover later that there are two thousand such oil wells in the Paris basin. Even so, together with wells in Aquitaine, they only supply one per cent of France's petrol needs.

Morsains stands on top of a small hill on the main road. The chateau is next door to the church and opposite the *mairie*. Down the hill to the south is a large field which was probably where André's regiment stopped for a while. Some of the chateau dates back to the sixteenth century although most of the building went up in the early part of the eighteenth. The rough-cut church with a wooden porch snuggles up alongside it. There would have been very little room for a company of two hundred men there. On the other side of the church from the chateau was a farmhouse advertising bed and breakfast. I decided to have a look because I wanted somewhere to stay after my walk was over. It was also possible that André's men used it during their brief stay.

It did not take me long to realize that reserving a room here might be a mistake. I understood that the owners advocated respect for the environment but nothing prepared me for what I found. The courtyard cluttered with children's toys and dog turds might be overlooked, but a medieval room which consisted of a lean-to along the nave of the church was too much. I stooped inside to fall over the toilet pan at the end of the bed. Apparently the owners did not believe in cesspits and flushing toilets. I was expected to relieve myself and then shovel wood chippings into the dry toilet from a nearby box. If I felt damp in this cave the switch for the dehumidifier was at hand. A shower meant tramping through the long grass into the main house. The only alternative was to take an entire gîte on the other side of the courtyard at increased expense. Here I was likely to break my neck going down an unlit staircase. I discovered an adequate hotel nearby which was more comfortable and cheaper and took the obvious decision.

André's company was ordered to re-join the regiment in a field by the road four kilometres south of Morsains. They slept on bales of hay under the stars. I would rather have rested with André in that field than brave the smells in a medieval cave. About midnight André set off again to the south. His legs were tired so he accepted his captain's offer of a horse for a while. He was not an experienced horseman and felt uneasy. The horse knew he was only a chance rider. Day dawned and after passing through Montceaux-lès-Provins they reached a village called Villiers-St.-Georges, fourteen kilometres north of Provins.[27]

After Morsains I continued "à travers champs" as André would say. At one point my planned route along *chemins d'exploitation* ran out and I stumbled across a sea of ploughed earth towards the hamlet of Condry on the Montceaux-lès-Provins road. On my right were the fields where André slept under the stars. At Neuvy further down the *route départementale* I turned off to cross the Grand Morin which, like its little sister, played such a part in the battle to come. Wider than the northern river it is nevertheless a modest stream between lush banks of grass and trees, a French version of the River Kennet perhaps. A green lane ran out on the edge of a field just before the Château de Nogentel.

I walked down the drive to be confronted with a fairy tale building: decorated Gothic-style dormer windows, two towers with pointed roofs like witches' hats and tall chimneys with the intertwined letters CA (Comtesse d'Ambrugeac). It would not have looked out of place in the Loire valley. The elevation was perhaps too great for the width and the north-facing central courtyard between the two wings got very little light. I walked nervously past the grille and across the lawn, casting a glance at a fishing lake, ruined tower and farm buildings on one side and a park of self-catering chalets on the other. In front of the chateau itself Florence the young *châtelaine* greeted me, all charm and desperate to please. She, her husband and brother-in-law had bought the chateau six years before with the proceeds of the sale of a timber business in Courgivaux nearby. Now they were running it as an enterprise and repairing the building bit by bit. The middle range had fourteenth-century origins but most of it was built or restored in the nineteenth.

Florence led me up a grand staircase to my room in one of the towers. Large and circular it had a heavy panelled bed and every comfort except somewhere to hang my clothes. My rucksack and anorak looked out of place draped over so much carved woodwork. I have always wanted to live in a tower, however, so this brief visit was the next best thing. While chewing my way through supper in a cavernous salon I was disturbed by a large man with a broad country accent. A tree surgeon from Lorraine he slurred his words so that I was struggling to keep up. He had work to do here on fourteen hectares of woodland, no doubt enough to keep him busy for a few days. He nearly dropped his *pastis* when I mentioned casually that I had walked all the way from Belgium. Sipping the rest of a bottle of Beaujolais I wondered how I could justify the expense of staying here when the subject of my book had to make do with pigsties and fields. This, however, was the only accommodation available near Esternay and I could not have reached Provins that night.

Next morning I strode across the fields which saw some of the early fighting in the Battle of the Marne. It seemed a miracle to me that the chateau had survived undamaged with shells falling all around. Had this agricultural landscape of open fields changed much since the battle started? I very much doubted it. Changes in tree cover may have altered the views. Crops like maize were not grown in 1914. In essence, however, it is much as it was. The commemoration of the sacrifices made was also minimal: a cemetery at Montceaux-lès-Provins with a brief mention of the village's liberators, one or two small plaques and a crumbling Michelin signpost on the main road. Most of the villages around here were almost destroyed and had to be rebuilt after the Great War. Seventy-five per cent of Montceaux was reduced to rubble and the village was awarded the Croix de Guerre. Three villagers were killed and the rest fled. The church is in immaculate condition but the village has gone back into the deep sleep from which it was briefly awakened one hundred years ago. There are a few modern houses, trucks pound down the main road and a mobile phone mast underlines how far communications have developed in the last century. Elsewhere wooden-framed barns crumble among the weeds.

I rested under the sculpted trees next to the sturdy church. A nave from the eleventh century, a squat bell tower from the twelfth and an apse from the fifteenth spoke of unchanging rural France. Montceaux is on a knoll perhaps twenty metres higher than the surrounding plain. If you look back from the open farm land to the south it is easy to see the church. The *chemin* between fields running parallel to the road to Villiers-St.-Georges crosses one of the bleakest landscapes in Western Europe. East and west there is not a hedge or any break in the expanse of ploughed earth save the lines of trees on the roads. The land hardly rises or falls. As a scene of slaughter it is too terrifying to contemplate. The track ran in a straight line without deviation for four kilometres until a kink brought me to the settlement of Champcouelle. I crossed a stream and battled up a slope towards the cemetery in Villiers-St.-Georges. This was the end of my retreat.

*

André recounts that the regiment stopped in a large orchard. He describes how they took up action stations on 5 September in a field of sugar beet behind a crest. Germans shells burst to their left not very far away. Rifle fire came from that direction too. Some of the men went to get water in a small group of houses ahead but that had to be stopped in case they gave their position away to enemy artillery. Dinner was meagre with almost no bread because their supply trains had departed for Provins. At last they settled down for the night; sleeping on hay gathered in a field where the grass had recently been scythed. The sky was clear, the moon shone and it was not too cold.[28]

Before heading for Provins and the comforts of a hotel I had one more piece of detective work to do. Where were the orchard and the field where they slept? The village is located around two right-angled bends in the otherwise straight road to Provins. There is a single line of houses along the road with some modern buildings towards the disused railway on the eastern side; also a grain silo, an old people's home and a college. The gardens behind contain a number of fruit trees, perhaps the remnants of the orchards which flourished around many French villages in the nineteenth century. Beyond this mop of green leaves lies the agricultural desert. Just north of town there is a slight rise in the ground shown on the map as the Butte de Champcouelle. I like to think that André and his men rested there facing north with the German First Army's shells exploding to the north-west as they made a last effort to catch the Fifth Army in the flank. The houses where they fetched water might have been in the hamlet of Champcouelle itself.

André says that they faced north (at last!). The parenthesis speaks volumes. They had just been told they would soon be advancing in that direction. André's captain went to get orders from divisional HQ in the rear and came back with the news: "We are going to turn round. It is the end of the retreat!" André comments "Ouf! Voilà une nouvelle qui nous ravigote!" (That is news to perk us up!) An English understatement if ever I heard one from the mouth of a Frenchman.[29]

The Allied troops hear the plans to attack

The relief was palpable right down the Allied line as the troops were told of the great attack the next day. Some of the commanders were concerned that the soldiers were not ready. Rouquerol met General Hache commanding the 3rd Corps at the chateau in Esternay. Hache told him the attack would start on the 6th and Rouquerol replied that this was madness. The men were not ready.[30] Joffre issued his final order to make it clear that not an inch of ground must be conceded and that weakness would not be tolerated.[31] It has been said, however, that the advance northwards welled up from deep within the armies themselves. We have seen that the troops frequently felt they had the measure of the Germans and could not understand why they kept retreating. Now the anxiety and the waiting were over. However difficult, everyone knew what they had to do.

La Chaussée was at Escardes from which the 5th Division was to launch one of the Fifth Army's first attacks. He says news of the advance was received with joy. He wondered how they had survived the retreat, particularly with so many reservists who were not fit. Now they were battle hardened and ready to move forward.[32] Sergeant Omnès from Catholic Brittany went to confession at the church in Sézanne. He noted that several priests were talking quietly to the soldiers.[33] There were some who were furious when Joffre's order was read out. Antoine Guasson with the Fourth Army near Vitry-le-François later wrote: "What a pain! Not to retreat... But what we are being asked to do is impossible. We are shattered. Some cry and kiss each other, others are furious. I am one of the latter. The major wins us over with kindness. He appeals to our courage. We bend before his will; but it is hard!"[34]

Among the British troops there was a feeling of optimism. Lieutenant Edgington of the Royal Field Artillery described the joy at the change of direction on 6 September.[35] Bernard Denore noted in his diary on 5 September that his unit marched thirty kilometres to a place called Chaumes which was crowded with staff officers. "We bivouacked in a park, and then had an order read to us that the men who had kept their overcoats were to dump them, as we were to advance at any moment. Strangely, a considerable amount of cheering took place then."[36] Sergeant Bradlaugh Sanderson wrote in his diary for 6 September: "What a glorious day! Instead of going to Paris, we are to take the offensive, and we are going back. There wasn't half a cheer. Perhaps they heard it in Paris. Someone started the Tipperary song and 'Rule Britannia!' To use a Tommies' term, 'we did give it socks'... Today we had read out to us the Kaiser's statement about us being 'a contemptible little army', and it made us mad. Just let us get a chance at them."[37]

At 8 pm on the 4th Charles Péguy and his soldiers were told that the French Armies were changing direction; the moment had come to rid the country of the enemy.[38] His comrade Victor Boudon includes at this point a paean of praise in honour of the *union sacrée*; the unity of all Frenchmen, previously so divided, in defence of France: "but today, at this supreme moment when France and the principles it stands for must triumph or perish forever, all that (discord) has disappeared. The enmities have dissolved in this unique concern, the only hope of everyone: 'the darkness must not triumph over light!' This horrible war, criminally unleashed by an odious imperialism, must be the last of all wars! They must not pass."[39]

The cheering did not last for long as machine guns and artillery started to take their toll. Joffre had set in motion 980,000 French and 100,000 British soldiers with 3,000 guns against a German line of 750,000 men and 3,300 guns all the way from Verdun to Paris. He had taken every step to ensure the Allies had numerical superiority in the west where his attack would be launched. But as he knew, the outcome from the River Ourcq near Meaux to the gates of Nancy would be on a knife edge. He had made his decision. If his troops failed it could be 1870 all over again. All he could do was exhort from the sidelines and wait.

7: THE BATTLE OF THE MARNE AND ITS CONSEQUENCES

It has been said that the outcome of the Battle of the Marne depended on successful manoeuvres. It cannot be considered on its own but was the outcome of the movements of the different armies during the previous month. To use an analogy with the sonata form of classical music, the opening theme of the Marne was the German war plan involving the violation of Belgian neutrality. The second theme was the initial concentration of the French Armies in the Ardennes and Lorraine. In the development section we see how these two themes interacted to produce the retreat of the Allies and the formation of new armies in the west and the centre. The coda of this symphonic movement is the Battle of the Marne itself. It is impossible to describe the retreat without saying something about the conclusion. Here we will consider the key developments and the fortunes of the witnesses whom we have followed thus far.[1]

The Battle of the Marne commenced a day earlier than Joffre intended. Manoury's columns started their move forward from Paris on 4 September. Reinforcements were still being despatched to this sector including Paul Lintier, the artilleryman from the east, who on the evening of the 4th transferred by train to Paris. On the 5th the German 4th Reserve Corps, guarding von Kluck's flank north of Meaux, spotted the masses of French infantry and opened fire. A full-scale confrontation quickly developed. The French infantry tried to attack the

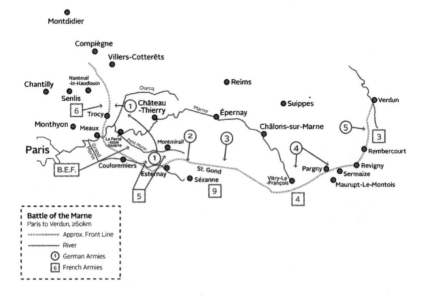

Battle of the Marne
Paris to Verdun, 260km
.... Approx. Front Line
———— River
① German Armies
⑥ French Armies

148

Germans on a hill at Monthyon. By the end of the day the war had taken one of its most renowned casualties. Charles Péguy was shot dead, upright in a hail of machine gun fire, leading his troops from the front.

The Battle of the Marne consisted of four individual clashes in very different sorts of terrain, each of which, however, impacted on the others: the struggle on the River Ourcq near Paris between Manoury's Sixth Army and von Kluck's First; the advance of the Fifth Army against von Bülow's Second supported by the British Expeditionary Force on its left; the attempts by the left of von Bülow's Army and von Hausen's Third to break the French centre under Foch around the Marshes of St. Gond; and the struggle in Lorraine.

The Ourcq

This battle took place on a hilly plateau west of the River Ourcq and north of the Marne and the town of Meaux. Subsequent development makes it seem much closer to Paris than it would have been in 1914. Planes taking off from Charles de Gaulle airport will occasionally disturb visitors to the battlefields today. Even so, there are still enough small villages, orchards and fields of grain to create the atmosphere of that August one hundred years ago. Three streams cut through the chalky soil of the Paris basin between gentle wooded slopes. It was not easy ground on which to manoeuvre.

Joffre had hoped that the advance against the flank of the German right would come as a complete surprise to his opponent. The early clash on 5 September robbed the French Sixth Army of that advantage. Von Kluck instantly focused his forces on the threat from the French. He instructed two corps to march a long distance north with the aim of turning the French left flank.

The fighting on 6 September produced a stalemate despite every effort by the French to push forward. Manoury renewed his attacks the next day but his army was hard pressed even to hold its positions. And then the taxis came to the rescue.

This episode has become synonymous with the whole Battle of the Marne. Galliéni made use of the taxis because there were not enough trains to transport troops to the front outside Paris. Four hundred taxis arrived at the Esplanade des Invalides near Napoleon's last resting place and not far from the Eiffel Tower during the night of 6-7 September. Here they picked up troops from the 7th Division and deposited them just behind the front. Some got lost on the way. Between 6 and 8 September some 4,000 troops were driven to Nanteuil-le Haudouin, a distance of fifty kilometres. The drivers were paid on the meter but at only 27 per cent of the rate paid by individual civilian passengers. After discount each trip cost 35 old francs, the equivalent of £85 in today's money. In reality Galliéni's action was of limited significance but it demonstrated to soldiers and civilians alike the will to resist.

On 8 and 9 September the French Sixth Army faced more crucial tests. Von Kluck now brought the full weight of his regrouped forces to bear, recalling two more corps who had been supporting the right wing of von Bülow's Second Army. They had to march ninety kilometres in just over twenty-four hours. One of these units was the Brandenburg Grenadiers in which Walter Bloem was serving. Bloem had a premonition that all was not well when, on 7 September, his men were ordered to march north. "North! Backwards, in fact! Most strange." The order specified that they would be returning to places they had already passed through, so the men were to be told that this must not be regarded as a retreat. Having thrown back the enemy who was opposing it from the south the First Army was now to advance against the east front of Paris to guard against hostile operations from that place. Bloem did not entirely believe these explanations. He and his comrades felt anxious.[2] Having moved a short distance they were ordered to turn about. They spent the rest of the 7th continuing to fight the French Fifth Army at Sancy near Montceaux-lès-Provins and only set off north again on the 8th. The march was exhausting in the heat. They were all distressed by the stench of dead horses near La Ferté-Gaucher on the Grand Morin. During a brief midday halt the regiment lay prostrate in a field. Bloem remarked: "And so it went on apparently for hours. Whoever was asking his troops to do what we were doing must have been in desperate straits, staking his all on it; for it was almost a superhuman demand. We became just

French infantry firing sheltered behind their sacks at Étrepilly during the Battle of the Marne (Archives départementales de Seine-et-Marne FRAD077_42Fi68_300)

a flock of helpless sheep pattering along in the dark. What did it matter? What did anything matter? We were losing spirit; it was too much."[3] The hill out of La Ferté-sous-Jouarre on the Marne was the last straw. One after another men collapsed into the ditch. They found some filthy billets at midnight and after three hours' rest were off again.[4] Eventually they reached the battlefield near the River Ourcq on 9 September where they occupied trenches near a village called Trocy. The shelling was intense and Bloem realized that this time they were fighting to save their country from defeat.

All thought of a French advance had evaporated by now. It was just a question of maintaining existing positions. The French were constantly on the edge of a major collapse as the Germans tried desperately to turn their left or northern flank. On the morning of 9 September, however, von Kluck received disturbing news that the British and also French cavalry were on the Marne at Charly, the home of André's parents. He decided to retract his left wing to counter this danger. Manoury now had more room to manoeuvre, either to join the British or to reinforce his left. The encirclement of Manoury's Army had become impossible and in any case he had a second line of defence to which he could retreat. Now the only option for von Kluck was a successful assault in the north on Manoury's left.

Exploiting the gap

Von Kluck's regrouping of his scattered forces to counter-attack Manoury on the Ourcq opened up a gap between the First Army and von Bülow's Second Army. Opposite this gap stretching from Montmirail to Meaux stood the left flank of

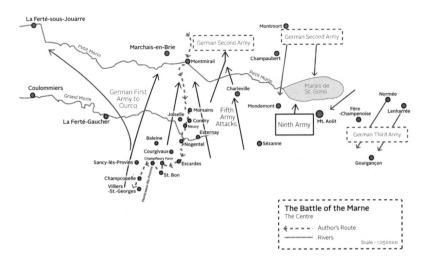

the French Fifth Army and the British Expeditionary Force. The Fifth started its advance from a line stretching north-east from Provins. Its front stretched all the way from Sézanne in the east to a point south of Coulommiers in the west, a distance of fifty kilometres. At first it had von Kluck's men to contend with as well as elements of von Bülow's forces. On 6 September the German First Army attacked the flank of the 18th Corps west of Coulommiers. There was some fierce hand to hand fighting.

In the centre the 5th and 6th Divisions of the 3rd Corps attacked Escardes and Montceaux-lès-Provins respectively. André in his field near Villiers-St.-Georges watched events unfolding. He saw the artillery duel with French heavy 120s firing from behind them. No shells landed in his vicinity, however. One infantry regiment went into the attack and then later came back with its wounded. André and his men were feeling sleepy because they had had nothing to eat. He remembers chewing some raw sugar beets but the taste was bland and they irritated his throat. He wondered whether the retreat might start again, but no. Behind them were waves of infantry who marched past towards the battle.[5]

Escardes lies in open farmland on a slight ridge to the south of the Esternay to Paris road. There are several small woods in the vicinity and today some of these obscure the view down to Courgivaux, which was the 5th Division's objective. At Escardes the 39th Infantry Regiment from Rouen and Dieppe pushed back German attacks. Charles Mangin, commander of the division, then set up his HQ here and directed his men forward. A plaque on the *mairie* records his presence. Walking across the ground between Escardes and Courgivaux it is difficult to imagine how men could have crossed it under fire without sustaining enormous casualties. It is almost flat and there is very little natural cover apart from the scattered woods which are some distance apart. Mangin believed in massive bombardments by the artillery before an attack. In 1918 he made his name with the technique of the rolling barrage which moved forward just ahead of the advancing infantry and kept the enemy's heads down. At the end of the day Courgivaux was in French hands.

On Mangin's left the 6th Division was ordered to capture Montceaux-lès-Provins. Its commander was Philippe Pétain, later the hero of Verdun and Marshal of France. It was typical of the man that he prepared the ground for his infantry as carefully as he could, ensuring close cooperation with the artillery and thorough reconnaissance including the use of aeroplanes. But ultimately the men had to move forward over open ground under hostile fire. The fighting started at St. Bon and Champfleury farm nearby. Today St. Bon is a small hamlet; a manor house, a church, one or two new buildings, two farms and a cemetery. The soldiers hesitated before launching their attack. At this point Pétain pushed through the ranks to a point several metres in front of the first line of men and marched straight towards the barrage of German 105 mm shells. His men surged forward. André noted: "Four kilometres in front of us the village of St. Bon, which crowns a ridge, is the scene of bitter fighting. We see soldiers twice charge with their bayonets, houses burn and the Germans finally being driven out."[6]

Before the division could reach its main objective at Montceaux it had to secure its right flank by driving the Germans out of Champfleury farm one and a half kilometres to the north-east. The troops advanced under the protection of a rise in the ground between the village and the farm. I stood by a water tower on the top of the hill. The farm was now a few hundred metres away. How could the French infantry have got close to the walls? The open field in front of me seemed to offer no cover. The woods behind the farm were probably not so extensive in 1914. Despite these conditions the farm was bombarded by the artillery, rushed and captured.

Once the farm was taken the division could move on to attack Montceaux-lès-Provins itself. To do this they had to advance across another kilometre of open ground. There was no alternative. I walked up the farm track from St. Bon between huge wheat fields, heading straight for the outskirts of Montceaux. The land rises slightly then dips again before the last approach. The intensity of fire from the German fortified positions on the knoll of Montceaux-lès-Provins must have been awesome. At the edge of Montceaux Pétain's troops, in cooperation with the 18th Corps, had to tackle the entrenched German defenders in the railway station and the walled house called Les Chataigniers. Today weeds grow over the railway track but the walls of the house still look formidable standing some three metres above the road below. The French artillery opened up again virtually reducing Montceaux to rubble. Aerial reconnaissance spotted a German battery behind the village and it was eliminated. The Germans defended their positions with rifles and machine guns but after repeated attacks the French occupied Montceaux one hour before midnight. The cost was high. In the 11th Brigade alone 600 men were killed. The small cemetery near the station contains a few individual graves of soldiers killed that day and on the 7th, when the Germans counter-attacked. Some remains may be in the ossuary containing 200 bodies.[7]

The French Fifth Army moved forward cautiously, consolidating its positions after each effort before advancing again. The network of dense woods, tree-lined fields and the occasional ravine hampered their movements. Three rivers—the Grand Morin, the Petit Morin and the Marne itself—lay across their line of attack. After the battle for Montceaux-lès-Provins the next objective was to take Esternay, the key to the first river crossing at the Grand Morin. German heavy artillery ravaged the ranks of the 1st Corps but eventually the town was captured. By the evening of 7 September some units had reached the village of Joiselle five kilòmetres north of Esternay.

On 7 September Sergeant Omnès in the 10th Corps was engaged in fighting north-east of Sézanne. A regiment from another corps fled through his lines. He relates that General Franchet d'Esperey was standing just behind him with a colonel. Franchet said: "We must go forward whatever the cost!" Then they both gripped their revolvers. They passed close to me saying: "Follow me with your men." Omnès and his colleagues advanced under heavy enemy shell fire. Luckily, however, they did manage to find some *eau-de-vie* in a village, which cheered them up. They fired on the Germans from a garden wall and the latter started to flee. Omnès and his comrades climbed into a house from which they could shoot at the Germans more effectively. Fortunately again, the house had some good bottles in the cellar. "The glory of the good wine of France was never celebrated in song with so much fervour as it was by exhausted soldiers to whom it gave the strength to fight for the liberation of the sacred soil of the Patrie! Between two shots everyone emptied their glass and soon bursts of laughter mixed with the sound of shells exploding. Oh, the happy character of the French!" By the evening they had reached a village called Charleville about nine kilometres north of Esternay. Omnès records how the Germans were pushed back even further and he saw more and more German corpses. He took some German eagles as trophies of war. Some prisoners pleaded to be spared because they were Alsatian.[8]

As von Kluck pulled his four main corps towards Paris the German position weakened. Von Bülow started to retract his right wing for fear of being outflanked. Before von Kluck recalled his 3rd and 9th Corps on 8 September von Bülow had already started to move them behind the Petit Morin, a retreat of fifteen to twenty kilometres. A gap of thirty kilometres between the German First and Second Armies was enlarged to forty-eight. The Second Army was left on its own to deal with the French Fifth and the British Expeditionary Force. Von Bülow's men were exhausted. They had started the campaign with 260,000 soldiers but this number was now reduced to 154,000, the difference accounted for by men lent to other German Armies as well as the killed, wounded and missing. Now both flanks of the German Second Army were under threat and the French advanced more confidently.

André relates that towards the end of the afternoon of 6 September his unit moved forward a short distance to a hamlet where they found something to eat: some chickens barbecued over a fire on their bayonets, bottles of wine, tuna and pears cooked in wine but without sugar. All the soldiers clearly had to think of their stomachs. At 10 pm the official food distribution arrived and the men devoured the bread they had been lacking. They slept comfortably on straw.

On the morning of the 7th they realized that the front had moved forward and they advanced across the fields. On a crest they dug trenches and later went on to Montceaux-lès-Provins passing huge craters caused by German shells and some dead French soldiers. They carried on marching north and came across a place where French shells had destroyed a German battery (perhaps the battery north of Montceaux which had caused the French attackers so much trouble on the 6th). The company had to create defensive works on the edge of a wood facing north, probably the wood I observed south of Baleine where André's unit now rested.

He remarks that it was a poor little village where only two inhabitants were left. The Germans had departed in a hurry in the morning. The battalion bivouacked in a field because all the houses were in ruins. They were poor dwellings anyway, dirty and full of atrocious smells. The men cleared the remains of the last German meal out of a house, installed their own cooking stove and made a soup with vegetables from the garden. The night was spent on some straw in a hangar with no doors. The next day some of the men were sick, probably because of the dirty water they drank at Baleine. The regimental journal confirms this, and the soldiers were advised to boil drinking water in future. The settlement today still seems insignificant and undistinguished with a few farm buildings including two barns where André could have slept.[9] Baleine lies in an oasis of green meadows surrounded by woods. The ground is perfectly level with no high point to catch the eye. It is typical of the countryside south of Montmirail through which the Fifth Army now had to advance.

On 8 September the 18th and 3rd Corps successfully cleared the way into Montmirail, the fortress on the Petit Morin. The former also crossed the Petit Morin five kilometres to the west and pushed on to Marchais-en-Brie where they were in sight of Napoleon's column. Brunel de Pérard talks about the large numbers of German prisoners taken in this advance, many of whom said they had not eaten properly for five days.[10] Von Bülow pulled back his right even further so that his army now faced more west than south. The gap had now widened to sixty kilometres. At this stage a fresh army might have driven forward more vigorously and caused the Germans real problems. Not only were Franchet's men tired; they had also contended with determined German resistance in their fortified positions on the hills surrounding first Esternay and then Montmirail. On 9 September Conneau's cavalry crossed the Marne at Château-Thierry but a commander found one regiment of infantry slumped by the roadside. It took an attack by the Zouaves from North Africa to drive out the remaining German garrison.

On the morning of the 8th André was not unduly hurried. He had time to write two postcards and look around the garden as if he was on holiday. One has the impression that Franchet d'Esperey deliberately kept the group of Reserve Divisions back from the front line during the battle. He would have been party to the view of senior officers that these troops were not likely to be reliable in serious fighting. André's section set off and soon saw smoke from the fighting around Montmirail appearing over the tops of the woods. They passed a French artillery post destroyed by enemy shelling and saw corpses of men and horses and broken crates of ammunition. It started raining but as they were not being asked to hurry they found time to shelter in a wood. Later they saw inhabitants returning to their farms. The rain came down harder and the mud in the fields stuck to their boots. They stopped for the night in a little hamlet. The men complained about sleeping out in the rain while the colonel's horses were made comfortable in a stable. Even the officers who found shelter were wet through. There was no fire. The farmer and his family came back and the officers moved out of their rooms, sleeping on the floor where they had dined.

On the morning of the 9th they got dry, had some food from a regular distribution and set off. Many corpses and the debris of battle littered the roadside: big piles of shell cases, tyres, empty petrol cans, broken bicycles and other abandoned equipment. They crossed the valley of the Petit Morin and climbed up to the main road not far from Napoleon's column, eventually dossing down in Villemoyenne among yet more debris. This is another ordinary little settlement like Baleine. I took a picture of a barn with old walls where André's men might have slept and also of the house next door which was possibly used by the officers. Small unkempt meadows, where the rest of the regiment bivouacked, surrounded the house.

On the 10th André advanced towards the Marne on the same route he had taken seven days before, only this time he felt more at ease. He passed many dead horses in the fields with swollen stomachs and stiff legs. They smelt very strongly. When walking past he worked out the wind direction and calculated how long to hold his breath. Other horses were in a bad way waiting to die. Dead horses in their hundreds were a common sight during the retreat and the battle. André's section arrived at Crézancy, the other side of the river from Mont-St.-Père, and took over the house of a M. Lamarre whom André knew. The door had been broken down, the window panes smashed and in the drawing room books, music and other objects were scattered on the wooden floor. However, this damage was minimal compared with what they had seen over the last few days. The Germans had only left at 9 am that morning.[11]

While the Fifth Army was making slow if steady progress the British Expeditionary Force was proceeding at an even more leisurely pace. Starting from a line north-east of Melun they advanced forty kilometres between 6 and 8 September against minimal opposition. There were perhaps 10,000 German troops to impede the progress of the 100,000-strong British Army. On 6 September Haig's 1st Corps lost only seven men killed. Caution was still the watchword on the 7th, however, and it was only in the evening that advance guards reached the Grand Morin at La Ferté-Gaucher close to the French Fifth Army. On 8 September they continued this slow move forward across the Petit Morin, not reaching the Marne between La Ferté-sous-Jouarre and Château-Thierry until the next day. By this time the Germans had managed to blow most of the Marne bridges but not the one at Charly-sur-Marne, the home of André's parents. There the Grenadiers found the bridge intact, although prepared for detonation. They were told the Germans were too drunk to finish the job. The Guards entered the town unopposed to find bombastic German inscriptions chalked in huge letters on the walls of houses.[12]

Why were the British so slow? The German rearguards fought skilfully and the wooded country around the Petit Morin impeded progress. At La Ferté-sous-Jouarre it took time for the artillery to destroy the last pockets of German resistance and for the engineers to re-build the bridge.[13] Some in the British Expeditionary Force were frustrated at the slow progress. The troops felt in better shape than during the retreat. Distribution of food was more regular and fewer of the men were footsore. There was a natural desire to get at the Germans.[14] Yet there can be little doubt that Sir John French was following the old adage, once bitten, twice shy. He believed that the French had failed to inform him of their retreat while he faced the full force of von Kluck's Army at Mons. In the Battle of the Marne he tested the water carefully, making absolutely sure the French were

English infantry hidden near Meaux in a brickworks during the Battle of the Marne. (Archives départementales de Seine-et-Marne FRAD077_42Fi142_300)

supporting him on either flank. He did not want to expose his precious army to unnecessary risks and receive another near fatal mauling as at Le Cateau. In German minds the British posed a significant threat to their perilously stretched line. If a more energetic and less risk-averse commander had driven hard into the flanks of the German First and Second Armies perhaps the outcome of the battle, and of the war, would have been different.

The marshes of St. Gond

Foch had been given command of the new Ninth Army with the task of holding the French centre around the marshes of St. Gond, the source of the Petit Morin. He had two corps, the 9th in the centre and the 11th on his right. On the left were the crack troops of the 42nd Division. He was facing the left of von Bülow's Army and the Saxons of von Hausen's Third Army. There was a gap in the line between his right and the Fourth Army's left, covered by cavalry. Foch had about 95,000 men at his disposal against approximately 150,000 Germans, although some of von Hausen's men were supporting the German Fourth Army. The marshes stretched sixteen kilometres west-east between two hills; the northern one occupied by the Germans and the southern by the French. Four narrow causeways, each approximately three kilometres long, traversed this boggy ground which was intersected by drainage ditches. This was not exactly easy terrain to cross under fire. In 1914 the marsh was more extensive than it is today but because of the hot weather in August 1914 the water table was relatively low. To the west lay the chalk escarpments of the Paris Basin; to the east the plain of *la Champagne pouilleuse* dominated by one or two hilly outcrops.

A devout Catholic from the Pyrenees, Foch had been a brilliant teacher at the École de Guerre. Autocratic and frequently bad-tempered, his clipped orders were sometimes difficult for his subordinates to understand. He believed that attack was often the best form of defence and that generals sometimes talked themselves into defeat. Yet he did not support a senseless doctrine of the offensive in all circumstances. Morale was important but so was careful analysis of any situation.

Foch started the battle in his sector by launching the Moroccans of the Blondlat Brigade across the marshes at night. They crept silently forward but searchlights, machine guns and heavy rifle fire confronted them when they reached the northern edge. Not surprisingly many of them did not return. This set the scene for two days of fierce fighting, of attacks and counter-attacks, around the marshes and on the escarpments to the west. All along the line Foch's forces were under huge pressure and losses were high. At 5 pm on 7 September Foch ordered an attack on his left with the help of the 10th Corps released by Franchet d'Esperey and some reinforcements whom Joffre had despatched from

Lorraine. It ended in disastrous losses inflicted by superior German firepower.

Von Hausen observed the battle with increasing frustration. His colleagues to right and left were constantly asking for help from his troops, which limited his ability to make progress on his own sector of the front. He felt put upon by his neighbours, the ambitious von Bülow, commander of the Second Army, and Prince Albrecht, Duke of Württemberg, in charge of the Fourth. Now from hesitation he swung to decisive action, but with hindsight perhaps too late. In the dark on the morning of 8 September he launched the Prussian Guard into a silent attack at the point of the bayonet. They easily overran the French positions at Normée and Lenharrée. Soon the French were streaming back southwards, retreating eventually twelve kilometres on a twenty-kilometre front. At Lenharrée today a small stream passes through the village in the middle of a shallow depression surrounded by trees. After a few hundred metres you reach the crushing immensity of the Champagne plain. The dry and dusty chalk is never far below the surface of the gently undulating soil. There are no vertical lines; the world is horizontal as far as the eye can see.

The 114th Infantry Regiment had been fighting hard near Nancy until 4 September when it was pulled out of the line to rest. After a short time in Troyes, on 6 September it was deployed to Foch's right wing at Normée. The diary of André Bourgain, a corporal in the 8th Company, records the moment when their sentries were surprised by the German attack and many of the men in the French trenches fled. Some of them ran away in their shirts, abandoning their equipment. After this rout they retreated twelve kilometres to a ridge behind the village of Gourgançon.[15]

The threat to Foch's position was severe and became more so when a German division in the centre finally managed to establish itself on the southern edge of the marshes. And then the Prussian Guard's offensive on the plain ground to a halt for a while; they were tired and very hungry. The Germans tried to press on again and Foch launched counter-attacks, asking for a last effort from his exhausted soldiers. The fighting from hillock to hillock and from farm to farm became confused. Meanwhile Foch was holding the Germans on the south of the marshes in check with artillery firing from the hills above.

On 9 September the Germans pressed forward again on the plain and also captured the vital hill of Mont Août rising one hundred and fifty metres on the edge of it. Now Foch's flank had in effect been turned. He had already realized the danger and allegedly uttered his famous phrase about counter-attacking when his men were falling back. This was one of the myths of the Marne. He responded by asking Franchet to protect his left while he pulled the 42nd Division across his army to counter-attack on his right. At the same time he had to deal with one last threat to his centre. The Hanoverians broke through to the

Château de Mondemont on top of the hill of the Marne monument at 6 am on 9 September. The Moroccan Division launched ferocious attacks with infantry which were all repulsed by the German machine gunners with heavy loss of life. Eventually the French succeeded in bringing up two 75 mm field guns and opening fire from 300 metres away. They virtually demolished the chateau and the few Germans who survived crawled back down the hill.

The struggle between Vitry-le-François and Nancy

The fighting further east raged unabated while the armies in the west manoeuvred for advantage. No one in Lorraine achieved a breakthrough and the result was a stalemate. The German Fourth and Fifth Armies commanded by Prince Albrecht and the Kaiser's son launched repeated attacks on the French Fourth and Third Armies on a front stretching north-east from Vitry-le-François to Verdun. The 107th Infantry Regiment of Captain Campagne fought the Germans at close quarters, back and forwards, in the town of Vitry itself.[16] Guasson was stationed in a position nearby as part of the French Fourth Army. Most of the deaths in his sector were the result of devastating shelling. Each night he went out to help pick up the wounded. On 8 September he recalls running into a party of Germans doing the same.

> After covering a kilometre we arrive between the two lines. It is dark and we trip over the corpses. We call out to the wounded in a low voice. The Germans are there looking for their wounded. Many of them speak French. They show us where our wounded are lying. We exchange cigarettes and tobacco. All night we pick up our wounded, many die in the wagons... This task is very painful. The wounded are heavy because they can't help themselves. Some complain, the others gasp for breath. We would like to collect them all but it is impossible.[17]

On the 9th they tried to advance, ran up against German machine guns and had to withdraw. It was useless. On the 10th they tried it again with the same result. "Major Castellane, a sabre in his hand, puts himself at the head of his unit and shouts '*Mes enfants*, follow me, have courage. I have seven children but this action is necessary.' He has only gone a few metres when a bullet hits him right in the forehead. He falls without a cry. His orderly throws himself on him weeping. The men are electrified and hurl themselves forward screaming at the enemy. The Germans retreat and leave us with equipment and prisoners." Despite the German artillery they advance between five and six hundred metres.[18]

Joffre was so concerned about the security of the French front between Vitry-Le-François and Verdun that he threw two more army corps into the breach, one directed at the gap between Foch and Langle de Cary's Fourth Army on the Champagne plain, and one at the gap between Langle de Cary and Sarrail's Third Army. In response to German pressure Joffre also told Sarrail that if necessary he could move his army south to link up with the Fourth Army, even if it meant breaking off contact with the fortress of Verdun. Sarrail refused to take this step and thus the gap to the left of his line near the village of Revigny was vulnerable until reinforcements arrived. The German Fifth Army stormed the Revigny heights on the Côtes de Meuse on 8 September although without the support of the Fourth Army on their right.

Maurice Genevoix was in position at Rembercourt, south of the Revigny Gap. The fighting which he describes was particularly brutal. On 6 September his unit advanced in a rush. "I feel excitement taking me over. I feel as if I live in all these men whom I push forward with a gesture in the face of bullets which fly towards us looking for chests, foreheads, living flesh... A stifled cry on my left; I just have time to see a man falling on his back, twice pushing his legs forward. In a second his whole body stiffens. Then it relaxes and becomes inert, dead flesh which the sun will decompose tomorrow."[19] A fold in the ground gives them shelter. He is about to find a more permanent place of safety when a German bombardment starts. "A comrade, I saw him quite clearly as his body suffered the full impact of a shell. His hat flew off with his cape and an arm. On the ground there lies an inchoate mass, red and white, an almost naked body, squashed. Without a chief his men scatter."[20]

On the 8th Genevoix contemplated "a large and desolate plain, torn up by shells, littered with corpses whose clothes are torn, their face turned to the heavens or stuck in the earth, their guns having fallen alongside them."[21] Two days later, the Germans launched a desperate charge, their bayonets reflecting the flames consuming the grass around them. "They shout like savages; the sound of their rough voices clearly heard over the top of the firing, interrupted by shells exploding, carried on the wind with squalls of rain."[22] Like Guasson he was witness to carnage, with no advantage gained by either side. Attack and counter-attack led to stalemate. The German attack on the Revigny heights ended in failure.

Meanwhile the battle around Nancy was reaching its climax following Joffre's instruction to Castelnau to hold firm. On 7 September the Bavarians three times stormed the north front of the Grand Couronné, finally resorting to brutal bayonet charges at night. They almost broke through, but not quite. By now 8,200 German bodies littered the slopes. Again Castelnau wavered but Joffre stiffened his resolve. On the 10th he launched a number of counter-attacks which began to take their toll on the Germans. They abandoned their positions around Lunéville, leaving behind their wounded as well as arms and ammunition. The line of the Meurthe was now secure and Nancy had been saved.[23]

The intervention of Colonel Hentsch and the end of the battle

By the morning of 9 September the battle had reached a critical phase. On the Ourcq Manoury's left was yielding to German pressure. The British Expeditionary Force and the French Fifth Army were advancing steadily into the gap between the German First and Second Armies. Would von Kluck be able to break the French Sixth Army's resistance before the threat to his flank from the British became severe? How long could Foch hold on in the centre? These were the critical issues.

The Battle of the Marne ended on 9 September when the Germans decided to withdraw to the north. How did this happen? Here we come to perhaps its most controversial episode. Von Moltke, Chief of General Staff in Luxembourg, was very concerned by the gap between the First and Second Armies and the possibility that it could be exploited by the Allies. At this moment of crisis he did not go to visit the battlefield himself but on 8 September sent a trusted staff officer, Colonel Richard Hentsch, Chief of the Intelligence Section of General Headquarters, with full powers to reach a decision on his own as to the best course of action.

Hentsch started by visiting the Fifth, Fourth and Third Armies who were nearest to Luxembourg. There did not seem to be any grave concerns in their sectors of the front. Why he did not start in the west, where reports indicated the greatest threats lay, is not clear. He only reached von Bülow's HQ at the Château de Montmort north of the St. Gond marshes at 6.45 pm on the 8th. In discussions overnight von Bülow explained his fear that his right flank would be turned. He was also worried about the pressure on his left. Von Kluck's constant refusal to cooperate made him very angry. Why had von Kluck ignored Moltke's instruction not to cross the Marne ahead of the Second Army? Von Kluck alone was responsible for the current predicament of German forces. Von Bülow believed that his colleague should close the gap between First and Second Armies by moving his forces east even if this meant breaking off the battle with Manoury. Shortly after Hentsch left von Bülow received more bad news and ordered his whole army to retreat before von Kluck had been consulted. He made no effort to contact his colleague by telephone, which would have been perfectly possible. Von Bülow alone was responsible for setting the withdrawal of the whole German Army in motion.

In the morning Hentsch drove over to von Kluck's HQ, making a long detour to avoid the advancing Allies. The chaos that he witnessed on the way unnerved him. When he reached First Army he met only Hermann von Kuhl, the Chief of Staff, even though von Kluck was a mere three hundred metres away in his command post. Hentsch concluded his presentation by saying that the Second

Army had been reduced to "cinders" and that with the full authority of von Moltke he ordered the First Army to retreat. Von Kuhl was amazed but felt he had no option but to comply. He made no effort to contact the Second Army or Army Headquarters. After Hentsch's visit he simply informed von Kluck of the new orders which the latter accepted with great reluctance. It seems incredible that so grave a decision could have been taken in such a careless manner. Neither the Second Army nor First Army was in danger of imminent defeat. Fresh forces released by the capitulation of Maubeuge were on their way. Von Kluck could have continued the assault on Manoury's left a little longer although a successful outcome was already less likely. The decision to retreat or not was finely balanced. Von Kluck took the safe option and obeyed orders.

Once von Bülow and von Kluck pulled back the others had to follow. Von Hausen was perplexed after his success on the plains of Champagne. It took two more days for the fighting between Vitry-le-François and Verdun to cease. By 11 September all the German Armies who had fought in the battle were pulling back. Suddenly they had gone.

Casualties

The first two months of the war produced carnage unparalleled up to that time. The French official history set losses at 206,515 men in August (20,253 killed, 78,468 wounded and 107,794 missing including prisoners) and 213,445 (18,073 killed, 111,963 wounded and 83,409 missing including prisoners) in September, the highest monthly casualties in the Great War. Of the 191,203 missing approximately 125,000 were taken prisoner. A later enquiry into losses undertaken by the Service Historique de l'Armée lists 313,000 killed, disappeared or prisoners for August and September. If you add this number to the Official History's figure for those wounded, but deduct wounded who subsequently died in hospital (16,000), the total casualty figure for the two months including 174,431 long-term wounded comes out at 487,431.

The Battle of the Marne itself may well have accounted for 85,000 French casualties in an army numbering around 900,000. The German casualties were around 100,000 out of 750,000. British casualties were 1,700 out of 100,000 troops; far fewer than the 7,800 that the 2nd Corps lost in one day at Le Cateau in August and on a par with losses at Mons. Casualties were also heavy among the horses although no reliable figures exist.[24]

Aftermath

It was an orderly withdrawal. There was bewilderment at the turn of events but discipline was maintained. Walter Bloem wrote: "This was a retreat then, pure and simple. Not a shadow of doubt about it now. Retreat!... a great vast melancholy and misery hung over us all, seemingly over the whole world. That was, for us, what is now called the Battle of the Marne."[25] Within the First Army a company of Brandenburg Grenadiers had time to drink ninety bottles of claret on the march. They left the empties for the French to collect. Like von Moltke before them the French General Staff were now asking, "where are the prisoners?" Major Pierre Bréant, serving with the cavalry between the left of the Fifth Army and the British, remarked on 10 September that the enemy was said to be beaten but that there was no evidence of a rout.[26] The Germans sent their Pioneer Corps ahead to prepare defensive positions on the line of the River Aisne fifty kilometres to the north. They selected positions on the steep northern bank, flanked to the north-west by the Forest of Compiègne. To the south-east their line ran along the hills of Reims and then into the woods of the Argonne towards Verdun. By 13 September the First and Second Armies were safely across the river. The army corps released by the fall of Maubeuge filled the gap between the two, joined a day later by troops withdrawn from Alsace. The Germans also made some tactical retreats around Nancy and further south.

The Allied pursuit of the retreating Germans was slow and by the time the need for more energy was recognized it was too late. On 11 September the unusually hot weather broke and rain hampered the Allies. By 13 September the French Fifth Army had reached Reims and the British were across the Aisne. The French cavalry pushed into the gap between the German First and Second Armies but later withdrew when German reinforcements arrived. Allied attacks against positions prepared by the Germans made little progress. On 14 September Joffre switched tactics from all-out pursuit to more methodical attacks but the German line held. The war of the trenches had begun.

The last throw of the dice that might have enabled either side to achieve a quick victory was the so-called race to the sea in the autumn of 1914. Each side tried to outflank the other by manoeuvring new forces into position in the gap between Compiègne and the Channel ports. Both failed and a new line of trenches was established ending in the mud of Flanders around Ypres. The Germans launched their major offensive at Ypres in mid-October in a last desperate attempt to achieve a breakthrough in 1914. It ended in stalemate but was the graveyard of the Old Contemptibles, the British professionals who had fought all the way from Belgium to the Marne and back.

Consequences of the Battle of the Marne

So the Marne did not result in total victory for the Allies but a stalemate which lasted until the new war of movement in 1918. For their part the Germans had invaded France with the intention of annihilating her armies within forty days. This plan ended in total failure. Strategically they had suffered a major setback although they never admitted it openly. Italy, a former alliance partner of Germany's, had already decided to remain neutral. This meant that France did not have to leave troops guarding the Alpine frontier. Clearly the war was going to last longer than anyone thought.

As we have seen in the Introduction, many explanations have been offered for the failure of the Germans to land a knock out blow in the west. They made the fatal mistake of underestimating their opponents. On this occasion, unlike in 1870 and 1940, the French High Command was much more effective than its German counterpart. Joffre was the organizer of victory. He recognized his mistakes in the Battle of the Frontiers and held the French Armies together during the retreat. With Galliéni's help he developed the plan to attack the Germans on von Kluck's flank. He exuded an air of calm in the gravest crisis. Some later questioned whether he personally won the battle. He commented that if France had lost he knew who would have been blamed. In his memoirs Foch, his lieutenant and eventual successor in 1918, recognized Joffre's unique achievement.[27]

The Marne was a French battle in which the British played a supporting role. Without the "contemptible little army" the victory of the Marne would not have been possible, even if they could have pursued their enemy with more vigour. Their very existence caused a German loss of nerve, the only way to describe their over-hasty retreat. It was the last time French forces played such a preponderant role. As the war dragged on they needed British and American manpower to hold the line and then turn the tide in 1918.

The Marne was a victory for France but also paradoxically a tragedy. Apart from the enormous loss of men caused by industrialized slaughter the country also sacrificed seventeen per cent of its territory for four years together with the industrial production of the Nord and Lorraine. In the occupied territories controlled by the German Army civilians' homes were destroyed and farmers lost their livelihoods. For those left on the wrong side of the German lines the retreat meant four years of deprivation, exactions and forced labour.

The German Army, on the other hand, never accepted that it had lost the chance of total victory within weeks of the Great War starting. After the Armistice four years later the myth of the stab in the back was born. The fruits of this myth became apparent after Hitler came to power. It was only thirty years later that Germany renounced the dream of total hegemony and a new European order was born. Taking a wider perspective, the failure by either side to achieve a final victory on the Marne led to thirty years of unrest, death and destruction in Europe.

It was been said many times in Britain that France has never fought hard to defend itself and has relied on British help. The Marne was emphatically one occasion when this was not the case. The French soldiers put up with the hardships of the retreat and then turned about, often exhausted and without adequate food, to counter-attack successfully. General von Kluck recognized the enormity of this achievement. "But that men who have retreated for ten days… that men who slept on the ground half dead with fatigue, should have the strength to take up their rifles and attack when the bugle sounds, that is a thing upon which we never counted; that is a possibility that we never spoke about in our war academies."[28]

The Marne was in one sense a battle of another age, fought by infantrymen marching long distances. When Franchet d'Esperey recalled Napoleon's victories against the Prussians at Champaubert and Montmirail exactly one hundred years before, he underlined this point. This was a battle fought between soldiers with aching limbs and very sore feet. Two million soldiers marched a long way in the searing heat of an unusually hot summer. Many of the German troops started in the west of their country near the Belgian border, a distance from the Marne battlefield of over six hundred kilometres.

Downhearted and disorganized after defeat on the French frontiers the British and French soldiers did not give up. Their morale held and they marched together out of danger, fighting off the Germans as they hurried south. Frequently they had to scavenge in the countryside for something to eat as supply arrangements broke down. They threw away their packs of over 25 kilos and surplus clothing better suited to winter weather. When the order came to turn about there was a great sense of relief. The hardships of the retreat had not been in vain.

8: WHAT HAPPENED TO ANDRÉ BENOIT?

The retreat to the Aisne

André's unit continued marching and eating and after 11 September they frequently got wet. On the evening of 13 September the regiment arrived at Cormicy north-west of Reims and east of the country they had passed through during the retreat. They crossed the canal from the Aisne to the Marne and took up positions on the edge of a wood on the far side, facing north-east. The very next day they were involved in heavy fighting, far more serious than anything André had seen to date. They retreated back to Cormicy and it is at this point that he mentions digging very basic trenches for protection from German shells and covering them with doors, planks and shutters ripped from houses. For the next week or so they suffered the cold and damp and also stiff knees, crouching down in a confined space which was nothing more than a glorified hole for a few men.

The Germans shelled them sporadically. André had to patrol the front line beyond the canal. On the 22nd engineers arrived to erect the first barbed wire in front of the French positions. He could see bodies in no man's land and on one occasion his men managed to rescue a wounded German soldier.

On 23 September André was involved once again in a full-scale attack on the German lines towards a hill named Côte 100. This was situated two kilometres from the canal side settlement of La Neuville and four kilometres from Cormicy. Advancing under heavy rifle and shell fire he hit the ground when the German machine guns opened up. After a long time lying flat with bullets whistling just over his head he crawled back on his stomach, using his spade and sack for protection. He remarks that the sword that all officers carried got in the way. At a meeting with the colonel afterwards there were only three officers left in his battalion—his friend Lefebvre, one other lieutenant and himself. Since 19 August they had lost the commander, four captains and five out of eight lieutenants, either killed or wounded. The captain of André's company, a man called Évrard, had received a bullet in the knee. He eventually returned to active service as commander of a battalion in the 67th Infantry Regiment but was killed in Champagne in May 1915.

André was given command of the remnants of two companies other than his own until new officers arrived. After the fighting they spent some time learning how to improve their shelters and make them more comfortable. He cut his beard for the first time since 9 September. He also notes approvingly that the men had a wash. The cook produced some decent hot meals. He and several of the men suffered from dysentery and were given opium pills.

On 3 October the regiment moved east. The march was difficult, firstly because their legs were stiff after a long period in the trenches and secondly on account of continual stops to cope with the effects of dysentery. Later they travelled by lorry, eventually reaching a position thirty kilometres south-east of Amiens and not far from Montdidier. On 5 October he watched a French fighter pilot shoot down a German plane. Fifty years later he had an opportunity to meet the pilot.

*

On 22 June 1964 André happened to see a TV programme which included an item about former fighter pilots of the Great War. One of them was introduced as having been the first to shoot down an enemy plane, on 5 October 1914. André looked up his war journal and realized that this aerial combat must have been the one he witnessed when Sergeant Joseph Frantz shot down a German plane. He left a letter with the TV station and a short time later received a reply from Frantz, now President of the Vieilles Tiges, an association of old war pilots. The reply pointed out that André and Roland Dorgelès, author of one of the best-known French war novels *Les Croix de bois* (The Wooden Crosses), were among the few witnesses of the fight. André was invited to the commemorative cocktail party on 5 October 1964 at the Aero-Club. Also present was Gabriel Voisin, the creator of the Voisin bi-plane involved which had been armed with a machine gun. André heard an account of the duel and was asked, along with Roland Dorgelès, to say a few words about what he saw.

*

The French and German Armies were now engaged in the race to the sea. André's contribution, with his men, was to spend some time digging trenches. He was delighted, meanwhile, to sleep in a bed alongside Lefebvre for the first time since 14 September and to take his shoes off. On 12 October two young women, who ran the farm where they were staying, organized a special meal for his 26th birthday: napkins, flowers, and birthday kisses.

On 13 October they were off again, back in the direction from which they had come. After a night spent in lorries they arrived at Braine and marched north to cross the Aisne. They saw English troops playing football and the Tommies offered them cigarettes. They arrived at the Ferme du Metz on the Canal de l'Aisne à l'Oise at 1 am. They were not far from the village of Soupir and right under the steep east-west escarpment on the north bank of the Aisne River with the Chemin des Dames running along the top. The canal ran in a valley with undulating fields and woods climbing up either side until it entered a tunnel under the main ridge.

The company took over English trenches in this area from the Royal Berkshire Regiment; some in the front line and André and his section in the second line. The English had dug individual holes for shelter under some apple trees just below the farm. They were near a lock and a bridge leading to Moussy on the east bank. André and his men spent some time remaking their shelters and also helping the front line units improve their trench. There was not a lot of firing but they realized the Germans could see their every movement so they had to be cautious. The English had left them many tins of corned beef and potatoes. The company's men were very happy to receive parcels from home containing tobacco, chocolate and woollen clothes. They also got a chance to read a newspaper for the first time. The cooks brought them hot meals.

At 10 pm on 19 October they relieved the men in the front line trench, which ran from the next lock north across a field on the west bank. It was six hundred metres from the Ferme du Metz. André's section occupied the eastern end right up against the canal embankment and he had a small command post on the bank itself. The German positions were only eight hundred metres away, on the other side of the canal and sited on a wooded slope higher up. The German front line on the south-facing slope of the Chemin des Dames ridge had a commanding view of the Aisne valley below. Sited uphill from any attackers it occupied a superb defensive position. André's men improved the trench to give themselves more protection from German enfilading fire. The cooks brought them food after dark when it was safe to move around. André went out at midday on 22 October to eat with Lefebvre and a shell blast knocked him off his feet. He learnt to keep close to the ground in future.

André's section was relieved at 10 pm on the 22nd and enjoyed a night at the Moussy lock over a kilometre away. Mulled wine, a meal, coffee and a cognac in front of a warm fire, followed by a good sleep on a mattress, all did a lot for their morale. The next three days were fairly quiet and they enjoyed a period of rest in Soupir. André went to mass just as a few shells fell near the church. The young military chaplain delivered a short sermon which André thought was very good. He also noticed the graves of some English soldiers who had fallen in the recent fighting.

On the night of the 25th they went back to the front line trench. Somebody was on watch all the time; one man stood guard while another slept. André did his rounds to check the sentries were awake. The night of the 26th was quiet apart from half an hour's barrage by the French artillery at 11.30 pm. It was so loud that André's teeth chattered nervously. A corporal and three men undertook a night patrol and realized that they had come very close to some German soldiers who were speaking softly. On the 27th it rained and the trench became very muddy. During the night there was some firing off to the right. The next day they were relieved again and went back to the English holes near the farm. They could not move out of them by day as it was too dangerous. Lefebvre told the colonel that the front line trench was too far forward relative to others on the far side of the canal.

At 2 am on the 31st they returned to the front line and created a parapet of sacks filled with earth. André was observing the enemy lines when a German fired at him. The bullet came to rest three quarters of the way through the sacks. During the day the Germans dug a trench from the wood down towards the canal bank and André's men fired at them occasionally. On 1 November the Germans bombarded the Ferme du Metz. The relief of André's section was postponed for another 24 hours.

On 2 November André took his meal with Lefebvre before daybreak. At first light the Germans subjected the extensive buildings of the Ferme du Metz to an intense bombardment. Through his spy-hole André could see that this was more serious than any previous exchange in the sector. To the left he heard the tic-tac of machine guns. His men looked at him anxiously. Then shells fell on the centre of the trench and two men were killed. He decided to rescue some vital

Bridge, Metz lock, Canal de l'Aisne à l'Oise, where André Benoit ran for his life. The bridge with a stone parapet mentioned by André in his diary was replaced after the war. (Terry Cudbird)

items from his command post. The Germans turned their machine gun onto the trench itself and more French soldiers arrived to try and shelter in it.

An order arrived from Lefebvre to retreat to the Ferme du Metz along the canal because the Germans had forced their way into the higher end of the trench by the road. André now saw that they could not get out through the earthworks onto the canal bank because the Germans had got that exit covered with the machine gun. The only option was to take a narrow path underneath the canal embankment. When they emerged outside they saw several lines of German infantry coming down the flank of the hill towards the French second line trenches at the Ferme du Metz. They were almost completely trapped between the Germans and the canal.

In a split second André decided that their only hope was to run for the bridge over the river just beyond the farm and put the canal between themselves and the advancing Germans. As they set off the enemy opened fire at close range but André made it to the lock. Bullets scattered chips of brickwork around his feet. He reached the bridge but did not clear the chain across it and fell flat on his face. Crawling to the stone parapet he picked himself and kept running up the road towards Moussy. He remembered the Englishman showing him the deep water channel used for regulating the level of the canal and aimed straight for it. He got thirty metres up the road when a massive blow to his head stopped him in his tracks. He collapsed on his back thinking he had been shot in the head. He said to himself: "it is easy to die, but it is a shame." He was suffocating and a red veil crept over his eyes. His body went rigid. He shouted for help and then passed out.

*

André came round lying on his stomach. He had lost his pince-nez so he could not see very well. His head was bleeding profusely and he could not staunch the flow even after applying a bandage. A soldier lay dead on the road in front of him; another had thrown his leg across André's body and was delirious in his agony. A man nearby warned André to keep down or the Germans would fire again. Fortunately they were protected by a small bank on the side of the road. They lay there and waited.

Some German soldiers arrived. One took André's revolver and sack and helped him get up. André walked to the bridge supported by two of his own men. The Germans put a large bandage on his head while others of their number fired from the parapet. He was taken to the courtyard of the ruined Ferme du Metz and given coffee. The Germans were considerate. Two of them moved to keep the sun off his head. He told them about his missing pince-nez and that there was a spare in his sack. They went to get this for him and also brought his hat. The bullet had torn through the seam of the peak. He fell asleep with other prisoners in a shelter in an old quarry.

Later he heard that the Germans had advanced some way into the valley of the Aisne. The regimental journal records that two companies were captured by the Germans but the rest escaped south towards Soupir. André and his fellow prisoners started marching north escorted by two soldiers. A Pole in German uniform told him that he would rather not be serving in the Imperial Army. In a wood André noticed the bodies of several English soldiers which had been there three weeks. He arrived at a very well-equipped medical station. When asked to step forward he indicated that the men should go first. A doctor examined the wound and said that, although the bone had been damaged, it was fairly superficial. He put on a proper bandage and André was installed in a tent where a sympathetic German gave him a pillow. In the night he vomited blood.

When morning came he was asked to pick out some men from his group to dig a grave for a French soldier who had died in the night. There was nothing to identify the corpse, but his purse contained a small religious medallion. André said a short prayer over the body. Then he set off with his fellow prisoners to march slowly north to the Chemin des Dames. Passing the Fort de la Malmaison they came to a settlement called the L'Ange Gardien (Guardian Angel) where there was a farm and an inn at the junction of the Chemin des Dames and the Laon to Soissons road. (I tried to find it, but it was wiped off the face of the earth in 1917.) This was some kind of German HQ. Officers with a profusion of military decorations stood around in grey cloaks. One of them interrogated André, asking him whether he was with the "Negroes". (Senegalese troops had been fighting around Vailly on the same front.) The officer shouted at him, "They are not men. They are animals, monkeys!" Given the German Army's treatment of natives in the German colonies in Africa this remark was not surprising. André's group was put in a room where his comrades said he started to become incoherent. At nightfall they were taken by road to the station at Anizy-le-Château and from there to Germany.[1]

A prisoner of war

At the beginning of the war prisoners were often put into makeshift accommodation but this changed as the numbers increased. At the end of the war there were over 500,000 French prisoners in Germany. Officers were interned in camps separate from other ranks. André was sent to Krefeld between November 1914 and January 1915. There the commander of the camp asked for French volunteers, who were Catholic and behaved well, to go to the annex of a Franciscan convent at Werl, a small town in North Rhine-Westphalia east of Dortmund. Officers in the town of Werl came from France, Russia, Belgium,

Serbia and Greece. Werl also housed prisoners who were civilian deportees from occupied France and Belgium, as well as officers' orderlies. André's name appears in a list of over 2,000 prisoners compiled in 1915 along with his friend Armand Lefebvre. Lefebvre was the last to leave the front line trench when he also was made a prisoner. In August 1916, while André was still in prison, the French Army made him up to full reserve lieutenant as opposed to second lieutenant. Even though a prisoner of war he was still regarded as being on active service.

The Germans had more respect for officers. Conditions in their camps were better than for the men and the deportees. They had beds rather than straw-filled palliasses, used separate dining rooms and were exempt from forced labour. One of the main burdens of camp life was the tedium. Activities like sport, concerts, plays, lectures and reading were allowed. André participated in a choir which sung regularly at mass. Encouraged by several of his comrades he set about organizing various adult education courses in subjects like mathematics, which he taught himself, accounting, English and German. He himself learnt the German language. He managed to find suitable teachers from among the prisoners and the German commandant lent them a room, presumably on the basis that well-occupied officers were less likely to cause trouble. The Belgian officers arranged

André Benoit as a prisoner of war. He is wearing the uniform of the 267th Infantry Regiment in which he served in 1914. (Courtesy of Dr. Monique Burtin and Mme. Anne Moreau-Vivien)

a dinner in his honour and sent him an invitation as "Monsieur le Recteur Magnifique de l'Université de Werl". Food was very poor, the staples being vegetable soup and bread made from bran and potatoes. Matters became worse as the Allied blockade of Germany intensified, and escaping malnutrition after 1916 was a daily preoccupation. Items like soap and fats completely disappeared, according to André. Officers received parcels and letters from home, including food and warm clothing, either directly or via the Red Cross. André observed that these parcels from home fulfilled an urgent need. They really kept morale up, especially when he knew his parents had had to make sacrifices to send things which must be in short supply in France. Lack of hygiene and associated diseases were also an issue. According to André's family, he was not ill-treated during his imprisonment and he did not suffer from any serious illnesses although he did get depressed occasionally because of the endless inactivity.

During their imprisonment André and Armand assembled the notes they had both taken between August and November 1914, searched their memories and worked out the basis of the book now known as *Trois mois de guerre au jour le jour: 1914, journal d'un fantassin* (Three Months of War from Day to Day: 1914, Diary of a Soldier), eventually published in 1967. No doubt compiling this record occupied many tedious hours in captivity. Yet without this period of enforced idleness the book might never have been written when the two friends' memories were relatively fresh. There were no other sources for this work, as far as I am aware, such as letters written home.

It seems that André did not intend his diary for publication. It only appeared when André Vuibert of Librairie Vuibert in Paris saw the manuscript by chance fifty years later in 1967. We shall see how the book was published below.

In November 1917 André transferred again to another camp called Schwarmstedt where conditions were tougher. As a precaution he entrusted the manuscript of his book to the nuns at Werl and retrieved it from them after the war was over. Schwarmstedt was more like a concentration camp, with a barbed wire perimeter fence. After a few weeks there he then moved yet again to Höchst where he remained until July 1918. Meanwhile he had parted company with Lefebvre who in 1917 asked to transfer to a different camp to try and improve his morale which was by now at a very low ebb.

In July 1918 André left Germany and went to Switzerland. The Germans had signed an agreement, under the aegis of the Red Cross, to allow some prisoners to do this if they were ill or severely wounded or sometimes if, as in André's case, they had been in captivity a long time. They were "interned" in Swiss institutions, which took responsibility for them. These, however, were nothing like the German camps. Internees could go out and receive visitors. André was sent to the Hotel de l'Europe in Interlaken.

Here there was a dramatic change in his fortunes. He met twenty-one-year-old Odette Bonafons, the daughter of Jacques Bonafons, a doctor and property owner in Nice. Odette was staying in Interlaken in the same hotel with her mother and her sister to be near her brother Marcel, also a French officer who had been interned in Berne. Odette's family originated in Corsica, where the Buonafontes had owned land. A contemporary photograph shows a young woman with a dark Italianate beauty and lustrous eyes. They fell in love and decided that they wanted to get married and live together in Switzerland, which they could do even though André was an internee. At this stage they did not know that the war was near its end. With the support of the Red Cross they had set their wedding day for 7 December, and then the armistice intervened on 11 November. They went ahead with their wedding in Fribourg and returned to France afterwards. The marriage was subsequently registered in France in September 1919, according to the records of Charly-sur-Marne. Odette later gave birth to a daughter, Jacqueline.

André Benoit after the war

André's army record indicates that he arrived in France on 15 December 1918 and returned to an army depot on 27 February 1919. He would have been given a medical examination and interrogated by the French Army. His record includes a note of his bullet wound—seven centimetres over his left eye—but does not mention any other medical problems. We do not know the details of his interrogation, but questioning of prisoners of war was not a formality. They were to some extent suspect. A military panel would ask them questions such as: how did you become a prisoner of war, did you work for the Germans and why didn't you try to escape? After this André was put on indefinite leave and officially demobilized back to the Reserve in July 1919. He must have started studying mathematics immediately because he sat again for the prestigious *agrégation* at a special session in October 1919 and this time was successful.

He accepted a post as a senior mathematics teacher at the French Lycée in Mainz in Germany. It is true that Mainz was in the French occupation zone from the end of the war until 1930. Yet whatever André's experiences in Germany during the war, they did not put him off from returning there for ten years until 1929. Apart from teaching mathematics André also helped prepare those students who wanted to take the entrance exam to the elite St. Cyr military academy, the French equivalent of Sandhurst.

While in Germany André did not cut his links with the Army. He was in any case on the reserve officers' list. In September 1920 he was transferred to the 82nd Artillery Regiment and promoted to reserve artillery captain at the end of 1924. André seems to have been a conscientious officer for whom his service in the reserve was important. His record says he undertook training courses every year between 1928 and 1935 including in anti-aircraft gunnery. Between 1928 and 1930 he served as President of the Association of Reserve Officers of the Rhine Army.He obtained the highest possible praise from his senior officers during this period, the only criticism being that he could sometimes be too meticulous.

In 1929 André returned to France, taking up a post as senior mathematics teacher at the Lycée Condorcet in Paris. This very prestigious school is one of the four oldest in the capital. The list of former pupils is a roll-call of famous names in literature and the arts including Proust, Verlaine, Cocteau, Alfred de Vigny, Paul Valéry, Toulouse-Lautrec, Claude Lévi-Strauss and Henri Bergson, as well as leading industrialists like Louis Renault, André Citroën and Marcel Dassault and a host of political leaders. This was a top job for a pedagogue. Over the next twenty-four years André not only taught mathematics there but also published numerous textbooks on mathematics for secondary schools, working closely with Henry Vuibert of the Librairie Vuibert in Paris, a firm which still exists today. There are references to 61 editions of his books in the catalogue of the Bibliothèque Nationale in Paris. He was very popular with students and particularly with his Jewish students, some of whom were persecuted during the Occupation. He gave them what support he could. Jean-Claude Herz, a

Rue Émile Morlot today, the site of the Benoit family home in Charly-sur-Marne. (Terry Cudbird)

Jewish student at the Lycée Condorcet between 1941 and 1942, spoke with much warmth of André whom he described as lovable.

André maintained his links with Charly-sur-Marne. He had always been fond of his maternal grandparents, Alexandre and Marguérite Camus, who lived in Charly when he was young. A photograph shows them as ordinary country folk in costumes of another age. He used to visit his parents regularly during the holidays. They lived in rue Émile Morlot in the centre of Charly, where his father had his workshop. Frequently André worked on his books in a hut on an allotment his parents owned at Monthuys, to the west of Charly. It cannot have been very comfortable because it also served as a tool shed.

Jules and Clémence Benoit had a neighbour called Garousse, who became Jules Benoit's apprentice carpenter and subsequently set up his own business. M. Garousse's son Daniel remembers Jules Benoit as a craftsman with "gold in his hands who had no machines but only worked with his hands, using the tools available at the time". Jules Benoit died in 1928 but Clémence remained in the family house in Charly for another 28 years, dying in 1955. A curious anecdote concerns the American General George Patton who as a young officer during the Great War lodged in Jules' and Clémence's house. He returned at the Liberation in 1944 to see it again.

André already had the Croix de Guerre. In 1931 he was decorated for his military service as a Chevalier in the Légion d'Honneur. The documents in support of his nomination include his citations for bravery during the war: firstly the 138th Brigade commander said he maintained absolute calm in his section when under fire in the action on 23 September 1914. He was very close to the enemy near La Neuville on the Canal de l'Aisne à la Marne. By the order of the Army he was given a further citation in 1920, noting that he was "seriously wounded and taken prisoner on 2 November 1914 and that during captivity he had given proofs of devotion in continuing to serve his country. In this way he voluntarily exposed himself to the serious consequences which could have resulted for him." It was unusual for soldiers to be given citations for their correct conduct when prisoners of war. Sometimes they were commended because they had carried out acts of sabotage, had tried to escape or had been engaged in some kind of intelligence gathering activity. In André's case he passed on useful intelligence to France, which he describes in his unpublished diary:

> We can, now, send two letters and two postcards home each month, always written in pencil. A new arrival at the camp asked me to agree to give up from time to time one of these postcards home for the benefit of a French information network. I accepted. With a pen moistened with saliva you write on the card, in the spaces within a specially designed template, the words you are given. Then you write in pencil over the

top of this across the whole card anything you like, for example the sort of letter you might write to a cousin. I am told what I must write as an address for the recipient and this changes every time.

His army records confirm his relationship with the information network.

André continued his service as a reserve artillery captain throughout the 1930s. In 1937 he was retired from the reserve officers' list because of his age. He could have asked to continue, but typically he thought he was not experienced enough in artillery matters to do so. His colleagues said he was too scrupulous, so eventually he had second thoughts and applied successfully to be reinstated. On 22 August 1939, aged over fifty, he reported for war service for the second time in his life. He was assigned to an Intelligence Centre in Paris and worked on the surveillance of attacking enemy aeroplanes. At this time he published a short and humourous book of mathematical riddles in the form of poems under the pseudonym Captain Calk (Capain Calculus). After the German invasion in May 1940 he was involved in another retreat, this time in the direction of Bordeaux. A third army citation describes his exemplary conduct: "He was an officer of the highest moral standing and completely devoted to his duties. Having carried on with his work at the Paris Information Centre as long as he possibly could, between 12 and 25 June he fell back with his unit and continued to keep it operating during the greatest difficulties."

In this retreat he ended up at Lacaussade in the Lot-et-Garonne, south-east of Bordeaux, in an army vehicle. He was officially demobilized at Gabarret, not far away in the Landes, on 16 July and returned to his work at the Lycée Condorcet for the rest of the war.

An academic decoration was conferred on André in 1930 when he was nominated as an Officier de l'Instruction Publique. In 1952 he received further recognition for his work as an educator when he was created an Officier in the Légion d'Honneur as opposed to a Chevalier. The report which led to his nomination includes the following reference from the Proviseur of the Lycée Condorcet: "A mathematics teacher of the first rank, he is a well-established authority on the subject, and his reputation is justified by the value of his teaching as well as the active interest he takes in his pupils to help them find careers. He is always dedicated, affable and smiling. He is esteemed by all his colleagues and merits having his career crowned with this distinction. He is the author of manuals which are widely used and he is single-mindedly devoted to his work as a teacher." The document contains a note revealing that the Ministry of Education had made enquiries about his morality and attitude during the Occupation of 1940-44 and that nothing had been discovered which prevented his being admitted to the Légion d'Honneur.

André retired from the Lycée in 1953 but continued to be very active.

In the 1930s he had lived in the fifteenth *arrondissement*, one of the outer districts on the left bank in Paris. After the Second World War, however, we find him a little nearer the centre in an apartment at 39 Avenue de Saxe in the seventh *arrondissement*, not far from the École Militaire and the Invalides, where Napoleon is buried. After his mother died in 1955 he bought a second home on the Breton coast where he enjoyed family holidays. His granddaughters remember him from this time as a very genial older man, a great story teller and a natural optimist about life who also enjoyed telling jokes. His book on the war was published by André Vuibert in May 1967, a year after the death of his great friend Armand Lefebvre at Chantilly, near Paris, in June 1966, aged eighty-two. André's wife Odette died in October 1967. He survived to the age of eighty-four and died on 9 March 1974 at the same address.

War played a large part in André's life. He also lived to see France recover from the two World Wars, make peace with Germany and enjoy the fruits of the *trente glorieuses*, the period of rapid economic growth between 1945 and 1973. He started off as the son of a carpenter from a family who had been settled in a small area of the Aisne for generations. He ended up as a respected teacher at one of the most prestigious lycées in France, living at a smart address in the seventh *arrondissement* of Paris. His life was typical of many in his generation but remarkable none the less.[2]

Author's note

I had some incredible pieces of luck while compiling this brief biography of André Benoit. My hosts at Gland on the Marne, Éric and Danièle Debaize, put me in touch with M. Tony Legendre, the Secretary of the Société Historique et Archéologique de Château-Thierry. He in turn referred my inquiries about André to Mme. Nicole Jobe, who organized an exhibition about Charly-sur-Marne during the Great War some years ago. Mme. Job spoke to Daniel Garousse, the son of Jules Benoit's apprentice, who remembered Jules and also André. M. Legendre also introduced me to Mme. Marie Josée Ulmet, President of the Cercle Généalogique de l'Aisne in Château-Thierry. She furnished me with much of the information, including the dossier concerning the award of Légion d'Honneur decorations to André Benoit. She also put me in touch with the surviving family. André Benoit had a daughter and in turn three granddaughters who remember him with great affection. Mme. Anne Moreau-Vivien and Dr. Monique Burtin kindly gave me access to André's papers and photographs, including the photographs of André as a young soldier. The reader can imagine that, having walked in André's footsteps with his diary, it was wonderful at last to see his face. I can say that his appearance is entirely consistent with how I had imagined him from what he wrote: kind and compassionate, intelligent and precise, with a sense of humour. It was a great pleasure eventually to meet Mme. Moreau-Vivien and Dr. Burtin in Paris and to toast the memory of André Benoit with a glass of his favourite champagne from a village only a few kilometres from Charly.

9: REMEMBERING 1914

The memory of the retreat and the "miracle" of the Marne made a lasting impact both at a national level and in the lives of those who took part. On the German side there were recriminations. In France the unexpected victory deceived military leaders into believing that one more push, one more manoeuvre could, with the *poilu*'s resilience, drive the Germans from France altogether. The costly attacks in 1915 were the direct result. In the longer term the events of 1914 were used by the nationalist right to trumpet France's special destiny.

Joan of Arc and the Miracle of the Marne

For some years before 1914 a debate had raged among intellectuals about the true significance of Joan of Arc, who saved France in another hour of her greatest need. Had she, as many Catholics claimed, been sent by God to bring France back to the fold of the Church, or was she, as the left and anti-clericals argued, a victim of the clergy, abandoned to her fate by both the monarchy and the Catholic hierarchy? Charles Péguy wrote two books about her in which he sought to prevent her memory being perpetuated by either of these extreme views. To Péguy, Joan was an example of putting faith into action.

On 22 December 1914 Maurice Barrès, the nationalist intellectual, novelist and politician, wrote an article in which he was the first to refer to the victory of the Marne as a miracle in that it seemed almost inexplicable that France had managed to snatch victory from the jaws of defeat after the German invasion, the losses on the frontiers and the long retreat. He attributed this miracle to Joan of Arc: "the eternal French miracle, the miracle of Joan of Arc". Her presence still inspired the French, he insisted, and she should be acknowledged both as a national heroine and as a patron saint. Barrès talked about her as "that mysterious force, that divine force from which hope springs". He rather glossed over the fact that Joan had been burnt by the English, an embarrassing fact in view of the Anglo-French alliance. Joan was duly canonized by the Catholic Church in 1920 and the first national festival dedicated to her was held on 8 May 1921.[1] Statues of Joan appeared on many memorials for the fallen in French churches after the First World War. In 1937 veterans of the Battle of the Marne were presented with a medal on which Joan of Arc's effigy appeared.

Others had attributed the miracle of the Marne to the Virgin Mary or St. Geneviève, the patron saint of Paris. A few soldiers claimed to have seen them during the battle, while some Catholic bishops spoke of supernatural allies who helped the soldiers. In 1916 a Catholic Missal of the miracle of the Marne embodied these ideas in a series of engravings: Christ on his cross hovering over the battlefield; St. Geneviève protecting the city of Paris. However, the preface

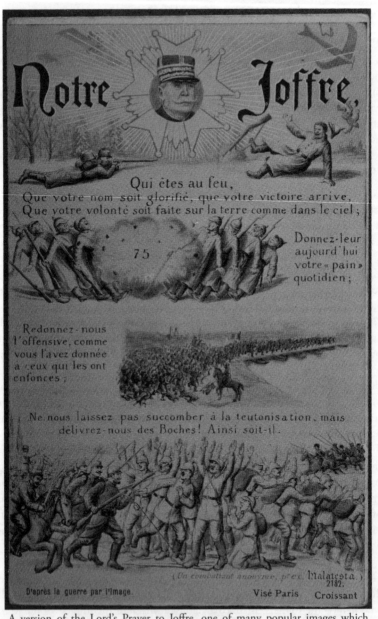

A version of the Lord's Prayer to Joffre, one of many popular images which perpetuated his memory. (Historial de la Grande Guerre – Péronne (Somme) et © Yazid Medmoun)

suggested that the Marne was not a miracle without a rational explanation. It was more a question of God stepping in to help the French soldiers who gave an example of bravery and prayed for divine aid. There was a risk that the idea of a totally supernatural miracle in September 1914 diminished the real reasons for the success on the Marne—the stamina of the Allied soldiers, Joffre's strategic concept for a counter-attack and the fatigue and divisions among his opponents.[2]

A more populist view of the Marne is to be found in a poster produced by the Imageries d'Épinal, the cheap and widely distributed series of pictures which sold in their hundreds of thousands in the nineteenth and early twentieth centuries. A poster entitled *La Victoire de la Marne* shows a female figure striding to battle with her dress high on her legs and advancing ranks of French soldiers behind. Joffre appears as a reassuring fatherly figure leading two children in the traditional dress of Alsace and Lorraine back to their national family. The allegorical woman suggests both Marianne, the Republican symbol, and a winged Victory.[3]

Monuments

The main French monument commemorating the victory of the Marne at Mondemont has a touch of the supernatural, even though no religious symbols appear on it. A sculpture of a winged Victory rests on top of a huge column. Surrounded by large clouds from which trumpets announce the triumph of the armies, Victory is passing through a storm and pushing aside shafts of lightning. The column itself is 36 metres high and with its deep foundations weighs over two thousand tons. The finish is pink, which is supposed to resemble the rock commonly found in the Vosges Mountains, reminding people of the return of Alsace to France after 1918. The sheer size of the monument is meant to convey the superhuman courage of the soldiers and the scale of the threat they faced. It certainly dwarfs the sculptures of the generals and a *poilu* at the bottom.

The inscriptions on the monument, apart from listing the armies which took part, include three more general statements. Firstly: "At Joffre's command the retreating French Army stopped and faced the enemy. This was the start of the Battle of the Marne which took place on a front seventy leagues long [about 280 kilometres] from Verdun to the gates of Paris. After a heroic struggle lasting several days the enemy retreated in all sectors along the whole front and VICTORY passed." This statement seems to be a deliberate attempt to rehabilitate Joffre who had been relieved of his command halfway through the war. It also links the battle to the sculpture of Victory on top of the column. The second statement is Joffre's order of the day on 6 September stipulating that every solider must hold his ground. There was no question of looking back. The third inscription links this battle to previous attempts to resist invasion: "To all those who formed a barrier against invasion of our land from the earliest times." In the canon of war memorials across France it is more than patriotic. It is unashamedly nationalistic, especially in the symbolism of the winged Victory.[4]

The story of the erection of the monument was less than glorious. On 6 September 1917 an official ceremony to commemorate the victory was held at Mondemont, presided over by the President of the Republic, Raymond Poincaré. This took place not long after the mutinies in the French Army in that year and was particularly appropriate in view of Joffre's words about no weakness being tolerated on the Marne. Joffre was present with Foch and other leading generals. In 1920 the National Assembly voted funds to construct a monument at Mondemont, which was chosen because it stood at the strategically vital centre of the Allied position. It was not, however, until 1929 that the Académie des Beaux-Arts ran a competition for a design which was finally agreed in 1930. The monument was finished in 1933 but the sculpture was not completed until 1938. During all this time the "carrot", as it came to be called locally, was covered in scaffolding. The official inauguration was fixed for 19 September 1939 but did not take place because of the outbreak of the Second World War. Unlike other war memorials in France the Germans left this one untouched during the Occupation. It was finally inaugurated in September 1951; thirty-seven years after the victory it was intended to commemorate and when all the generals sculpted on the bottom were dead.

In terms of commemoration, the Battle of the Frontiers, the retreat and the victory of the Marne were overshadowed by all that took place subsequently. This is certainly the impression I gained when walking across the sites where many of the events of August-September 1914 took place. There are war cemeteries of course: at Charleroi, Guise, Le Cateau, Mons, Villers-Cotterêts, Montceaux-lès-Provins, Escardes and Villiers-St.-Georges and also at Vitry-le-François, where there are 4,000 graves. Their size does not strike us as so terrible as those at Ypres, the Somme, Verdun, Tyne Cot and the Chemin des Dames. In August and September 1914 the fighting was dispersed over a wider area than the later battles.

The inscriptions or monuments specifically referring to this period are unimpressive. Yet the opening months were the bloodiest of the whole war. There is the large chapel at Dormans on the Marne dedicated to the memory of the fallen in both the battles in this area, in 1914 and in 1918. The monument to the Battle of Guise was inaugurated on 28 April 1929. It stands between two busy roads, is difficult to get at and seems rather neglected. Some vegetation was growing between the cracks in the façade when I visited it. There is nothing similar at Charleroi. There are monuments commemorating the fighting on the River Ourcq near Paris but very few paying tribute to the enormous efforts made by the Fifth Army; merely a few brief references to the Marne in communal graveyards or on local war memorials, e.g. Montmirail, Escardes, Montceaux-lès-Provins, Villiers-St.-Georges. There are also two commemorative plaques on the *mairies* in Montceaux and Escardes. In the sector between Vitry and Verdun there is a chapel in the former and monuments at Sermaize-les-Bains, Maurupt-le-Montois and Pargny-sur-Saulx. This was the sector which Maurice Genevoix described so graphically. There are also some local monuments in the Ardennes on the Belgian border where some of the bloodiest fighting took place.

Perhaps the most prominent reminder of the Marne is the statue of Joffre on horseback right outside the École Militaire in Paris, near the spot where Galliéni was based during the battle and not far from the Eiffel Tower. André probably walked past it many times because it is also close to the appartment he occupied in the Avenue de Saxe. On the plinth are inscribed not only Joffre's order of 6 September but also his assessment of the results of the battle delivered five days later. On the back are the names of subsequent battles with which he was associated—Marne, Flanders, Champagne, Somme, Verdun. The huge losses in these frontal assaults eventually led to his being replaced as commander-in-chief. There is no doubt that the Marne was his finest hour.It is strange that he is mounted on a military steed which later in his career he only used on ceremonial occasions. The motor car in which he drove all over the front might have been more appropriate. Also he is dressed in an immaculately tailored uniform whereas for most of the battle he wore loose fitting clothes to disguise his portly figure.

The British commemoration of the Retreat from Mons, the Battle of the Marne and the subsequent struggle on the Aisne seems to be much better served. Apart from many local plaques there is the cemetery and monument at St.-Symphorien for Mons. There are also monuments at Le Cateau, Villers-Cotterêts and Néry. The Imperial War Graves Commission built four monuments to commemorate the missing of World War One: at Thiepval for the Somme, at Soissons for the 1918 offensive, at Neuve-Chapelle for the Indian Army and at La Ferté-sous-Jouarre "to the glory of God and the lasting memory of 3,888 British officers and men whose graves are not known, who landed in France in the month of August 1914 and between then and October fought at Mons and Le Cateau and on the Marne and the Aisne," as the inscription says. British forces passed through La Ferté on the Marne before and after the battle. The names of all the missing are recorded on the monument which is decorated with fairly conventional imagery: a sarcophagus, a flag, bayonets, a helmet, wreaths, crowns, swords, urns and the coat-of-arms of the British Empire. The monument was inaugurated in 1928 in a formal ceremony.

Writing about the Marne

The events of August-September 1914 were viewed through the distorting mirror of each participant's experience. This book is based on diaries and memoirs. It is important to understand something about the writers if we are to understand the retreat and the Battle of the Marne correctly.

Some of what was written during the war cannot be considered as impartial. Military censors looked at soldiers' letters from the front. The newspapers were also limited in what they could say. Information about defeats or the hardships faced by the troops was regarded as bad for the morale of the civilian population. The soldiers themselves felt that the triumphalist propaganda in the press was mere *bourrage de crâne* (brainwashing).

After 1918 the main actors in the drama of August-September started to publish their versions of events. Naturally enough they sought to justify their own actions. Joffre and Galliéni published their memoirs. This led to an argument about which of them conceived the plan which led to the German retreat. Lanrezac published his account to put the record straight following his dismissal. He felt he was not to blame for Joffre's mistakes, for example in underestimating the disposition of German forces in Belgium.

For an understanding of what the 1914 retreat was like for the infantry we have to go to published and unpublished diaries which started to appear in the 1920s and which are still being printed for the first time to this day. Many have been written by British and French soldiers, a few by Germans. We have to remember, however, that many of these diarists' descriptions of events were influenced by their own preoccupations.

Long marches every day and fighting rearguard actions did not allow the retreating soldiers much time to make more than a few scribbled notes. There are many fewer diaries and letters for this period than for the trench warfare later on. Those that have survived were often written up several months or years later. Memory is faulty, and it was difficult to recall exactly what happened. The participants went on to different careers and this influenced how they wrote. The diaries of events became books about the war. Their authors were looking back on a formative period in their lives and trying to make sense of it in their own way. So they try to make sense of their common experiences as soldiers; for example, the baptism of fire; death, mutilation and killing others; the physical hardships of the march; witnessing the plight of refugees. Sometimes they draw a moral from their story about the tragedy of war and its effect on human beings. The texts cover all aspects of the retreat but vary enormously in tone and are written from many different angles. What follows is an analysis of the main sources for this book, bringing out the variety of approaches taken.

French diaries

André Benoit

André Benoit's book does not pretend to be a literary work. It is a daily diary written in plain prose and short paragraphs in which the rhythm of the sentences does not vary very much. It has an almost cinematic quality like a newsreel. He is very precise about the times at which certain events took place and the distances between objects. Is it fanciful to see in this characteristic the influence of his joiner father and his own mathematical training? He gives the reader a very clear idea of how the soldiers lived in their bivouacs, how they marched and how they fought. The features of the landscape stand out in sharp relief. For example, when following his account of the action at the Battle of Guise I found his description of the topography very accurate.[5] He picks out many small details among all the things that happened to him. When he is retreating towards La Fère, for instance, he goes into a farm to look for something to eat, "having taken care to push the bolt on the large door to the courtyard back into place"—presumably to prevent the flood of soldiers on the road following his men in.[6] Clearly his memory had not failed him.

In his book André does not explore his motivation or that of his comrades. He says little about the events of the campaign of 1914, the context for the actions of his own unit. On a personal level he rarely reveals his feelings. His granddaughters explained that he was not the sort of man to publish material of a personal nature. Right at the beginning he does admit to disappointment when it appeared that he might be kept in the depot and not go to war.[7] It is therefore not surprising that he jumps at the chance to join Captain Évrard on campaign.[8] He is proud when he is the first to execute a deployment with his section as they near the Belgian frontier. "This pride was mixed up with a little emotion."[9] When the captain tells him that the retreat has ended, his reaction sounds typically cool.[10] He sees several dead bodies, both French and German, on 7 September but makes no remark other than to record the fact. Perhaps Antoine Guasson and Célestin Brothier in the armies further east went to the other extreme.

André says little about himself, but we can deduce certain things from the text. He was a believer and a practising Catholic who took the opportunity to go to mass whenever possible. He mentions this several times in his narrative. On 13 August he visits the basilica of Notre-Dame-de-Liesse with his friend Lefebvre, lights a candle and drinks some water from the spring which is supposed to perform miracles. This is still an important Marian shrine receiving over 50,000 pilgrims a year. The Black Virgin refers back to the daughter of a Sultan who saved the lives of three Crusaders and then came to France to marry the son of a French king. André records going to mass on 15 August and also at Soupir on 25 October, when he remarks on the sermon.

He lets slip other revealing details. He seems to have been regarded as young to be an officer because the captain at one point calls him *petiot* or tiny, although he was in fact nearly six feet tall. This term must refer to his age of 25 years.[11] As a reservist he was not very fit and found the long marches trying. He says on 28 August that he was unconscious with fatigue after a long march. He wears a pince-nez, which must have been a nuisance on active service. One gets broken on 11 September and another falls off as he is running for his life from the Germans on 2 November. We can deduce from the descriptions of the actions in which he was involved that he was brave and resourceful when he had to be. We know he did not speak English well enough to talk to a British officer without an interpreter during the take over of the British positions near the Ferme du Metz.[12]

He says nothing about his family although he does mention a friend at Condé-en-Brie with some affection and also someone else he knew at Crézancy nearby.[13] It is clear that Lieutenant Lefebvre was a close personal friend who probably remained so all his life. Overall we get an impression of a sociable man who enjoyed his food, loved a joke and was interested in and concerned about the men in his section.

The book is full of references to food and drink, understandable perhaps given the privations of the march: downing several anisettes in La Petite Rue and taking away a flask of Cointreau[14]; digging his hand into a bottle of prunes saturated with sugar syrup[15]; toasting France's eventual victory with champagne at the exorbitant price of twelve francs a bottle while eating pork chops (this would be a price of at least 100 euros today)[16]; enjoying a party on his 26th birthday[17]; the simple pleasure of a cup of hot chocolate[18]; a mulled wine, a coffee and a good cognac in the inn at Moussy lock in front of a fire.[19] He gives us a host of details about his soldiers, always with a touch of humour: the strong man Favrie from Les Halles in Paris who helped him out digging a hole[20]; the cook who drank the officers' Pernod[21]; the alarm clock which goes off in his rucksack as he is marching[22]; the drunken men being admonished by the captain[23]; the soldier expressing annoyance at one man's death on the battlefield because he was carrying the squad's coffee grinder.[24]

Captain La Chaussée

How does André's straightforward human approach compare with that of other witnesses? Captain Julien La Chaussée of the 3rd Corps, 5th Division, wrote a lively diary of the doings of his unit taken from what he calls his "Mémoires de guerre" written for his children. It has a more literary form than a simple daily journal, with episodes written up with recreated dialogue. It is interesting that he later published some poems on the war and his native Normandy as well as a novel. The war poems seem very conventional in their metre and sentiments. One deals with his regiment's action at Escardes on 7 September. The remainder cover the painful defeat of 1940.[25]

He does not seem to have any particular interests or concerns to bring to his account. He writes clearly and imaginatively but while he includes all the horrors of war his emotions are relatively restrained. At the beginning he remarks that his book is not meant to be heroic, merely sincere in its portrayal of the events he witnessed. He dedicates his book not only to his comrades dead and alive but also to all innocent people struck down in the war and to the cause of human fraternity. His story ends near Verdun in June 1916 when he was taken prisoner.

La Chaussée's account shows more awareness of the situation of the whole Fifth Army. For example, his regiment understood that they had to retreat after the Battle of Charleroi because their left wing was threatened by the enemy.[26] After Guise they were told the retreat had to continue because the English on their left were outnumbered and retiring. "How can the Germans have so many troops," he asks "enough to stretch all the way from Switzerland to northern France?" He tried to explain the retreat to his men but found it difficult to do so after the apparent success of Franchet d'Esperey's advance near Guise.[27] André would never have made remarks like this. La Chaussée had the advantage of being in a unit in the front line rather than with the reserves

Sergeant Omnès

Albert Omnès' work is a short account of the Campaign of 1914 written for himself and his family. It was published by the Association de Bretagne 14-18 in 1988. Omnès was brought up in Dinard in Brittany and obtained a Bachelor of Science and Philosophy degree. He studied and taught English for a time before the war. He also took part in sports and gymnastics and was a trained shot. As a result he obtained a military aptitude certificate which allowed him to choose his regiment when he was called up for military service in 1911. He went to the 47th Infantry Regiment at St. Malo near his home. Because of the extension of military service from two to three years passed by the National Assembly in 1913, he served until the outbreak of war and subsequently until 1919. He was promoted sergeant in 1913. He suffered a serious face wound in Artois on 4 October 1914 and was not fit enough for front line duties for the rest of the war. He received various decorations including the Croix de Guerre and the Légion d'Honneur. After the war he worked at the lycée in Quimper and subsequently at a college near Dinard until his retirement. Despite the wound, which still troubled him after the war, he lived to the age of ninety-one.

In his journal Albert Omnès comes across as a different character from André; more emotional, more obviously concerned about his parents and perhaps more light-hearted. He describes the captain talking to his men on 1 August in these terms: "He made a speech which went right to our hearts. The thought of the old people remaining in some thatched cottage in the crack of a cliff or a heathland hollow caused tears to cloud the eyes of the brave little Bretons, even though they disguised them as much as possible."[28] While Omnès is getting everything ready for departure his father comes to see him. "Emotion gripped my heart when I saw my dear father crying."[29] He describes a drinking session as they fired on the Germans during the Battle of the Marne.[30] He is fishing in a stream on 17 August and swimming in the Meuse on 21 August not long before the Battle of Charleroi.[31] Food, drink and tobacco seem to play a prominent part in his wartime experiences as we have already noticed.

Like La Chaussée he is very willing to comment about events in other sectors of the front. On 31 July he mentions hopes for peace and an international agreement among the great powers.[32] On 1 August he is pleased to note that Russia is mobilizing in the east and that Germany will have to fight on two fronts.[33] On 8 August he talks about the French capture of Mulhouse.[34] Overall, like André, he gives us a good feel for what the retreat and the fighting were like.

Robert Porchon

We find more straightforward diaries like Omnès' among soldiers fighting in Lorraine. André Bourgain in the 114th Infantry Regiment or Robert Porchon, a 2nd lieutenant in the 7th Company of the 106th Infantry Regiment, are good examples. Maurice Genevoix, who served as a 2nd lieutenant in the same company, was Porchon's friend. Porchon died in the attack on Les Éparges on the Côtes de Meuse near Verdun on 20 February 1915. His letters to his mother and his diary, which is no more than some hastily scribbled notes, give an unadorned account both of his own emotions and of the reality of all-out fighting. He describes 10 September as the most frightening day of his young life. He realized that his unit was outflanked and came face to face with a German. Before the latter could strike with a bayonet, Porchon shot him with his revolver. Later he writes to his mother that he had been very worried how he would cope with his baptism of fire—rifles, machine guns and cannon—but that he has not experienced much fear. Later in the same letter, however, he admits that an individual of a nervous disposition could not cope with what he saw during a night attack.[35]

Célestin Brothier

In some of these personal diaries certain themes keep recurring like a leitmotiv. One such is the journal of Célestin Brothier, the brigadier in the gendarmerie who was mobilized to the front in Lorraine at the age of forty-one. He died the following year of wounds and disease resulting from his service. The gendarmerie had special responsibilities during wartime which put them in constant contact with the front. They investigated offences against military law, carried out reconnaissance to bring back information on enemy troop movements and arrested marauders, particularly those who looted items from corpses on battlefields. They made sure bodies were properly buried and the effects of the deceased returned to their families. They also had to protect German prisoners from reprisals.

Brothier had to deal with men who deserted their posts, such as men in the 17th and 11th Infantry Regiments who fled the battlefields in the Sedan sector on 23 August.[36] It is not surprising that he gives some detailed and harrowing descriptions of dead bodies on the battlefields, as we have already seen. On 6 September he also witnessed the distress of the wounded, particularly when he was evacuated to hospital himself because of dysentery.[37] He was a sensitive man who sympathized with the suffering of others, for example the distress of families parting with soldiers leaving for the front.[38] He does not recount the horrors to glorify war but simply to tell it how it was.

During August Brothier also had to deal with people suspected of being German spies. While there were undoubtedly some civilians helping the Germans, there were many wild rumours and it was not easy to separate fact from fiction. He made some arrests. He recognized that on the eastern frontier there were families with divided loyalties, with relatives in Alsace for example who had to fight for Germany.[39]

He also reports frequently on German atrocities—the burning of villages, the killing of children and the rape of women. On 14 August his comments are based on second-hand reports by villagers near the frontier who were demonstrating against German prisoners. On 24 August he presents the evidence of Belgian gendarmes. On the 26th he reports the destruction by fire of the French village of Noményy. On 1 September he alleges that the Germans use French civilians as human shields.[40] From this comes a hatred of Germany and everything it stands for, which he identifies with Prussian militarism. When he is in hospital he has time to vent his feelings on this subject at greater length. He admits that war has led to barbaric acts by many people but believes that the Germans are the worst. The dominance of the military in their society has corrupted the German character. Their soldiers are treacherous while the French are open and trustworthy. The sheer size of the German war machine is proof of this inordinate militarism, although he does admit that the French have learnt a lot about warfare from their enemy. He also rages against Wilhelm—Attila the Hun—and his dictatorship. He thinks about the carnage which is probably taking place all over Europe as he closes his eyes in his hospital bed.[41] We have seen that some of these stories of German atrocities were well-founded.

Robert Deville

Clearly the role played in the Army could affect a diarist's point of view.[42] Originally from the part of Lorraine annexed by Germany in 1871, Robert Deville was a second lieutenant on the staff of the lieutenant-colonel commanding the 17th Regiment of Field Artillery (2nd Corps). He described the Battle of Virton in Luxembourg and the subsequent retreat until he lost his arm on 13 September. He gives a precise account of military events and can appear unemotional compared with other witnesses. His detachment is no doubt due to his not being in a fighting unit as well as to his character. He offers few general opinions on the war. Naturally enough he talks frequently about artillery matters. While he admits that the Germans are better provided with heavy artillery, which can be devastating, he believes in general that German fire is nothing like as effective as that of the French. Most of his own batteries would have consisted of the rightly feared 75 mm field guns. One cannot help feeling, however, that there is an element of wishful thinking here.[43] Deville admits to being by nature optimistic, and this trait appears in his comments after the battle on the frontier on 22 August. In his sector the day was not good, but not as bad as the French had feared. The infantry moved forward a little but did not pierce the line of German trenches and suffered heavy casualties. The Germans wasted their ammunition and his regiment sustained few losses despite heavy machine gun fire. He thanked God for the beauty of the sky in the evening; after one of the worst days of carnage in French military history.[44]

Général Gabriel Rouquerol

Rouquerol, the artillery general in the 3rd Corps of the Fifth Army, was more aware of the infantry's plight. He wrote two orthodox histories of the Battles of Charleroi and Guise, but his *Le Troisième corps d'armée de Charleroi à la Marne* is a more genuine personal reflection on everything he saw. He emphasizes right at the beginning what the infantry had to put up with: thirty to forty kilometres marching per day, beginning before dawn and finishing after dusk; lack of regular meals or rest; making do with unplanned bivouacs; constantly trying to escape from the enemy; the sounds of cannon firing even after dark.[45] He observes the effect on men of facing the enemy: "fixed stares of haggard men, that I had noticed among all those who had just experienced the first shock of the enemy, animal looks..."[46] He notices with sympathy the abandoned farmhouses and the refugees on the road.[47] Although it was upsetting he had to ask the pathetic groups of women, old people and children to stand aside while the cannons went past on the road. They did not complain but their silence was more poignant than an insult.[48] Rouquerol observes that the retreat was a fine example of endurance and discipline. He believes that the German High Command thought an army like the Fifth, which had been through such an ordeal, would never be able to display any energy again.[49]

Jacques Brunel de Pérard

Some witnesses had literary ambitions but were cut down before they could achieve anything. Brunel de Pérard was one of these.[50] A baron born in Arromanches-les-Bains in the Calvados, Normandy, he was a second year student at the École de Droit and the École des Sciences Politiques. In 1913 he made his literary debut with three well-regarded articles in the *Paris Journal*, including *Lettres à un débutant* and *Portraits de Paris*. He also wrote for *Le Nouveau Mercure*. At the age of nineteen he was already an accomplished public speaker and had founded a Bonapartist review called *Imperia* which he intended to revive when the war ended. In October 1913 he started his military service in the 43rd Artillery Regiment based at Rouen and this service continued after war was declared. The diary he kept was for his own personal use and was not intended as a literary work for publication. Despite this he was one of the few witnesses of the retreat of the Fifth Army whose writing was eventually published. He was killed by a German shell on 27 September 1914 aged twenty, five days after receiving his first promotion from private to corporal. His *Carnet de route* was published in 1915.

We can see in what he wrote that he had literary ambitions. At the very beginning he refers to his professional concern for correct composition even though he is scribbling rough notes.[51] He admits that he has several novels in his thoughts and that he is an admirer of Oscar Wilde's *The Picture of Dorian Gray*.[52] He enjoys having a few admirers of his literary talent[53] and likes to drop artists' names into his diary. He compares some leaves he sees to a painting by Fragonard.[54] A view of Reims cathedral, seen from a distance, reminds him of an engraving by Gustave Doré.[55]

He also admits to enjoying the good life of a young man about town, perhaps like Dorian or Oscar. He describes going to sleep on some straw, which, he says, smelt like tea in the Ritz.[56] Occasionally he hankers after luxuries: a theatre trip, a supper in a good restaurant, white linen, cigarettes giving off blue smoke.[57] A fellow writer at *Le Nouveau Mercure* described him in 1915 as an elegant *flâneur* (stroller or loafer), a refined dandy, an artist and a dilettante.[58]

We sense his immaturity in the number of times he records highly improbable news of French and Allied successes as if they were facts.[59] Maybe he lacked a critical or cynical spirit. He also tended to see the war as a series of theatrical events, rather than getting to the heart of what it was like. Early in the diary he wonders if he lacks sensibility when he feels little for dead soldiers he does not know. Yet, in his last words—although he could not have known that this was what they would be—he imagines how he would feel if the war ended suddenly: "From certain strictly personal points of view… I would regret these two months which I have just lived through and which have brought great hardships but have also allowed me to experience a wonderful variety of rich emotions. Although I do not fear death it would be a shame not to come back. Up to now I have learnt how to cope with war."[60] The sacrifice of his early promise provides a patriotic moral, in a sense encouraging other young men to follow his fine example.

Paul Lintier

Paul Lintier was another young man with a future as a writer whose life ended prematurely at the age of twenty-three.[61] At least he had time to write two substantial books of war memoirs, one of which *Ma pièce* (*My 75*) enjoyed considerable popularity after his demise on the battlefield in 1916. The Académie Française awarded *Ma pièce* a prize in recognition of its literary quality.

He was brought up in Mayenne but studied law in Lyon where his uncle was a professor. While there he founded a student magazine called *Lyon-Étudiant*. Before the war he also wrote three short books including a novel. He joined the 44th Regiment of Artillery in 1913 and was wounded on 22 September 1914, returning to the front ten months later. He died in March 1916 at Jeandelaincourt, 32 kilometres north-east of Nancy.

Lintier achieved the immediacy of a diary but structured his material into a coherent narrative. The evocative powers of the young writer are immediately obvious. Here is one of his vivid descriptions, this time of an enemy shell flying towards his battery:

> From far off came a sound at first resembling the whirr of wings or the rustle of a silken shirt, but which rapidly developed into a droning hum like that of hundreds of hornets in flight. The shell was coming straight at us, and the sensation one then experiences is indescribable. The air twangs and vibrates, and the vibrations seem to be communicated to one's flesh and nerves—almost to the marrow of one's bones. The detachment crouched down by the wheels of the ammunition wagon and the drivers sheltered behind their horses. At every moment we expected an explosion. One, two, three seconds passed—an hour. The instinct

of self-preservation strong within me, I bent my shoulders and waited, like an animal flinching from death. A flash! It seemed to fall at my feet. Shrapnel bullets whistled by like an angry wind.[62]

His poetic treatment of the countryside is equally arresting; for example, a passage about the forest near the Belgian frontier.[63] Even more impressive is his ability to analyze the feelings of soldiers as we saw in earlier passages. He evokes so well their fears—of the next day, of death—and their desire to see the sunrise one more time. In view of his appreciation of everything around him it is hardly surprising that he wrote: "Ah! If only I escape the hecatomb, how I shall appreciate life! I never imagined that there could be an intense joy in breathing, in opening one's eyes to the light, in letting it penetrate one, in being hot, in being cold—even in suffering. I thought that only certain hours had any value, and heedlessly let the others slip past. If I see the end of this war, I shall know how to suck from each moment its full mead of pleasure, and feel each second of life as it passes by, like some deliciously cool water trickling between one's fingers."[64] We retain an image of a sensitive patriotic young man who was prepared to give up the life he loved so much to the national cause.

Étienne Derville

Étienne Derville was another young man cut down before he could realize his early promise, although he was different in character from Brunel de Pérard and Lintier. The Abbé Evrard notes in his introduction to Derville's account of the war that before 1914 he felt a sense of vocation for the Church. First of all he wanted to found a factory on the principles of social Catholicism and resolve the conflict of capital and labour. He had to abandon this and also plans to be a Catholic missionary abroad. After a first degree he did start a year at the Catholic Faculties in Lille, but his spiritual struggle seems to have affected his health and he gave up this course of study.[65] He was an intense young man who felt alone.[66] He started his military service with the 33rd Infantry Regiment on 7 October 1912 and was promoted sergeant a year later. (The 33rd Infantry Regiment was home to another Catholic young man from the north of France—Charles de Gaulle.) Derville was eventually killed in action in 1918. We can see his Catholic conscience in his writing: when he regrets not leaving payment for some jam taken from a deserted home,[67] and in his description of thefts from sacks[68], even though he is sympathetic to the sick men who probably did it.

Maurice Genevoix

The literary lion among all these early writers on the war was Maurice Genevoix. He was brought up in the Loire region, went to the lycée in Orléans with his friend Robert Porchon and from there to the École Normale Supérieure in Paris. He only had to do one year's military service before the war because this obligation was reduced for those who went to one of the elite *grandes écoles*. In August 1914 he was called up to the 106th Infantry Regiment in Ruffey's Third Army and served in the Verdun sector. He fought in the Battle of the Marne and early in 1915 was involved in the dreadful slaughter around Les Éparges on the Côtes de Meuse south-east of the great fortress. He was seriously wounded on his left side on 25 April 1915, losing the use of his left hand, and did not return to the front.

Because he had seen so much death he set about writing a series of war memoirs collected together under the title *Ceux de 1914* (Those of 1914). These made his literary reputation. He went on to write a series of novels based on his love of the countryside of the Loire valley and the Sologne region south of Orléans, as well as travel books. His regional novel *Raboliot* won the Prix Goncourt in 1925. He was elected to the Académie Française in 1946 and became its Secretary from 1958 to 1974. When not in Paris he loved to live in the Loire region of his upbringing and he bought a house near Orléans. A man of enormous resilience despite his war experiences, he lived to the age of ninety and was still writing up to his death in 1980.

Although Henri Barbusse and others wrote widely acclaimed novels based on their experiences in the trenches, many consider Maurice Genevoix to be France's finest writer on the Great War. Those who participated in the fighting thought he told it how it was without the exaggeration and literary flourishes despised by hardened veterans. He was a realist in the grand tradition of nineteenth-century writers like Stendhal and Tolstoy. His writing has a remarkable precision based on his phenomenal memory. He was not able to make many notes so exact recall of events was critical. Perhaps the violence, the emotions, the danger and closeness to death imprinted the details on his mind. He was also a fine stylist who always seemed to find the right word or expression to bring a scene to life. His writing has a pace which carries the reader through the traumatic events recorded. Some may consider, however, that his organized narrative does not fully reflect the chaos of sensations experienced by soldiers in combat.

Reading Genevoix is like watching a film on a big screen. He builds up a sweeping picture of the battlefield based on an accumulation of small details. We can see his technique at work in his description of the fighting around Rembercourt during the Battle of the Marne[69]; the death of a man shot and left hanging over barbed wire, hand to hand fighting with the Germans, the working of a French artillery battery: "They move with a speed, a precision, an energy which strikes me... The artillerymen exert themselves, run, jump, and gesticulate around their guns..."[70] It has been said that he is the writer of death and there are many examples in his book of how he tackles this without sentimentality and without dwelling unnecessarily on the details. On one occasion he sees some French soldiers relaxing in the October sunshine and enjoying a game of cards. He could hear their voices and their laughter.

> Two of the players smoked a pipe. I could make out the blue puffs of smoke which were slow to disperse in the calm air. A shock struck the crest; just one of those 77 shells which we pretended to despise. It fell right in the middle of the card players. Its black smoke hung around for a long time on the lips of the crater and in the pine branches. When at last it dispersed we saw a lacerated torso, half a man stuck on the lower branches of a tree, and next to the other half of this man—his two legs torn apart—a wounded soldier writhed slowly about in the grass. We were silent on the edge of the small road when the stretcher passed.[71]

On 10 September 1914 he killed some German soldiers in battle. This became a defining experience for him and he agonized about his own personal responsibility for their deaths as he wrote up different accounts of the same incident during his lifetime.[72]

Genevoix concentrates on bringing alive the experiences of the men at the front, not the actions of the generals. He once wrote: "Napoleon and Caesar were good captains. Tolstoy, having served in the army in the Caucasus, knew that pity, reflection, care for what is just and what is not could contribute to success in battles. This is because, if the ordinary soldier lacks confidence, he will quickly cry 'we are lost!' and flee when under fire."[73] When he realizes that the Battle of the Marne has ended in victory he describes how the men pushed forward to read the announcement. "They all had grey faces with hollow cheeks covered with stubble; their cloaks had traces of dust from the roads, of mud from the fields, of water from the sky... most of them seemed absolutely worn out and miserable... But they were the victors! And I wanted to tell each one about the surge of affection I felt for all of them, soldiers who deserved the admiration and respect of the world because they had made a sacrifice without shouting about it, without even understanding the greatness of their heroism."[74]

Marc Bloch

For Marc Bloch the experiences at the front in 1914-15 helped him develop his historical and philosophical ideas. He was born in 1886 into a Jewish family who after 1870 decided to opt for emigration from Alsace-Lorraine to France to keep their French citizenship. He had already taken his *agrégation* at the École Normale Supérieure in Paris, completed his doctoral thesis and taught for two years when he was called up as a reserve sergeant in August 1914. He served in the 272nd Reserve Infantry Regiment and kept a *carnet de route* of jottings which he later turned into his *Souvenirs de guerre* for the years 1914-15. These were not published until after his death in 1969. Together with *L'Étrange défaite* (*Strange Defeat*), his analysis of the collapse of France in 1940, they represent his personal reflection of the impact of war on his life.[75]

What emerges is the importance of personal courage and responsibility and the necessity of freedom. When we read his memoirs of the Great War we discover a very active intelligence, self-awareness and a patriotism which is not vainglorious. On 11 September, after witnessing fighting and dying on the previous day, he analyzes his own feelings with honesty. He admits to being content to be alive. "It was not without a secret pleasure that I contemplated the large gash in my canteen, the three holes in my coat made by bullets that had not injured me." But he was also elated because of the victory the colonel had mentioned. "I had little comprehension of the battle. It was the victory of the Marne, but I would not have known what to call it. What matter, it was victory. The bad luck that had weighed us down since the beginning of the campaign had been lifted. My heart beat with joy that morning in our small, dry, devastated valley in Champagne."[76]

In this short book we also sense the critical faculties of the historian interrogating his sources, i.e. himself. Discussing 10 September he wrote: "My recollections of that day are not altogether precise. Above all they are poorly articulated, a discontinuous series of images, vivid in themselves but badly arranged like a reel of movie film that showed here and there large gaps and the unintended reversal of certain scenes."[77] During the retreat from the frontiers he was disturbed by the lack of explanation for what was happening: "We knew absolutely nothing. I suffered acutely from this ignorance. I stand bad news better than uncertainty, and nothing irritates me more than the suspicion that I am being deceived."[78]

Between the wars Bloch earned an international reputation as a historian of the Middle Ages and was co-founder with Lucien Febvre of the academic journal *Annales*, a seminal influence in historical studies. He was also critical of the leadership of the country when confronted by the threat from Nazi Germany. In 1940 as a Jew he had to give up both the editorship of *Annales* and residence in Paris. All these experiences reinforced the qualities evident in the young man in the trenches. He became a leader of the Resistance in Lyon and in 1944 was caught by the Gestapo, tortured and executed by firing squad. His last words were "Vive la France!"

Antoine Guasson

Others, unlike Bloch, took a more overtly political stance in their work. Thus, while individual details of events in their books are useful to build up our picture of the retreat, we have to be aware of their point of view when considering the whole period. Antoine Guasson took an explicitly pacifist, anti-war stance in his book *Heures maudites: journal de route d'un soldat de la guerre 1914-1915* (Accursed Hours), published by the Librairie du Travail in 1936. The title itself is almost a statement of belief. He introduces us to his horror of war right at the beginning of the book when he sees a young German scout dead in a ditch on 22 August. "A violent feeling grips me. I cannot stop myself crying in a loud voice. Now I understand the horror of war. My comrades' faces betray the same emotion."[79] His book is full of such distressing scenes portrayed in a way intended to repel the reader. He describes the horrific experience of visiting a military hospital on 24 August, where many of the dying were left in a field outside: "What a sight! A writhing mass of tangled bodies, dying men dragging themselves towards the haystacks, dead men stuck together. Blood. Death rattles. The wind blows out our candle. Our teeth chatter. We run away frightened by this vision of death." Not long afterwards the Germans arrive and Guasson and his comrades have to leave the seriously wounded and fight their way to safety.[80] On 3 September at Suippes he describes wounded soldiers in the ambulances: "many had been wounded in the buttocks which caused green diarrhoea to run onto their shoes... The smell is atrocious." The mayor and Guasson look at a dead soldier: "The stomach is open, the entrails have fallen out and unwind in a spiral... the mayor does not want to see any more. He runs off, his hands over his eyes."[81]

His words on the battlefield on 11 September after the victory are intended to produce a stock emotional response: "The spectacle is tragic. Dead men, everywhere dead Frenchmen. Tears run down our cheeks. While passing we cover the ravaged or appallingly mutilated faces with their cloaks."[82] He also becomes aware of the similar fate which has befallen the German troops. Gradually he becomes more sympathetic towards his enemies. He and a comrade defend a German prisoner who is being maltreated.[83] On 14 December he meets a German patrol at night and they exchange cigarettes and biscuits. They agree they will both take water from the same spring.[84] He is wounded on 5 April 1915 in Champagne and lies among other wounded and dying soldiers including one man pierced in the stomach who says he will die. A German with a crushed leg crawls over to Guasson and offers him water. Together they comfort the dying man.

> During this atrocious death the hands of the German touch mine. We look into each other's eyes and there is mutual understanding. We are the flotsam and jetsam of the war, bearing its stigmata on our poor bodies. We who only asked to live, to keep our strength and our youth, why do

we fight each other so cruelly? Yes, why?

Aren't we just the unhappy idiots sacrificed for a cause which seems obscure and vague? We who enjoy life in peace, happy with our lot, without any ambition, find ourselves thrown against each other. The infernal whirlwind has crushed us.

In the starlit night two soldiers reflect. One is German, the other French. For them there is no longer hatred or enmity. They are poor creatures, two men. Their hearts are awakened and join together. Their distress is infinite. Instinctively they lie side by side and they embrace each other to struggle against death, united in a fraternal gesture.[85]

Guasson came from Tulle in the remote Corrèze *département* where he was a cabinet maker. After the war he worked in the arms factory at Tulle where he became secretary of the trade union and delegate to the Commission Exécutive de la Fédération des Établissements Militaires. He had been a socialist since 1912 and after the Tours Congress of 1920, when the Parti Socialiste split, he joined the communists with all the socialists from the Corrèze. He was a communist candidate at local elections and continued with his union activities. After 1945 he served as a municipal councillor, retiring in 1959. He died in 1969 aged eighty.[86]

Jean Galtier-Boissière

Jean Galtier-Boissière was another who wrote about the events of 1914 and later developed pacifist as well as anarchist tendencies. Before the war he had already worked as a journalist, apart from completing a degree and studying philosophy at the Sorbonne. He started national service in 1911 and this ran into the war years. During the war he founded a journal called *Le Crapouillot*, a popular term for the artillery. He also wrote for another journal, *Le Canard Enchaîné*, but later severed his connection because of the strength of communist influence there. Although a man of the left, in the Second World War he sided with the Gaullists and criticized those journalists at *Le Canard Enchaîné* who had accused him of being soft on fascism but who themselves were sympathetic to collaboration with the Nazis. He published works on contemporary history, journals and novels.

Galtier-Boissière wrote an account of his experiences during the retreat, *En rase campagne 1914*, which formed the basis for his 1928 novel *La fleur au fusil*.[87] He gives the impression that the soldiers were ordered to march without having any idea what was going on. The tone of the novel is satirical, ridiculing war and the way it was conducted. "The inhabitants of other planets, if they exist, must follow the movements of this great mêlée, where millions of men will disembowel each other, with the same smile, with a hint of scorn which I ascribe to the little red ants that climb to assault the mole hill."[88] He describes the march on 15 August in this manner: "the road is like a ribbon without an end. Our képis make us look like a flock of sheep. In front of my eyes is the everlasting rucksack, the mess tin of the imbecile in front who keeps stopping without warning. I will end up by breaking my nose on his entrenching tool. I swear at him but he never replies."[89] On the 24th we meet a general with a beard, to whom the colonel says he has not received any orders what to do with the regiment. The general strokes his beard and says in an ironic tone; "Don't worry; we will try to make use of you!" No wonder the men do not know where they are going.[90]

On another occasion he is flat on the ground to escape enemy fire. He can only see grass, two mole hills and an ants' nest. It is like looking at a virgin forest in miniature; a host of insects, golden beetles, green flies, grasshoppers, crickets and ants run around busily. He observes the comings and goings of his little world curiously, a world which understands that men are at war, and he thinks that he is very small in the huge struggle around him. He is a humble pawn on the immense chessboard of the battle.[91]

Galtier-Boissière depicts himself as being drawn along by a force over which he has no control, like the refugees he sees.[92] Sometimes orders are ridiculous. He goes into a farmhouse to find some food and meets the adjutant coming out with a bottle of liqueur under each arm. "Move on," says the adjutant. "You're not allowed to go into houses!"[93]

Victor Boudon and Charles Péguy

Some writers had a nationalist agenda and were looking for heroes. They found one in Charles Péguy, the poet killed on 5 September at the beginning of the Battle of the Marne. Victor Boudon's book *Avec Charles Péguy, de la Lorraine à la Marne, août-septembre 1914* (With Charles Péguy, from Lorraine to the Marne, August-September 1914) was published in 1916 with a foreword by the nationalist novelist and member of the National Assembly Maurice Barrès. It was probably Barrès who instigated the book. Boudon served in the section led by Péguy in the 276th Infantry Regiment and witnessed his death.

Charles Péguy was already a well-known poet before the Great War as well as a formidable polemicist. He had also written plays in blank verse and his review, *Cahiers de la Quinzaine*, was very influential. Aged 41 in 1914, he was a distinguished graduate of the École Normale Supérieure and an intellectual engaged in the issues of the day. During the years before the war he totally changed his beliefs. As a young man he had been a militant socialist, a supporter of Jean Jaurès although never a Marxist. He was also anti-clerical and a supporter of the campaign to establish the innocence of Alfred Dreyfus, the question which led to bitter divisions within French society. In 1908 he rediscovered his religious beliefs and became a devout Catholic. He was disillusioned with many aspects of the modern world including its materialism and valued the humility of people who worked patiently on the land and looked after their families. At the same time he moved closer to the nationalists as the threat from Germany seemed to loom larger. To some extent he fell between two stools, trusted neither by the Church nor by the left. Even so he was highly respected and his death seemed particularly tragic, like that of his friend, the author of *Le Grand Meaulnes*, Alain-Fournier, killed a few weeks later. Péguy's reputation was up for grabs.

In this context Boudon's book had a particular importance. For Boudon the Germans were the Barbarians who wrought havoc in Belgium and burnt part of the old town of Senlis, something he witnessed with his own eyes.[94] They also took the mayor and some members of the local council as hostages and later shot them. The battle which must come soon, said Boudon, is to save French families, their women, their children, their aged parents and "this great city of Paris, which the Barbarians covet and which they approach with a savage joy".[95]

He depicts Péguy as a kindly, almost saintly, leader in a series of small incidents. On 31 August the men are eating some unpalatable green apples they have picked on the road to assuage their hunger. Péguy asks for one of them and, when warned that they are of little use, remarks that in war you have to be content with little.[96] Péguy lights the men's way through the forest of Chantilly, like the Light of the World.[97] As they move towards the battle Boudon refers to Péguy and his companions in arms as having marked the place where the German advance stopped, where the avalanche was checked.[98]

In the final pages we see Péguy, upright while his men are on the ground, directing their fire with his lorgnette as the German bullets fly around them. His men beg him to get down too but he refuses. "He stood up defying the machine guns, seeming to call for the death which he glorified in his verses. In that instant a bullet broke his noble forehead. He fell on his side without a cry but with a muffled groan, having seen the ultimate vision of the victory he hoped for so close at last."

Boudon charges on and then looks back to see the body of their dear brave lieutenant. "Under the mourning shroud of the twilight, the golden beams of the setting sun make the most magnificent halo for all these heroes who have fallen on the threshold of victory, and the smoke of the fires which redden the sky, while the cannons scream death, climbs like incense from this field of sacrifice… They all sleep now, rocked to an eternal sleep by the sound of the battle."[99] And then he quotes Péguy's famous lines from his 1913 poem *Prière pour nous autres charnels* (Prayer for We Beings of the Flesh), which echoes Christ's Beatitudes:

Blessed are those who died in great battles,

Stretched out on the ground in the face of God.
Blessed are those who died on a final high place,
Amid all the pomp of grandiose funerals.

Blessed are those who died, for they have returned
Into primeval clay and primeval earth.
Blessed are those who died in a just war.
Blessed is the wheat that is ripe and the wheat that is gathered in sheaves.[100]

It is fiendishly difficult to translate this poem and still retain the sound and spirit of the original so I am including the French version of these verses.

Heureux ceux qui sont morts dans les grandes batailles,
Couchés dessus le sol à la face de Dieu.
Heureux ceux qui sont morts sur un dernier haut lieu,
Parmi tout l'appareil des grandes funérailles,

Heureux ceux qui sont morts, car ils sont retournés
Dans la première argile et la première terre.
Heureux ceux qui sont morts dans une juste guerre,
Heureux les épis murs et les blés moissonnés.

Boudon's book is a piece of propaganda written up after the events, not a true account of the nature of the fighting in 1914.[101]

German diaries

Walter Bloem

Like some of the French witnesses of the retreat to the Marne Walter Bloem also had literary ambitions. Born in 1868, he was the son of a senior lawyer in Germany. After studying at Heidelberg, Marburg and Bonn universities he practised as a lawyer but also started writing plays and novels. In 1912 he published his trilogy of novels about the Franco-Prussian War which made him famous throughout Germany and very popular with the Kaiser.

He went to war as a company commander in the 12th Regiment of Brandenburg Grenadiers and was wounded after the Battle of the Aisne in 1914. Subsequently he served on both the Western and Eastern Fronts including in the General Staff.

After the war Bloem was a very successful writer in Germany, although he lost much of his fortune during the economic crisis and inflation of the 1920s. When the Nazis came to power he supported the regime, playing a significant role in the cultural activities run by the government. He died in 1951.

Bloem was a careful observer with a photographic memory who had an opportunity to write his account after being wounded, when the events were still fresh in his mind. His aim in his book *The Advance from Mons 1914* (published in 1916) seems to have been to provide a good literary account of the war containing imaginative descriptions of the landscape and dramatic battle scenes, mixed with touches of humour and references to his own feelings at key turning points, e.g. the realization that the Germans were up against a formidable opponent in the British Army after Mons or the disillusion after the retreat from the Marne. While the strain of the march was the same for the Germans as the British and French, it was psychologically easier to cope with until advance turned into retreat. Bloem is typical of many in the German Army who did not accept that the Marne was any kind of victory for the Allies.[102]

His heavy humour emerges when German troops have discovered some good wine to drink. They sip Burgundy and smoke cigars, for example, while watching Soissons in flames.[103] The episode at Jolimetz is another example. His battle scenes are vivid such as his description of high explosive shells used on the Aisne:

> The high explosive shells hurtled through, burrowing deep into the sodden ground like blows from a colossal steam-hammer: the earth itself seemed to crack, and masses of smoke, bits of rock, clods of mud, and large chips of shell shot up into the air: now and again these monsters would undermine a tree, the explosion uprooting it and sending it twirling like a corkscrew through the air till it fell in a million splinters. A monotonous and incessant rumbling like the beating of a monster kettledrum in the distance formed the bass of the battle symphony. This and the screaming in the wood about me were constant, never-ceasing, but between the high notes and the low notes was a mad confusion of deafening uproar: like the yelpings of a giant dog gone mad and the rocks of the hills being burst asunder.[104]

Although Bloem does mention the sight of terrible wounds on the Aisne we never feel the pain of war.[105] Instead he describes the ecstasy of knowing he has conquered fear. He feels a sense of salvation, of release, of realizing that his failings have been forgiven. Metaphorically he hears a choir of angels: "Never before nor since have I experienced so intensely the joy of sacrifice, of surrendering things temporal for things eternal, but I know now how sweet and glorious it is. And I know, too, that if this is its prelude, then death must be merely as a joyous home-coming after an aimless journey."[106] This language seems to glorify war by making it into a quasi-religious experience.

After he is evacuated from the front he also describes his regret that he will never see his fellow soldiers again.[107] It is difficult to reconcile such expressions of solidarity, however, with his racist response to prisoners from the British Empire. Black soldiers are likened to gorillas. And these, he remarks with sarcasm, are the people summoned to Europe to save civilization from the Huns.[108]

Ludwig Renn

Ludwig Renn, on the other hand, came to the events of 1914 from a completely different standpoint. His book *Krieg* (War), which covers the retreat and the Marne, came out ten years after the conflict in 1928. It is a book describing episodes in his life as a soldier from 1914 right through to 1918 rather than a day by day diary. In a narrative with plenty of dialogue he characterizes the experiences of the men and ignores the officers. He does not deal with the bigger picture of the 1914 campaign. Unlike Bloem he does not glorify war in any way; the events are presented without his personal views. We do learn that he does not believe in a God but little else. However, it seems that the experiences of the war years changed forever this son of an aristocratic German. He joined the German Communist Party in 1928 and was twice arrested by the Nazis, once because of the supposedly anti-war conclusions of his book on the Great War. He escaped from Germany and commanded international brigades during the Spanish. Civil War. Having seen out the Second World War in Mexico he subsequently returned to the German Democratic Republic where he died in 1979.

British diaries

The British memoirs of the retreat from Mons to the Marne are entirely different in character. The British Expeditionary Force consisted of professional soldiers. Although over half were reservists they were very different from most of the reservists on the continent. The British had all served in the regular army for many years and therefore had many of the attitudes of professionals and their regimental loyalties. The French reservists had usually only served full-time for one to two years before being called back to the colours. Apart from the officers, the French full-timers and reservists in 1914 were all conscripts and brought with them their attitudes and beliefs from civilian life. They did not identify themselves as soldiers but as citizens who were carrying out their military obligations. This is reflected in the words of those of them who wrote down their experiences. It is not surprising that, unless they were career officers, they wrote very different books from those of their British counterparts.

Some of the writings of British witnesses are unpublished manuscript diaries intended for personal use or for families and friends. Others were published as books, but many of these are still in diary form. Few of them are continuous prose pieces intended to give an overall picture of the events in question. One exception is Arthur Corbett-Smith's *The Retreat from Mons, By One who Shared in It*, which takes the form of a popular patriotic history. Two others are *Old Soldiers Never Die* by Frank Richards, the private in the Royal Welch Fusiliers, and *Old Contemptible* by Harry Beaumont, the extraordinary story of his part in the Battle of Mons and his subsequent escape through occupied Belgium and Holland.

Whatever the form of their writing, there is a conspicuous difference between the approach taken by officers and their men. Whereas the former tend to take on an official military tone the latter are informal, livelier, full of humour and a willingness to make light of adversity. Frank Richards wrote the following as the British prepared for the engagement at Le Cateau: "At dawn we marched out of Le Cateau with fixed bayonets. Duffy said: 'We'll have a bang at the bastards today.' We all hoped the same. We were all fed up with the marching and would have welcomed a scrap to relieve the monotony."[109] H.J. Rowthorn's reminiscence of how he survived behind enemy lines is another splendid example, full of the joys of corned beef sandwiches, pots of tea and friendly advice from his comrades.[110]

Frederic Coleman gives many examples of this sort of humour and optimism in his book *From Mons to Ypres with French*, published in London in 1916. Coleman was an American who volunteered to work for GCHQ with his car, running errands. He was also a journalist whose colourful and convincing work no doubt appealed to an American audience. He roams over the whole theatre of operations and conveys the atmosphere of the retreat well without, however, describing the more unpleasant aspects of the fighting. His book is full of characters like the lantern-jawed soldier encouraging his men to keep marching at St. Quentin with "'Come on, you blighters! Don't block the road. You ain't no bloomin' army now, You're a forlorn 'ope, that's what you are. Nice-lookin' lot of beggars. 'Op it!' And they "opped it' to the music of his cheery abuse. God bless him!"[111]

Edward Spears was the British liaison officer serving in Lanrezac's HQ. His book *Liaison 1914* is in a class of its own, a serious account of the whole campaign by someone who was in a unique position to observe both the decisions of the generals as well as the conditions faced by the men. His style is readable and he is particularly good at pen portraits of the major actors in the drama. Consider these words on Joffre.

He had a big face, rather soft in texture, though not flabby, the hinges and sides of the jaw forming a bold outline. His chin was marked and determined. The whiteness of his hair, the lightness of his almost colourless blue eyes, which looked out from under big eyebrows the colour of salt and pepper, white predominating, and the tonelessness of his voice coming through the sieve of his big whitish moustache, all gave the impression of an albino. His cap was worn well forward so that the peak protected his eyes, which resulted in his having to tilt his head slightly to look at one.

A bulky, slow-moving, loosely-built man, in clothes that would have been the despair of Savile Row, yet unmistakably a soldier.[112]

Spears was motivated to write this long book after a visit to the French Senate where it was apparent little was known about the British contribution in 1914. Although he bases his work on his personal observations he also gives a clear picture of the overall military situation. This is the point at which memoirs become a serious work of history. Yet we must beware of his prejudices. For example, he included a much quoted anecdote about Lanrezac's sarcasm which was not strictly true. At a meeting on 17 August Sir John French asked the French general whether the Germans would cross the Meuse at a place called Huy, which with his very limited French he found fiendishly difficult to pronounce. Relying on a story from a British officer who claimed to be a witness, Spears reports that Lanrezac replied: "Tell the Marshal that in my opinion the Germans have merely gone to the Meuse to fish."[113] In fact, Lanrezac probably made a joke of what he would have liked to have said, at a mess dinner with his officers after Sir John had left. Spears later became close to French, who was godfather to his son. He absorbed the latter's sense of betrayal by Lanrezac and his negative view of the French general's leadership.[114]

Echoes of the past

One hundred years after 1914 interest in the First World War shows no signs of diminishing. The literature on the subject is enormous and new publications appear constantly from major histories to diaries of individual participants. Commemorations seem to divide along national lines. The French visit the sites where their soldiers fought and the British tend to go to the places associated with the Commonwealth and British Armies. Over two millions Britons are likely to cross the Channel in 2014 and there are now more visitor centres and museums to receive them.

The best way to recreate the dramatic retreat of 1914, however, is to visit the countryside where it took place—the hedges and ditches of the Thiérache, the meandering River Oise with the open plateau above, the Forêt de St. Gobain, the heights above the River Aisne, the curving hills of the Marne valley and the immense Champagne plain. Some of this has hardly changed at all in one

Joffre in 1917, a photograph by R. Melcy (Wikimedia Commons)

hundred years. Standing quietly by the St.-Quentin-La Fère road at La Guingette or in the square at Braine, I could hear in my head the sound of tramping boots, the clatter of gun carriages and the accents of Normans, Bretons, Gascons, Scots, Geordies and Cockneys as they struggled along under a blistering sun they knew not where; anxious about their homes, exhausted, hungry, thirsty, with sore feet, packs which cut into their shoulders and the enemy constantly at their backs.

There were times and places where the echoes from the past seemed real and immediate. Standing on the fields above Cousolre it did not take much imagination to see the smoke and flames of battle in the open vista towards Charleroi. The damp lanes near St. Aubin were redolent of pigs and muck. In the narrow street of La Petite Rue I could see men slumped on the sidewalks and crowding around the *estaminet*, with barbed wire and wagons blocking the road. At Wiège-Faty the soldiers seemed to step out of the fire pump shelters where they slept. Walking from Benay back to the St. Quentin road, the German guns which André saw appeared on the hill again—a corporal taken, a young lieutenant spared. Such were the chances of war. In a clearing in the Forêt de St. Gobain I could smell the horses of the refugees whom André met and conjure up the flickering light of their camp fires. The whispering of nuns reached me through the imposing walls of the Premontré Abbaye as they fussed over General Valabrègue taking his supper. On the bridge over the Marne at Mézy I could feel the crush of the infantry and horsemen desperate to escape from the advancing Germans. The narrow defile south of Condé-en-Brie seemed full of menace. I shut my eyes and saw the silhouettes of the French dragoons watching for the enemy.

In one hundred years the society in which the young soldiers in these pages grew up has changed out of all recognition. The national self-belief, the religious faith and the closely knit communities from which many of them came have gone for ever. However, we can still wonder at their resilience and fortitude and reflect on how this changed the course of history. We can also identify with the human emotions they experienced—the shared hardships, the pleasures of the table and the sense of humour which often kept them going. I end with two anecdotes, one French and one British, which illustrate how amusement got them through their ordeal in different ways: the French love of words, repartee and the grand gesture; the British gift for self-deprecation and a sense of the ridiculous.

Charles Vallé was a member of André's section who had been an actor in civilian life. Here he offers a poem in honour of Évrard, the Company commander. It is written in Alexandrines, twelve syllables to the line, the distinctive metre of French verse since the days of Corneille and Racine in the seventeenth century:

I follow Captain Évrard without hesitating,

Who, however, sometimes treats me as a straggler,
But he is a good chap; he has a merry sense of humour,
Occasionally enlivened by some bellicose notion.
When in a large field he cries out "form a firing line!"
I must confess, sometimes, I'd rather be somewhere else.
And then, it is marvellous; here I earn a penny!
Enough to pay for a little hole in the ground!
But, if the pay is meagre, the task is glorious
And I guarantee to you, that if we have to we can strike a blow,
Go on, Captain, place yourself before us,
Say to us "pass in that direction" and we will all follow you.

Je suis, sans hésiter, le capitaine Évrard,
Qui, pourtant, quelquefois, me traite de traînard.
Mais c'est un très brave homme; il a l'humeur joyeuse,
Agrémentée parfois d'une idée batailleuse.
Lorsque, dans un grand champ, il crie: "En tirailleurs!",
J'avoue que, quelquefois, je voudrais être ailleurs.
Et puis, c'est merveilleux; ici, je gagne un sou!
Je pourrai me payer en terre un petit trou!
Mais, si maigre est la paye, glorieuse est la besogne
Et je vous garantis que, s'il faut que l'on cogne,
Allez, mon Capitaine, placez-vous devant nous;
Dites-nous: "Passons là" et nous vous suivrons tous.[115]

Frederic Coleman listened to the Royal Fusiliers marching past after Le Cateau.

"You oughter know who *we* are," said the sergeant, somewhat haughtily. "We're the lot what was first in Mons and last out, *we* are."

"That's right," piped up a squeaky voice that came from a diminutive member of the squad; "buck, you beggar, buck. Tell'em the tale."

A grin on half a dozen faces told that the small one might be expected to produce some comment when occasion permitted. The sergeant turned. "What's ailin' *you*, Shorty?" he demanded.

"Tell'em the tale," croaked the little man. "Fust in Mons and last out. In at three miles an hour and out at eighteen. That's us, you bet," and he snorted as the squad roared in appreciative mirth.[116]

KEY DATES: JULY-SEPTEMBER 1914

28 June: Assassination of Archduke Franz Ferdinand in Sarajevo

28 July: Austria declares war on Serbia

30 July: General Russian mobilization authorized

1 August: French and German mobilization authorized

3 August: Germany declares war on France

4 August: Britain declares war on Germany

7 August: Fall of Liège citadel

8 August: French troops enter Mulhouse

15-17 August: British troops sail for France

20 August: Battle of Morhange in Lorraine between French Second Army and German Sixth and Seventh Armies

20 August: Germans occupy Brussels

21-23 August: Battle of Charleroi between French Fifth Army and German Second and Third Armies

23 August: Battle of Mons between British Expeditionary Force and German First Army

21-23 August: Battles in the Ardennes between French Third and Fourth Armies and German Fourth and Fifth Armies

24 August: French and British retreat begins

25-28 August: German attack on Nancy via Trouée des Charmes repulsed

28 August: German victory over Russian forces at Tannenberg in East Prussia

29 August: Battle of Guise between French Fifth Army and German Second Army

1 September: French Fifth Army crosses River Aisne

4-13 September: Battle for Nancy between German Sixth Army and French Second Army.

1 September: Battles of Villers-Cotterêts and Néry between British Expeditionary Force and German First Army

2 September: French government leaves Paris for Bordeaux

2-3 September: French and British Armies cross the Marne

6-9 September: Battle of the Marne

9 September: German forces retreat to the Aisne

14 September: Fighting commences along the Aisne

MILITARY LEADERS REFERRED TO IN THE TEXT

French
Commander-in-Chief: General Joseph Joffre
Commander Second Army: General Édouard de Castelnau
Commander Third Army: General Pierre Ruffey, later replaced by General Maurice Sarrail
Commander Fourth Army: General Ferdinand Langle de Cary
Commander Ninth Army: General Ferdinand Foch
Commander Fifth Army: General Charles Lanrezac, later replaced by General Louis Franchet d'Esperey
Commander Sixth Army: General Michel-Joseph Manoury
Military Governor of Paris: General Joseph Galliéni

British
Commander-in-Chief: Field-Marshal Sir John French
Chief of Staff: General Sir Archibald Murray
Deputy Chief of Staff: General Sir Henry Wilson
Commander 1st Corps: General Sir Douglas Haig
Commander 2nd Corps: General Sir Horace Smith-Dorrien
Commander Cavalry Division: General Edmund Allenby

German
Chief of Staff: General Helmuth von Moltke
Commander First Army: General Alexander von Kluck
Commander Second Army: General Karl von Bülow
Commander Third Army: General Max von Hausen
Commander Fourth Army: General Prince Albert, Duke of Württemberg
Commander Fifth Army: General Crown Prince Wilhelm Hohenzollern
Commander German Sixth Army: General Crown Prince Rupprecht of Bavaria

REFERENCES

1: The Outbreak of War

1 Benoit, André. *Trois mois de guerre au jour le jour:1914, journal d'un fantassin*. p.9; Archives de l'Armée de Terre, Vincennes, GR 8Ye 18878
2 Ed. Pedroncini, Guy. *Histoire militaire de la France: vol. 3 1871-1940*. p.272
3 Porchon, Robert. *Carnet de route*. p. 55
4 Omnès, Sgt. Albert. *Carnet de route, campagne de 1914*. p.2
5 Ed. Kocher-Marboeuf, Eric et Azaïs, Raymond. *Le choc de 1914*. p.39
6 Deville, Lt. Robert. *Carnet de route d'un artilleur*. p.3
7 Bloch, Marc. *Memoirs of War 1914-1915*. p.78
8 Benoit. pp. 9-10
9 Strachan, Hew. *The First World War: Vol.I To Arms*. p.107
10 Benoit. p.11
11 Ed. Ulrich, Bernd and Ziemann, Benjamin. *German Soldiers in the Great War*. p.28
12 Ed. Wedd, A.E. *German Students' War Letters*. p.1
13 Ed. Ulrich, Bernd and Ziemann, Benjamin. *German Soldiers in the Great War*. p. 25
14 Verhey, Joseph. *The Spirit of 1914*. Chapters 1 and 2
15 *Ibid*. pp.231-8
16 Quoted in Holmes, Richard. *Riding the Retreat*. p. 83
17 *Les Armées Françaises de la Grande Guerre* (AFGG). Tome 1 Vol.1, p.567 Appendices
18 Brunel de Pérard, Jacques. *Carnet de route*. p. 81
19 Ed. Pedroncini, Guy. *Histoire Militaire de la France: Vol.3 De 1871 à 1940*. pp.44-7
20 Herwig, Holger. *The Marne, 1914*. pp. 46 and 61; Strachan, Hew. *The First World War*. p.206
21 For details of kit carried by French, German and British soldiers *see* Lavisse, Commandant Émile-Charles. *Sac au dos*
22 MacMillan, Margaret. *The War That Ended Peace*. p.346
23 *The Cambridge Economic History of Modern Europe: Vol.2. 1870 to the present*, Leonard, Carol and Ljungberg, Jonas. Chapter 5 *Population and Living Standards 1870-1914*
24 Holmes, Richard. *Tommy: The British Soldier on the Western Front 1914-1918*. p.115. For the Tommies' living conditions generally *see ibid* pp.95-124
25 Strachan, Hew. *The First World War*. p.191
26 *Cambridge Economic History*. Broadberry, Stephen, Federico, Giovanni and Klein, Alexander. Chapter 3 *Sectoral Developments 1870-1914*; also Chapter 5 *op.cit*
27 Price, Roger. *A Social History of Nineteenth-Century France*. p.18
28 Gildea, Robert. *Children of the Revolution*. p.313
29 Price, Roger. *A Social History of Nineteenth-Century France*. p.90
30 For an insight into the French countryside in the late nineteenth century *see* Price, Roger. *Ibid*, pp.1-92; 143-196; Gildea, Robert. *Children of the Revolution*. pp.311-317; Planhol, Xavier de. *An Historical Geography of France*. pp.345-414.
31 Ed.Pedroncini, Guy. *Histoire militaire de la France: vol.3 De 1871 à 1940*. p. 83
32 *Ibid*, p.86
33 Price, Roger. *A Social History of Nineteenth-Century France*. p.331
34 Price, Roger.*ibid*, pp.331-6; Gildea, Robert. *Education in Provincial France*. p.369
35 Richards, Frank. *Old Soldiers Never Die*. pp.16-17

36 Craig, Gordon. *The Politics of the Prussian Army*. pp. 235-8
37 Ed. Pedroncini, Guy. *Histoire militaire de la France: vol.3 De 1871 à 1940*. pp.72-3.
38 Smith, Leonard V. *Between Mutiny and Obedience: The Case of the French Fifth Infantry Division during World War One*. p. 37
39 See Spears, Edward. *Liaison 1914*. p.24
40 Ed. Pedroncini, Guy. *Histoire militaire de la France: vol.3 De 1871 à 1940*. p.73 and p.76
41 Smith, Leonard V. *Between Mutiny and Obedience*. pp.37-8
42 Ed. Pedroncini, Guy. *Histoire militaire de la France: vol.3 De 1871 à 1940*. p.79
43 For NCOs *see* Ed. Pedroncini, Guy. *Histoire militaire de la France: vol.3 De 1871 à 1940*. pp.77-9; also Porch, Douglas. *The March to the Marne*. *passim*
44 Porch, Douglas. *ibid*, p.204
45 Porch, Douglas. *ibid*, pp.191-212; Smith, Leonard V. *Between Mutiny and Obedience*. pp.33-4. Indeed on the issue of recruitment and training of the infantry the whole of Chapter Two of his book, pp.20-38, repays careful study.
46 Ripperger, Robert M. "The Development of the French Artillery for the Offensive 1890-1914". *The Journal of Military History*, vol. 59 no. 4 (Oct. 1995) pp.599-618
47 For the origins of the Great War *see* MacMillan, Margaret. *The War That Ended Peace*; Clark, Christopher. *The Sleepwalkers*; McMeekin, Sean. *July 1914 Countdown to War*
48 MacMillan, Margaret. *ibid*, p.408
49 *Ibid*, p.158

2: The Battle of the Frontiers

1   Strachan, Hew. *The First World War: Vol.I To Arms*. p.207
2   Joffre, Joseph. *Mémoires du Maréchal Joffre*: T.1. 1910-1917. p.143
3   For war plans *see* Strachan, Hew. *The First World War*. pp.163-207 and Herwig, Holger. *The Marne, 1914*. pp.30-73
4   Strachan, Hew. *ibid*, p.206
5   Benoit. pp.13-18
6   Richards, Frank. *Old Soldiers Never Die*. p.11
7   Brunel de Pérard, Jacques. *Carnet de route*. pp.32-33
8   Benoit. p.18
9   Derville, Étienne. *Correspondance et Notes*. p.32
10 See Porch, Douglas, "The Marne and after: A Reappraisal of French Strategy in the First World War". *Journal of Military History*, vol. 53, no.4, Oct. 1989, pp.363-86
11 Grasset, Alphonse. *Vingt jours de guerre aux temps héroïques*. p.160
12 Grasset. *ibid*, p.169
13 Herwig, Holger. *The Marne, 1914*. p.150
14 Contamine, Henri. *La victoire de la Marne*. p. 120 in Baldin, Damien and Saint-Fuscien, Emmanuel. *Charleroi*. p. 117
15 Duménil, Anne. "Les combattants". In Audoin-Rouzeau, Stéphane et Becker, Jean-Jacques (dir.). *Encyclopédie de la Grande Guerre 1914-1918*. p.322
16 Spears, Edward. *Liaison 1914*. pp.46-7
17 *Ibid*, p.73
18 *Ibid*, pp.46-7
19 *Ibid*, p.82
20 Lanrezac, Charles. *Le plan de campagne français et le premier mois de la guerre*. p. 169

21 Omnès, Sgt. Albert. *Carnet de route: campagne de 1914*. pp. 8-9
22 Contamine, Henri. *La revanche 1870-1914*. p. 243
23 Lanrezac, Charles. *Le plan de campagne français*. pp.162-3 and p.169.
24 Baldin, Damien and Saint-Fuscien, Emmanuel. *Charleroi*. p.118
25 Spears, Edward. *Liaison 1914*. p.141
26 For a discussion of these issues see Baldin, Damien and Saint-Fuscien, Emmanuel. *Charleroi*. Chapters 8-11
27 Benoit. pp.20-22
28 Beaumont, Harry. *Old Contemptible*. p.32
29 *Ibid*, pp.32-35
30 For the Battle of Mons *see* Terraine, John. *Mons, the Retreat to Victory*. pp.86-108; also Murland, Jerry. *Retreat and Rearguard 1914*. pp.12-31

3: The Retreat begins

1   Lanrezac, Charles. *Le plan de campagne français et le premier mois de la guerre*. p.184 and p.199
2   Spears, Edward. *Liaison 1914*. pp.153-4
3   Derville, Étienne. *Correspondance et notes*. p.35
4   Lanrezac, Charles. *Le plan de campagne français*. p.197
5   Benoit. p.23
6   Benoit. pp.23-4
7   Omnès, Sgt. Albert. *Carnet de route: campagne de 1914*. p.9
8   La Chaussée, Julien. *De Charleroi à Verdun dans l'infanterie*. p.33
9   *Ibid*, p.37
10 Derville, Étienne. *Correspondance et notes*. p.36
11 *Ibid*, p.37
12 *Ibid*, pp.36-9
13 Benoit. pp.25-6
14 Lanrezac, Charles. *Le plan de campagne français*. p.200
15 Beaumont, Harry. *Old Contemptible*. pp.35-40
16 Private Papers of Harrop, Doctor IWM 8458. pp.38-49. *See also* Murland, Jerry. *Retreat and Rearguard 1914*. pp.38-40
17 Private Papers of Tower, K.F.B. IWM 11442. 24 August 1914
18 Private Papers of Spencer, A.V. IWM 1422. 24 August 1914
19 For the account of the BEF's movements on 24 August see Terraine, John. *Mons, the Retreat to Victory*. pp.112-121; also Murland, Jerry. *Retreat and Rearguard 1914*. pp.32-51
20 Ed. Craster, Michael. *Fifteen Rounds a Minute, the Grenadiers at War, August to December 1914*. p.39
21 *Ibid*, pp.39-40
22 Coleman, Frederic. *From Mons to Ypres with French*. pp. 12-13
23 Terraine, John. *Mons*. p.126; Murland, Jerry. *Retreat and Rearguard 1914*. p.62
24 Denore, Bernard John. "The Retreat from Mons". In Ed. Purdom, C.B. *Everyman at War*, p.3
25 Ed.Terraine, John. *General Jack's Diary*. p. 32
26 For accounts of the BEF's movements on 25 August see Terraine, John. *Mons*. pp.125-9, pp.134-140 and Murland, Jerry. *Retreat and Rearguard 1914*. pp.52-63
27 Rosenhainer, Lt. Ernst. *Forward March! Memoirs of a German Officer*. p.6

28 Ed. Baumgartner, Richard A. *Fritz: The World War 1 Memoir of a German Lieutenant.* pp.21-2; Bloem, Walter. *The Advance from Mons, 1914.* Chapter 9
29 Bloem, Walter. *ibid*, p.62
30 *Ibid*, p.63
31 *Ibid*, pp. 63-4
32 Galtier-Boissière, Jean. *La fleur au fusil.* p.97
33 Lintier, Paul. *My 75.* pp.91-2
34 Galtier-Boissière, Jean. *La fleur au fusil.* p.101
35 *Ibid*, p.103
36 Bloch, Marc. *Memoirs of War 1914-1915.* p.81. *See also* Bloch, Étienne ed. *Écrits de Guerre de March Bloch 1914-1918.* p.42
37 Grasset, Alphonse. *Vingt jours de guerre aux temps héroïques.* pp.250-279
38 Lintier, Paul. *My 75.* pp.138 and 155
39 *Ibid*, p.159

4: Le Cateau to Guise

1   Lanrezac, Charles. *Le plan de campagne français et le premier mois de la guerre.* p.197
2   Benoit. pp.26-7
3   For the action involving the Connaught Rangers *see* Murland, Jerry. *Retreat and Rearguard 1914.* pp.81-7
4   Bird, Antony. *Gentlemen, We Will Stand and Fight: Le Cateau, 1914.* p.102; Montgomery, Bernard Law. *The Memoirs of Field-Marshal Montgomery.* p.32
5   Bird, Antony. *Ibid*, p.117
6   *Ibid*, p.119
7   For an account of Le Cateau *see* Terraine, John. *Mons, the Retreat to Victory.* pp.136,145-154; Bird, Antony. *passim*
8   Benoit. pp.27-28
9   *Journal des Marches et Opérations* (JMO) 267e RI 26 août 1914; Archives de l'Armée de Terre 26 N 732/19
10 Ernest Lavisse. Discours à des enfants. 1907. p.35, quoted in Robb, Graham. *The Discovery of France.* p.324
11 Benoit. pp.28-9
12 Omnès, Sgt. Albert. *Carnet de route: campagne de 1914.* pp.10-11
13 Benoit. p.29
14 Benoit.p.29
15 Ed. Fossier, R. *Histoire de la Picardie.* pp.370 and 378
16 Weber, Eugen. *Peasants into Frenchmen 1870-1914.* p.110
17 Benoit. p.29
18 Benoit. pp.29-31
19 Terraine, John. *Mons.* p.157
20 Private Papers of Tower, K.F.B. IWM 11442. p.18
21 Terraine, John. *Mons.* pp.158-9
22 Richards, Frank. *Old Soldiers Never Die.* pp.20-22
23 Bird, Antony. *Gentlemen, We Will Stand and Fight.* p.152
24 Gaunt, F. *The Immortal First.* pp.28-9
25 Montgomery, Bernard Law. *The Memoirs of Field-Marshal Montgomery.* p.32
26 Bird, Antony. *Gentlemen, We Will Stand and Fight.* p.173
27 Private Papers of Rowthorn, H.J. IWM 15193

28 Van Emden, Richard. *The Soldier's War*. p.51
29 Ed.Terraine, John. *General Jack's Diary*. p. 42
30 Private Papers of Brereton, Cedric L. IWM 2615. p.VI
31 Richards, Frank. *Old Soldiers Never Die*. p.19
32 Gaunt, F. *The Immortal First*. pp.55-6
33 Private Papers of Rowthorn, H.J. IWM 15193
34 Van Emden. Richard. *The Soldier's War*. p.46
35 Bloem, Walter. *The Advance from Mons, 1914*. p.69
36 Von Kluck, General Alexander. *The March on Paris*. p.8
37 Renn, Ludwig.*War*. p.64
38 *Ibid*, pp.68-9
39 *Annuaire de la Société météorologique de la France*. Tomes 62-4 1914-1920. pp.205-6
40 Denore, Bernard John. "The Retreat from Mons". In Ed. Purdom, C.B. *Everyman at War*. pp.3-4
41 Corbett-Smith, Arthur. *The Retreat from Mons, By One who Shared in It*. p.116
42 Private Papers of Brereton, Cedric L. IWM 2615. p.VI
43 Murland, Jerry. *Retreat and Rearguard 1914*. p.103
44 Richards, Frank. *Old Soldiers never die*. p.20
45 Bloem, Walter. *The Advance from Mons, 1914*. p.65
46 Denore, Bernard John. "The Retreat from Mons". p.4
47 Private Papers of Richards, C.E.M. IWM 22368. pp. 4-5
48 Private Papers of Rowthorn, H.J. IWM 15193
49 Coleman, Frederic. *From Mons to Ypres with French*. p.41
50 Ed.Terraine, John. *General Jack's Diary*. p.42
51 Denore, Bernard John. "The Retreat from Mons". p.5
52 Private Papers of Edgington, W. IWM 563. 27 August 1914
53 Private Papers of Tower, K.F.B. IWM 11442. p.18
54 Terraine, John. *Mons*. pp.158-9
55 Denore, Bernard John. "The Retreat from Mons". p.6
56 Coleman, Frederic. *From Mons to Ypres with French*. p.30
57 Private Papers of Rowleston West, Roger. IWM 14546. pp.29-30
58 Murland, Jerry. *Retreat and Rearguard 1914*. pp.92-99
59 Private Papers of Spencer, A.V. IWM 1422. p.14
60 Joffre, Joseph. *Mémoires du Maréchal Joffre: T.1. 1910-1917*. pp. 319-325
61 *Journal des Marches et Opérations* (JMO) 267e RI 28 août 1914; Archives de l'Armée de Terre 26 N 732/19
62 Benoit. p.32
63 Benoit. pp.31-2
64 Murland, Jerry. *Retreat and Rearguard 1914*. pp.104-110; Terraine, John. Mons. p.171
65 For the account of the Battle of Guise *see* Lanrezac, Charles. *Le plan de campagne français et le premier mois de la guerre*. pp.214-42; Rouquerol, General Gabriel. *La bataille de Guise*; Terraine, John. *Mons*. pp.161-7 and 171-7. Herwig, Holger. *The Marne, 1914*. pp.183-190 presents an interesting reappraisal which sees the battle as a success for the German Second Army because they continued their advance the next day. Also Lanrezac failed to exploit opportunities on his right.
66 Omnès, Sgt. Albert. *Carnet de route: campagne de 1914*. pp.12-13
67 La Chaussée, Julien. *De Charleroi à Verdun dans l'infanterie*. p.44

68 *Ibid*, p.49
69 *Ibid*, p.50
70 Brunel de Pérard, Jacques. *Carnet de route*. p.66
71 Lanrezac, Charles. *Le plan de campagne français*. pp 231-2
72 *Journal des Marches et Opérations* (JMO) 267e RI 29 août 1914 ; Archives de l'Armée de Terre 26 N 732/19
73 Benoit. p.33
74 *Journal des Marches et Opérations* (JMO) 267e RI 29 août 1914 ; Archives de l'Armée de Terre 26 N 732/19
75 Benoit pp.32-5 for the whole of this episode
76 See Lanrezac, Charles. *Le plan de campagne français*. pp. 240-245
77 Deville, Lt. Robert. *Carnet de route d'un artilleur*. pp.29-46
78 *Ibid*, pp.56-63
79 Guasson, Antoine. *Heures maudites*. p. 29
80 Deville, Lt. Robert. *Carnet de route d'un artilleur*. pp.58-70
81 Guasson, Antoine. *Heures maudites*. p.31
82 Bloch, Marc. *Memoirs of War 1914-1915*. p.84
83 Genevoix, Maurice. *Ceux de 14*. p.14
84 Lintier, Paul. *My 75*. p.190
85 Strachan, Hew. *The First World War: Vol.I To Arms*. p. 243
86 Boudon, Victor. *Avec Charles Péguy*. pp. 69-78

5: Across the Aisne to the Marne

1   *Journal des Marches et Opérations* (JMO) 267e RI 29 août 1914 ; Archives de l'Armée de Terre 26 N 732/19
2   Benoit. pp.35-38 for this section
3   Bloem, Walter. *The Advance from Mons, 1914*. p.65; also quoted in Herwig, Holger. *The Marne, 1914*. p.220
4   Bloem, Walter. *Ibid*, p.69
5   Gaunt, F. *The Immortal First*. p. 32
6   Bloem, Walter. *Ibid*, p.70
7   *Ibid*, pp.70-1
8   Private Papers of Richards, C.E.M. IWM 22368. p.8
9   Private Papers of Rowleston West, Roger. IWM 14546. p.55
10 Private Papers of Brereton, Cedric L. IWM 2615. p.IX
11 Private Papers of Tower, K.F.B. IWM 11442. p.21
12 Ed. Craster, Michael. *Fifteen Rounds a Minute*. p. 50
13 Lanrezac, Charles. *Le plan de campagne français et le premier mois de la guerre*. p.247
14 Lanrezac. *Ibid*, pp.250-253
15 Rouquerol, General Gabriel. *Le 3e corps d'armée de Charleroi à la Marne*. p.6
16 Spears, Edward. *Liaison 1914*. p.306
17 For the account of what happened around Vauxaillon see Spears, Edward. *ibid*, pp.301-307
18 Benoit. pp.38-9
19 Benoit. pp.39-40
20 Brunel de Pérard, Jacques. *Carnet de route*. p.70
21 Lanrezac, Charles. *Le plan de campagne français*. pp.253-5
22 Pedroncini, Guy. "Les cours martiales pendant la Grande Guerre". *Revue Historique*

1974, 512 Oct-Dec., pp.393-408
23 Miquel, Pierre. *La bataille de la Marne*. pp.71-2
24 Lanrezac, Charles. *Le plan de campagne français*. p.255
25 *Ibid*, pp.255-6
26 Spears, Edward. *Liaison 1914*. p.293 and pp.318-9
27 Rouquerol, General Gabriel. *Le 3e corps d'armée*. p.7
28 *Ibid*, pp.2-3 and p.12
29 La Chaussée, Julien. *De Charleroi à Verdun dans l'infanterie*. pp.53 and 55
30 Terraine, John. *Mons, the Retreat to Victory*. p.185
31 Lanrezac, Charles. *Le plan de campagne français*. p.262
32 Guasson, Antoine. *Heures maudites*. pp.31-6
33 Ducasse, André; Meyer, Jacques; Perreux, Gabriel. *Vie et mort des français 1914-1918*. p.46
34 Ed. Kocher-Marboeuf, Eric and Azaïs, Raymond. *Le choc de 1914*. p.84
35 Boudon, Victor. *Avec Charles Péguy*. p.118
36 Coleman, Frederic. *From Mons to Ypres with French*. pp.63-4
37 For the account of Néry and Villers-Cotterêts *see* Murland, Jerry. *Retreat and Rearguard 1914*. Chapters 12 and 13
38 Denore, Bernard John. "The Retreat from Mons". pp.6-7
39 Terraine, John. *Mons*. p.195
40 Bloem, Walter. *The Advance from Mons, 1914*. p.77
41 Benoit. p.40
42 Von Kluck, General Alexander. T*he March on Paris*. pp.92 and 96
43 For events at Châtillon-sur-Marne, Mézy and Château-Thierry *see* Spears, Edward. *Liaison 1914*. pp.338-48; and Lanrezac, Charles. *Le plan de campagne français*. pp.265-6
44 Spears, Edward. *ibid*, p.347
45 Lanrezac, Charles. *Le plan de campagne français*. p.266

6: The Retreat's Last Phase

1 Denore, Bernard John. "The Retreat from Mons". pp. 7-8; Coleman, Frederic. *From Mons to Ypres with French*. pp.71 and 87
2 Ed. Craster, Michael. *Fifteen Rounds a Minute*. p.60
3 Denore, Bernard John. "The Retreat from Mons". pp.8-9
4 Ed.Terraine, John. *General Jack's Diary*. p.47
5 Spears, Edward. *Liaison 1914*. p.366
6 Rouquerol, General Gabriel. *Le 3e corps d'armée de Charleroi à la Marne*. pp.14-21
7 Spears, Edward. *Liaison 1914*. p.262
8 Von Kluck, General Alexander. *The March on Paris*. p.104
9 Ed. Horne, Charles F. *The Great Events of the Great War: Vol. II 1914*. pp.146-7
10 Rouquerol, General Gabriel. *Le 3e corps d'armée*. p. 19
11 Bloem, Walter. *The Advance from Mons, 1914*. p.81
12 *Ibid*, p.87
13 *Journal des Marches et Opérations* (JMO) 267e RI 3 septembre 1914 ; Archives de l'Armée de Terre 26 N 732/19
14 Benoit. pp.41-2
15 Benoit. pp.42-3
16 Joffre, Joseph. *Mémoires du Maréchal Joffre: T.1. 1910-1917*. pp. 370-2; Lanrezac,

Charles. *Le plan de campagne français.* pp. 276-7; Spears, Edward. *Liaison 1914.* pp.366-371

17 Spears. *ibid,* p.384

18 Strachan, Hew. *The First World War: Vol.I To Arms.* pp.251-3

19 Deville, Lt. Robert. *Carnet de route d'un artilleur.* p.86

20 Guasson, Antoine. *Heures maudites.* pp.37-55

21 Ducasse, André; Meyer, Jacques; Perreux, Gabriel. *Vie et mort des français 1914-1918.* pp.46-7

22 Galtier-Boissière, Jean. *La fleur au fusil.* pp.135-6

23 Herwig, Holger. *The Marne, 1914.* pp.204-218

24 Joffre, Joseph. *Mémoires du Maréchal Joffre.* pp.393-4

25 Spears, Edward. *Liaison 1914.* pp.413-18

26 Benoit. p.43

27 Benoit. p.44

28 Benoit. p.44

29 Benoit. p.44

30 Rouquerol, General Gabriel. *Le 3e corps d'armée.* p.21

31 Joffre, Joseph. *Mémoires du Maréchal Joffre.* pp.394-5

32 La Chaussée, Julien. *De Charleroi à Verdun dans l'infanterie.* p.62

33 Omnès, Sgt. Albert. *Carnet de route: campagne de 1914.* p.14

34 Guasson, Antoine. *Heures maudites.* p.58

35 Private Papers of Edgington, W. IWM 563. 6 September 1914

36 Denore, Bernard John. "The Retreat from Mons". pp.8-9

37 Van Emden. Richard. *The Soldier's War.* pp.51-2

38 Miquel, Pierre. *La bataille de la Marne.* p.99

39 Boudon, Victor. *Avec Charles Péguy.* p.125

7: The Battle of the Marne and its Consequences

1 For accounts of the Battle of the Marne *see* Herwig, Holger. *The Marne, 1914.* pp.225-306; Miquel, Pierre. *La bataille de la Marne. passim*; Blond, Georges. *The Marne. passim*; Strachan, Hew. *The First World War: Vol.I To Arms.* pp.254-280

2 Bloem, Walter. *The Advance from Mons, 1914.* p.87

3 *Ibid,* pp.93-4

4 *Ibid,* p.94

5 Benoit. p.45

6 Benoit p.46

7 Blond, Georges. *The Marne.* pp.143-48

8 Omnès, Sgt. Albert. *Carnet de route: campagne de 1914.* pp.15-17

9 Benoit.pp.46-8; *Journal des Marches et Opérations* (JMO) 267e RI, 7 septembre 1914 ; Archives de l'Armée de Terre 26 N 732/19

10 Brunel de Pérard, Jacques. *Carnet de route.* p.80

11 Benoit. pp.48-51

12 Ed. Craster, Michael. *Fifteen Rounds a Minute.* p.75

13 Ed.Terraine, John. *General Jack's Diary.* p.50; Ed. Craster, Michael. *Fifteen Rounds a Minute.* pp.69-75

14 Ed.Terraine, John. *General Jack's Diary.* p.49; Private Papers of Turnbull, D.R. IWM 18455. 7 September; Sgt. Bradlaugh Sanderson quoted in Van Emden. Richard. *The Soldier's War.* p.52

15 Ed. Kocher-Marboeuf, Eric and Azaïs, Raymond. *Le choc de 1914*. p.106
16 Ducasse, André; Meyer, Jacques; Perreux, Gabriel. *Vie et mort des français 1914-1918*. pp.47-53
17 Guasson, Antoine. *Heures maudites*. p.60
18 *Ibid*. pp.60-68
19 Genevoix, Maurice. *Ceux de 14*. p.31
20 *Ibid*, p.32 and quote p.33
21 *Ibid*, p.36
22 *Ibid*, p.42
23 Herwig, Holger. *The Marne, 1914*. pp.210-214
24 *Ibid* p. 315; Guinard, Pierre, Devos, Jean-Claude and Nicot, Jean. *Organisation de l'armée française, Introduction - Inventaire sommaire des Archives de la Guerre série N 1872-1919*. p.213
25 Bloem, Walter. *The Advance from Mons, 1914*. pp.100-101
26 Bréant, Commandant Pierre. *De l'Alsace à la Somme: Souvenirs du front (août 1914-janvier 1917)*. p.67
27 Quoted in Tyng, Seymour. *The Campaign of the Marne, 1914*. p.351
28 Quoted in Herwig, Holger. *The Marne, 1914*. p.311

8: What Happened to Andre Benoit?

1 For André's movements from 11 September 1914 to 3 November see Benoit pp.51-105 and also pp.110-111. *See also Journal des Marches et Opérations* (JMO) 267e RI, 13 octobre and 2 novembre 1914
2 This account of André Benoit's subsequent life is based on the birth, death and marriage records in the Archives Départementales for the Aisne; on a dossier on the award to him of membership of the Légion d'Honneur, which included his military records; on recollections of André Benoit from M. Daniel Garousse in Charly-sur-Marne; on published lists of French prisoners of war in Germany in the *Gazette des Ardennes*; on the catalogue of the Bibliothèque Nationale in Paris; on Albertini, Pierre. "Les Juifs du lycée Condorcet dans la tourmente". *Vingtième Siècle, Revue d'Histoire*, 2006/4 no. 92, pp.81-100. DOI:10.3917/ving.092.0081, for the reference to Jean-Claude Herz; on Andre Benoit's dossier in the Archives de l'Armée de Terre at Vincennes - GR 8Ye 18878; on information from Jean-Claude Auriol the author of several works on French prisoners of war in Germany during 1914-1918; on guidance from Dr. Heather Jones, Associate Professor at the London School of Economics; and last but not least on information from Dr. Monique Burtin and Mme.Anne Moreau-Vivien, granddaughters of André Benoit. I am also indebted to Éric and Danièle Debaize, to Mme. Nicole Jobe in Charly-sur-Marne for local memories of the Benoit family, to M. Tony Legendre, Secretary of the Société Historique et Archéologique de Château-Thierry and to Mme. Marie Josée Ulmet, President of the Cercle Généalogique de l'Aisne in Château-Thierry for details of the Benoit family history and the Légion d'Honneur dossier.

9: Remembering 1914

1 Gildea, Robert. *The Past in French History*. pp.160-1
2 Becker, Annette. *La guerre et la foi*. pp.70-1
3 Winter, Jay. *Sites of Memory, Sites of Mourning*. pp.129-130

4   Prost, Antoine. "Les monuments des morts". In Ed. Nora, Pierre. *Les Lieux de Mémoire: Tome I La République.* p.203

5   Benoit. pp.33-36

6   Benoit. p.36

7   Benoit. p.9

8   Benoit. p.11

9   Benoit. p.21

10 Benoit.p.44

11 Benoit. p.21

12 Benoit. p.89

13 Benoit. pp.42 and 51

14 Benoit. p.29

15 Benoit. p.42

16 Benoit. p.54

17 Benoit. p.87

18 Benoit. p.91

19 Benoit. p.94

20 Benoit. pp.67-8

21 Benoit. p.17

22 Benoit. p.20

23 Benoit. p.30

24 Benoit. p.61

25 La Chaussée, Capitaine Julien. *Poèmes de guerre.* pp.5-8

26 La Chaussée, Julien. *De Charleroi à Verdun dans l'infanterie.* pp 36-37

27 *Ibid,* pp.52-53

28 Omnès, Sgt. Albert. *Carnet de route: campagne de 1914.* p.2

29 *Ibid,* p.2

30 *Ibid,* p.16

31 *Ibid,* pp.6-7

32 *Ibid,* p.1

33 *Ibid,* p.2

34 *Ibid,* p.3

35 Porchon, Robert. *Carnet de route.* pp.75 and 78-9

36 Ed. Kocher-Marboeuf, Eric and Azaïs, Raymond. *Le choc de 1914.* p.65

37 *Ibid,* pp.103-4

38 *Ibid,* p.42

39 *Ibid,* pp.40, 55, 58, 93

40 *Ibid,* pp.55, 69, 72, 94

41 *Ibid,* pp.45 and 110-114

42 For Deville *see* Norton Cru, Jean. *Témoins.* pp.129-30

43 Deville, Lt. Robert. *Carnet de route d'un artilleur.* pp.44-5

44 *Ibid,* pp.42-5

45 Rouquerol, General Gabriel. *Le 3e corps d'armée de Charleroi à la Marne.* p.2

46 *Ibid,* p.7

47 *Ibid,* p.9

48 *Ibid,* p.9

49 *Ibid,* pp.9-10

50 For Brunel de Pérard *see* Smith, Leonard V. *The Embattled Self: French Soldiers'*

Testimony of the Great War. p.51; Norton Cru, Jean. *Témoins.* pp.100-1
51 Brunel de Pérard, Jacques. *Carnet de route.* p. 24
52 *Ibid,* p.42
53 *Ibid,* p.55
54 *Ibid,* p.28
55 *Ibid,* p.92
56 *Ibid,* p.44
57 *Ibid,* pp.68 and 93
58 *Ibid,* p.16
59 *Ibid,* e.g. pp.56, 61
60 *Ibid,* p.105
61 For Lintier, Paul *see* Smith, Leonard V. *The Embattled Self.* pp.56 and 58; Norton Cru, Jean. *Témoins.* pp.179-186
62 Lintier, Paul. *My 75.* p.81
63 *Ibid,* p.164
64 *Ibid,* p.182
65 Derville, Étienne. *Correspondance et notes.* p.12
66 *Ibid,* p.8
67 *Ibid,* p.33
68 *Ibid,* p.37
69 Genevoix, Maurice. *Ceux de 14.* pp 33-4, 36-37, 42
70 *Ibid,* p.52
71 Genevoix, Maurice. *La mort de près.* pp.49-50
72 Smith, Leonard V. *The Embattled Self.* pp.95-100
73 Genevoix, Maurice. *La mort de près.* p.38
74 Genevoix, Maurice. *Ceux de 14.* p.60
75 For a discussion of Marc Bloch's life and thought *see* Bloch, Marc. *Memoirs of War 1914-1915.* Introduction by Carole Fink pp.15-73
76 *Ibid,* pp.94-6
77 *Ibid,* p.89
78 *Ibid,* p.85
79 Guasson, Antoine. *Heures maudites.* p.15
80 *Ibid,* p.26 *et seq.*
81 *Ibid,* p.40
82 *Ibid,* p.69
83 *Ibid,* p.75
84 *Ibid,* pp.117-8
85 *Ibid,* pp.145-9
86 For Guasson's life *see* entry on Maitron database, CNRS, University of Paris 1
87 For Galtier-Boissière, Jean *see* Norton Cru, Jean. *Témoins.* pp.138-142
88 Galtier-Boissière, Jean. *La fleur au fusil.* p.94
89 *Ibid,* p.73
90 *Ibid,* pp.92-3
91 *Ibid,* pp.93-4
92 *Ibid,* p.117
93 *Ibid,* p.135
94 Boudon, Victor. *Avec Charles Péguy.* p.117
95 *Ibid,* p.124

96 *Ibid*, p.97
97 *Ibid*, p.118
98 *Ibid*, p.138
99 *Ibid*, pp.146-7
100 Cross, Tim. *The Lost Voices of World War One: An International Anthology of Writers, Poets and Playwrights.* p.269
101 Norton Cru, Jean. *Témoins.* pp.96-7
102 Bloem, Walter. *The Advance from Mons, 1914.* pp.104-5
103 *Ibid*, p.109
104 *Ibid*, pp.114-5
105 *Ibid*, p.114
106 *Ibid*, p.115
107 *Ibid*, p.124
108 *Ibid*, pp.106-7
109 Richards, Frank. *Old Soldiers Never Die.* p.17
110 Private Papers of Rowthorn, H.J. IWM 15193
111 Coleman, Frederic. *From Mons to Ypres with French.* p. 32
112 Spears, Edward. *Liaison 1914.* p.19
113 *Ibid*, p.75
114 Philpott, William. "Gone Fishing: Sir John French's Meeting with General Lanrezac 17 August 1914". In *Journal of the Society for Army Historical Research.* Autumn 2006. vol. 84, no. 339 pp.254-9
115 Benoit. p.19
116 Coleman, Frederic. *From Mons to Ypres with French.* p. 31

BIBLIOGRAPHY

Archives
Archives de L'Armée de Terre, Ministère de la Défense, Vincennes
Cotes 8Ye 18878 - dossier on Benoit, André.
Journal des Marches et Opérations (JMO) 267e RI, 11 août-10 décembre 1914;
Archives de l'Armée de Terre 26 N 732/19; available on
www.memoiredeshommes.sga.defense.gouv.fr
Archives Départementales de l'Aisne
Les registres paroissiaux; l'état civil. Charly-sur-Marne.
Cote 18 Fi BRAINE 186; carte postale Braine Rue St. Yved et les écoles Cote
18 Fi CHATEAU-THIERRY 115; carte postale Château-Thierry. Septembre
1914 effet du bombardement, Garage de l'Hôtel l'Éléphant.
Archives Départementales de Seine-et-Marne
Cote 42 Fi 68 carte postale Étrépilly, infanterie abritée derrière les sacs.
Cote 42 Fi 142 Bataille de la Marne, l'infanterie anglaise cachée dans une
briqueterie des environs de Meaux.
Historial de la Grande Guerre, Péronne, Centre de Documentation
Cote 3 APM 1.1 INVPHYS 007806-AB Boîte à musique Alliance Franco-
Russe.
Cote 15 FI 3360 INVPHYS 039747 Affiche Notre Joffre
Cote 2 PHO 2654.1 INVPHYS 024570 En Belgique. Août 1914. Colonne
d'Infanterie doublant le Ravitaillement du 43eme Artillerie sur la route de
Chimay à Rance. Auteur André Roussel.

Imperial War Museum Private Papers
Brereton, Cedric. L. 68th Battery, Royal Field Artillery. 2615
Charrier, Major P.A. 2/Royal Munster Fusiliers. 16488
Davies, Sgt. W.J.R. 129th RFA. 8102
Edgington, 2nd Lt. W. D Battery Royal Horse Artillery. 563
Harrop, Doctor. Duke of Wellington's Regiment. 8458
Richards, C.E.M. East Lancashire. Regiment. 22368
Rowleston West, Roger. Intelligence Corps. 14546
Rowthorn, H. J.   1/Northamptonshire Regiment. 15193
Spencer, Lt. A.V. 2/Oxfordshire and Buckinghamshire Light Infantry. 1422
Tower, K.F.B. 4/Royal Fusiliers. 11442
Turnbull, D.R. 1/Gordon Highlanders. 18455

Published Diaries and Other Primary Sources
Baumgartner, Richard A. (ed.). *Fritz: The World War 1 Memoir of a German*

Lieutenant. Huntington, USA, 1981.

Beaumont, Harry. *Old Contemptible.* London, 1967.

Benoit, André. *Trois mois de guerre au jour le jour:1914, journal d'un fantassin.* Paris, 1967.

Bloch, Étienne (ed.). *Écrits de guerre de Marc Bloch 1914-1918.* Paris, 1997.

Bloch, Marc. *Memoirs of War 1914-1915* (Translated with an introduction by Caroline Fink) Cambridge, 1988.

Bloem, Walter. *The Advance from Mons, 1914.* Solihull, 2011.

Boudon, Victor. *Avec Charles Péguy de la Lorraine à la Marne août-septembre 1914.* Paris, 1916.

Bréant, Commandant Pierre. *De l'Alsace à la Somme: souvenirs du front (août 1914-janvier 1917).* Paris, 1917.

Brunel de Pérard, Jacques. *Carnet de route (4 août-25 septembre 1914).* Paris, 1915.

Campagne, Colonel. *Le Chemin des croix.* Paris, 1930.

Coleman, Frederic. *From Mons to Ypres with French.* London, 1916.

Corbett-Smith, Arthur. *The Retreat from Mons, By One who Shared in It.* London, 1916.

Craster, Michael (ed.). *Fifteen Rounds a Minute, the Grenadiers at War, August to December 1914.* Barnsley, 2012.

Cross, Tim. *The Lost Voices of World War One: An International Anthology of Writers, Poets and Playwrights.* London, 1988.

Denore, Bernard John. "The Retreat from Mons". In Purdom, C.B. (ed.). *Everyman at War.* London, 1930.

Derville, Lieutenant Étienne. *Correspondance et notes (août 1914-juin 1918).* Publiés par l'abbé Eugène Evrard. Tourcoing, 1921.

Deville, Lieutenant Robert. *Carnet de route d'un artilleur: Virton, la Marne.* Paris, 1916.

Ducasse, André; Meyer, Jacques; Perreux, Gabriel. *Vie et mort des français 1914-1918.* Paris, 1959.

Galtier-Boissière, Jean. *La fleur au fusil.* Paris, 1980.

Gaunt, F. *The Immortal First: a Private Soldier's Diary of Experiences with the Original B.E.F.* London, 1917.

Gazette des Ardennes. 1915.

Genevoix, Maurice. *Ceux de 1914.* Paris, 1950.

Genevoix, Maurice. *La mort de prés.* Paris, 1972.

Grasset, Commandant Alphonse. *Vingt jours de guerre aux temps héroïques: carnet de route d'un commandant de campagne.* Paris, 1918.

Guasson, Antoine. *Heures maudites: journal de route d'un soldat de la guerre 1914-1915.* Paris, 1936.

Horne, Charles F. (ed.). *The Great Events of the Great War: Vol. II 1914.* National Alumni, USA, 1923.

Jack, General James; Terraine, John (ed.). *General Jack's Diary 1914-1918.* London, 2000

Joffre, Joseph. *Mémoires du Maréchal Joffre: T.1 1910-1917.* Paris, 1932.

Kocher-Marboeuf, Éric and Azaïs, Raymond (ed.). *Le choc de 1914.* La Crèche, Deux-Sèvres, 2008.

La Chaussée, Julien. *De Charleroi à Verdun dans l'infanterie.* Paris, 1933.

La Chaussée, Julien. *Poèmes de guerre.* Rouen, 1946.

Lanrezac, Charles Louis Marie. *Le plan de campagne français et le premier mois de la guerre (2 août-3 septembre 1914).* Paris, 1920.

Lintier, Paul. *My 75: Reminiscences of a Gunner of a 75mm Battery in 1914.* London, 1917.

Montgomery, Bernard Law. *Memoirs of Field-Marshal Montgomery.* London, 1958

Omnès, Sgt. Albert. *Carnet de route, campagne de 1914.* Lannion, Association Bretagne 14-18, 1998.

Porchon, Robert. *Carnet de route.* Paris, 2008.

Renn, Ludwig. *War.* London, 1929.

Richards, Frank. *Old Soldiers Never Die.* London, 1933.

Rosenhainer, Ernst. *Forward March! Memoirs of a German Officer.* Shippensburg, USA, 1999.

Rouquerol, General Gabriel. *Charleroi août 1914.* Paris, 1932.

Rouquerol, General Gabriel. *La bataille de Guise 29 août 1914.* Paris, 1925.

Rouquerol, General Gabriel. *Le 3e corps d'armée de Charleroi à la Marne.* Paris, 1934.

Société Météorologique de la France. *Annuaire. Tome 62-4 1914-1920* pp. 203-208.

Spears, Sir Edward. *Liaison 1914: a Narrative of the Great Retreat.* London, 1968.

Ulrich, Bernd and Ziemann, Benjamin (ed.). *German Soldiers in the Great War.* Barnsley, 2010

Van Emden, Richard. *The Soldier's War: the Great War through Veterans' Eyes.* London, 2008.

Von Kluck, General Alexander. *The March on Paris: The Memoirs of Alexander von Kluck, 1914-1918.* London, 1920.

Wedd, A.F. (ed.). *German Students' War Letters.* London, 1929.

Secondary Sources

Albertini, Pierre. "Les juifs du Lycée Condorcet dans la tourmente". *Vingtième Siècle, Revue d'Histoire* 2006/4, no. 92. pp.81-100.

Baldin, Damien and Saint-Fuscien, Emmanuel. *Charleroi 21-23 août 1914.* Paris, 2012.

Beau, G. and Gaubusseau, L. *Lanrezac a-t-il sauvé la France?* Paris, 1964.

Becker, Annette. *La guerre et la foi: de la mort à la mémoire 1914-1930.* Paris, 1994.

Becker, Jean-Jacques. *The Great War and the French People.* Leamington Spa, 1985.

Becker, Jean-Jacques et Annette. *La France en guerre 1914-1918, la grande mutation.* Brussels, 1988.

Becker, Jean-Jacques. *1914: comment les français sont entrés dans la guerre.* Paris, 1977.

Bird, Antony. *Gentlemen, We Will Stand and Fight: Le Cateau, 1914.* Ramsbury, 2008.

Blond, Georges. *The Marne.* London, 2002.

Bonneton Encyclopédies. Picardie. Paris, 2003.

Boüard, Michel de. *Histoire de la Normandie.* Toulouse, 1970.

Broadberry, Stephen and O'Rourke, Kevin (ed.). *The Cambridge Economic History of Modern Europe: Vol. 2 1870 to the Present.* Cambridge, 2010

Clark, Christopher. *The Sleepwalkers: How Europe Went to War in 1914.* London, 2012.

Clarke, David. *The Angel of Mons.* Chichester, 2004.

Contamine, Henri. *La revanche 1871-1914.* Paris, 1957.

Contamine, Henri. *La victoire de la Marne.* Paris, 1970.

Conte, Arthur. *Joffre.* Paris, 1998.

Craig, Gordon A. *The Politics of the Prussian Army 1640-1945.* New York, 1964.

Delumeau, Jean (ed.). *Histoire de la Bretagne.* Toulouse. 1969.

Duménil, Anne. "Les combattants". In Audoin-Rouzeau, Stéphane et Becker, Jean-Jacques (dir.). *Encyclopédie de la Grande Guerre 1914-1918.* Paris, 2004.

Fossier, R. (ed.). *Histoire de la Picardie.* Toulouse. 1974.

Gildea, Robert. *The Past in French History.* London & New Haven, 1994.

Gildea, Robert. *Children of the Revolution 1799-1914.* London, 2008.

Gildea, Robert. *Education in Provincial France 1800-1914.* Oxford, 1983.

Gudmundsson, Bruce. *The British Expeditionary Force 1914-1915.* Oxford, 2005.

Guinard, Pierre, Devos, Jean-Claude and Nicot, Jean. *Organisation de l'armée française, Introduction - Inventaire sommaire des Archives de la Guerre série N*

1872-1919. Ministère de la Défense, État-Major de l'Armée de Terre, Service Historique. Troyes 1975.

Guéno, Jean-Pierre and Pecnard, Jérôme. *Paroles de poilus.* Paris, 2003.

Hall, Isobel V. *Absolute Destruction: Military Culture in Imperial Germany.* Cornell, 2005.

Herwig, Holger. *The Marne, 1914.* New York, 2009.

Holmes, Richard. *Tommy: The British Soldier on the Western Front 1914-1918.* London, 2004.

Holmes, Richard. R*iding the Retreat: Mons to Marne: 1914 Revisited.* London , 1996.

Howard, Michael. "Men against Fire: the Doctrine of the Offensive in 1914". In Peter Paret (ed.). *Makers of Modern Strategy.* Oxford, 1986.

Lacouture, Jean. *De Gaulle the Rebel 1890-1944.* London, 1990.

Lavisse, Commandant Émile-Charles. *Sac au dos: étude comparée de la tenue de campagne des fantassins des armées françaises et étrangères.* Paris, 1907.

MacMillan, Margaret. *The War that Ended Peace.* London, 2013.

McMeekin, Sean. *July 1914 Countdown to War.* London 2013.

Maitron database, CNRS, University of Paris 1, for biography of Guasson, Antoine.

Ministère de la Guerre, État-Major de l'Armée, Service Historique. *Les Armées Françaises de la Grande Guerre* (AFGG) T.1 Appendices. Paris, 1922-

Miquel, Pierre. *Les poilus: le carnage de la Grande Guerre.* Paris, 2000.

Miquel, Pierre. *La bataille de la Marne.* Paris, 2004.

Murland, Jerry. *Retreat and Rearguard 1914: the BEF's Actions from Mons to the Marne.* Barnsley, 2011.

Norton Cru, Jean. *Témoins: essai d'analyse et de critique des souvenirs de combattants édités en Français de 1915 à 1928.* Paris, 1929.

Pedroncini, Guy (ed.). *Histoire militaire de la France: vol. 3 1871-1940.* Paris, 1992.

Pedroncini, Guy. "Les cours martiales pendant la Grande Guerre". R*evue Historique,* Oct-Dec, 1974.

Philpott, William. "Gone Fishing: Sir John French's Meeting with General Lanrezac 17 August 1914". In *Journal of the Society for Army Historical Research,* Autumn 2006, vol. 84, no. 339.

Planhol, Xavier de. *An Historical Geography of France.* Cambridge, 1994.

Porch, Douglas. *The March to the Marne.* Cambridge, 1981.

Porch, Douglas. "The Marne and After: A Reappraisal of French Strategy in the First World War". *Journal of Military History,* vol. 53, no. 4, October 1989.

Price, Roger. *A Social History of Nineteenth-Century France.* London, 1987.

Prost, Antoine. "Les monuments des morts". In Nora, Pierre. (ed.). *Les lieux de mémoire: Tome I La République*. Paris, 1984.

Ripperger, Robert M. "The Development of the French Artillery for the Offensive 1890-1914". *Journal of Military History*, vol. 59, no. 4, October 1995.

Robb, Graham. *The Discovery of France*. London, 2007.

Roland, André. *Régiments d'infanterie de la Grande Guerre*. 2 vols. St.-Cyr-sur-Loire, 2008.

Senior, Ian. *Home Before the Leaves Fall: A New History of the German Invasion of 1914*. Oxford, 2012.

Smith, Leonard V. *Between Mutiny and Obedience: The Case of the French Fifth Infantry Division during World War One*. Princeton, 1994.

Smith, Leonard V. *The Embattled Self: French Soldiers' Testimony of the Great War*. Cornell, 2007.

Smith, Leonard V; Audoin-Rouzeau, Stéphane; Becker, Annette. *France and the Great War 1914-1918*. Cambridge, 2003.

Strachan, Hew. *The First World War: Vol.1 To Arms*. Oxford, 2001.

Terraine, John. *Mons, the Retreat to Victory*. Barnsley, 2010.

Tombs, Roger. *France 1814-1914*. London, 1996.

Tombs, Robert. *Nationhood and Nationalism in France 1889-1918*. London, 1991.

Trénard, Louis (ed.). *Histoire des Pays-Bas français*. Toulouse. 1972

Tuchman, Barbara W. *The Guns of August*. New York, 1962.

Tyng, Seymour. *The Campaign of the Marne, 1914*. Oxford, 1935.

Verhey, Joseph. *The Spirit of 1914: Militarism, Myth and Mobilization in Germany*. Cambridge, 2000.

Weber, Eugen. *Peasants into Frenchmen 1870-1914*. Stanford, 1976.

Winter, Jay. *Sites of Memory, Sites of Mourning*. Cambridge, 1995.

Zeldin, Theodore. *France 1848-1945* 3 vols. *Intellect and Pride, Anxiety and Hypocrisy, Ambition and Love*. Oxford, 1979-1981.

INDEX